ARCHITECTURE

FORM · SPACE & ORDER

ARCHITECTURE:
FORM · SPACE & ORDER

FRANCIS D.K. CHING

 VAN NOSTRAND REINHOLD
NEW YORK

Published by Van Nostrand Reinhold
115 Fifth Avenue
New York, N.Y. 10003

Van Nostrand Reinhold International Company Limited
11 New Fetter Lane
London EC4P 4EE, England

16 15 14 13 12 11

Van Nostrand Reinhold
480 La Trobe Street
Melbourne, Victoria 3000, Australia

Macmillan of Canada
Division of Canada Publishing Corporation
164 Commander Boulevard
Agincourt, Ontario M1S 3C7, Canada

Library of Congress Cataloging in Publication Data

Ching, Francis D.K., 1943-
        Architecture: Form, Space & Order
        Bibliography: P. 388
        Includes Index.
        1. Architecture -- Composition, proportion, etc.
2. Space (Architecture) I. Title.
NA2760.C46   720'.1   79-18045
ISBN 0-442-21534-7
ISBN 0-442-21535-5 pbk.

I wish to acknowledge the following people for their valuable contributions to this work: Forrest Wilson, whose insights into the communication of design principles helped clarify the organization of the material, and whose help made its publication possible; James Tice, whose knowledge and understanding of architectural history and theory strengthened the development of this study; Norman Crowe, whose diligence and skill in the teaching of architecture encouraged me to pursue this research; Roger Sherwood, whose research into the organizational principles of form fostered the development of the chapter on ordering principles; Daniel Friedman, for his editing of the final copy and enthusiasm for the project; Diane Turner and Philip Hamp, for their assistance in researching material for the illustrations; and Larry Hager, Senior Editor at Van Nostrand Reinhold, for his patience while awaiting the final outcome.

Finally, I wish to dedicate this book to my wife, Debra, for without her unwavering support and encouragement, especially during the difficult times of the book's production, it would never have been fully realized.

PREFACE

This is a study of the art of architecture. It is a morphological study of the essential elements of form and space and those principles that control their organization in our built environment. These elements of form and space are the critical means of architecture. While utilitarian concerns of function and use can be relatively shortlived, and symbolic interpretations can vary from age to age, these primary elements of form and space comprise the timeless and fundamental vocabulary of the architectural designer.

This study emphasizes the element of form as the primary tool of the designer. It serves to lay out and classify for analysis and discussion basic forms and organizations of space and their generic transformations in a typological manner. It is ultimately the province of the individual designer to select, test, and manipulate these elements into coherent, meaningful, and useful organizations of space, structure, and enclosure.

A large portion of this work is devoted to images. These images span time and cross cultural boundaries. The juxtaposition of historical styles may appear to be abrupt at times, but is intended to force the reader to look for likenesses among seemingly unlike formations. Understanding these similarities among the wide range of historical examples should help clarify their differences.

The architectural examples used in this book are, of course, not exhaustive, nor are they necessarily the archetypes for the concepts or principles discussed. The wide range of examples is deliberate. Their selection is based on appropriateness and clarity and serve simply to illustrate fundamental ideas. These ideas transcend their historical context and encourage speculation: How might they be selected, analyzed, and reapplied to a wider range of architectural problems? This type of approach should help one better understand the architecture one experiences, the architecture one encounters in literature, and the architecture one imagines while designing.

Although presented in varying degrees of complexity, the elements and principles are discussed as discretely as possible. This book is merely a starting point. Readers are encouraged to use the book freely during the design process and to take note of additional examples recalled within the context of their individual experiences. As the elements and principles become more familiar, new connections, relationships, and levels of meaning may be established. The substance and manner of presentation seeks clarity in order to encourage the understanding of the art of architecture, the elements of form and space, and the ordering of our built environment.

Francis D.K. Ching

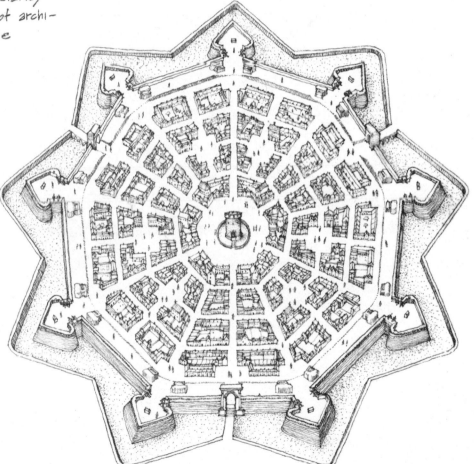

CONTENTS

4. ORGANIZATIONS

5. CIRCULATION

6. PROPORTION & SCALE

7. PRINCIPLES

CONCLUSION

BIBLIOGRAPHY

INDEX

INTRODUCTION

Architecture is normally conceived (designed) and realized (built) in response to an existing set of conditions. These conditions may be purely functional in nature, or they may reflect, in varying degrees, social, economic, political, even whimsical or symbolic intentions. In any case, it is assumed that the existing set of conditions - the problem - is less than satisfactory, and that a new set of conditions - a solution - would be desirable. The act of creating architecture, then, is a problem-solving or design process.

The first phase of any design process is the recognition of a problematic condition and the decision to find a solution to it. Design is, above all, a willful act, a purposeful endeavor. The designer must first document the existing conditions of a problem, define its context, and collect relevant data to be assimilated. This is the critical phase of the design process, since the nature of a solution is inexorably related to how a problem is perceived, defined, and articulated. Piet Hein, the noted Danish poet and scientist, puts it this way: "Art is solving problems that cannot be formulated before they have been solved. The shaping of the question is part of the answer." Designers inevitably prefigure solutions to problems they are confronted with. The depth and range of their design vocabulary will affect both their perception of a problem and the shape of its solution. This book concentrates on articulating elements of the design vocabulary, and presents a wide array of possible solutions to architectural problems. They are intended to enrich one's design vocabulary through exploration, study, and application.

As an art, architecture is more than satisfying the purely functional requirements of a building program. Fundamentally, the physical manifestations of architecture accommodate human activity. However, the arrangement and organization of the elements of form and space will determine how architecture might promote endeavors, elicit responses, and communicate meaning. These elements of form and space are presented, therefore, not as ends in themselves, but as means to solve a problem in response to conditions of function, purpose, and context - that is, architecturally.

The analogy may be made that one must know and understand the alphabet before words can be formed and a vocabulary developed; one must understand the rules of grammar and syntax before sentences can be constructed; one must understand the principles of composition before essays, novels, and the like can be written. Once these elements are understood, one can write poignantly or with force, call for peace or incite to riot, comment on trivia or speak with insight and meaning. It should be useful, therefore, for the student of design to recognize the basic elements of architectural form and space, understand how they can be manipulated in the development of a design concept, and realize their visual implications in the implementation of a design solution.

On the following pages is an overview of the basic elements, systems, and orders that constitute a physical work of architecture. These constituents can all be perceived and experienced. Some may be readily apparent while others may be more obscure to our senses. Some may dominate while others play a secondary role in a building's organization. Some may convey images and meaning while others may serve as qualifiers or modifiers of these images and meanings.

In all cases, however, the following elements and systems should be interrelated, interdependent, and mutually reinforcing to form an integrated whole. Architectural order is created when these elements and systems, as constituent parts, make visible the relationships among themselves and the building as a whole. When their relationships are perceived as contributing to the singular nature of the whole, then a conceptual order exists - an order that is, perhaps, more enduring than transient perceptual visions.

ARCHITECTURAL ELEMENTS

THE **ARCHITECTURE** OF	**SPACE** **STRUCTURE** **ENCLOSURE**	•organizational pattern, relationships, & hierarchy •spatial definition & image - qualities of • form, scale, & proportion • surface, shape, edges, & openings: • light, view, focus, & acoustics
EXPERIENCED THROUGH	**MOVEMENT** IN **SPACE·TIME**	•approach & entry •path configuration & access •sequence of spaces
ACHIEVED BY THE MEANS OF	**TECHNOLOGY**	•structure & enclosure •environmental comfort •health, safety, & welfare •durability
ACCOMMODATING A	**PROGRAM**	•user requirements, needs, & aspirations •legal restraints •economic factors •social/cultural factors •historical precedents
COMPATIBLE WITH ITS	**CONTEXT**	•site & environment •climate: sun, wind, temperature, precipitation •geography: soils, topography, vegetation, water •sensory: character of the place, views, sound

...& ORDERS

PHYSICAL

• **FORM & SPACE**
 SOLIDS & VOIDS
 INTERIOR & EXTERIOR

SYSTEMS & ORGANIZATIONS OF:

• SPACE
• STRUCTURE
• ENCLOSURE
+
• TECHNOLOGY

PERCEPTUAL

• Sensory perception and recognition of the physical elements by experiencing them sequentially in time.

• APPROACH & DEPARTURE
• ENTRY & EGRESS
• MOVEMENT THROUGH THE ORDER OF SPACES
• FUNCTIONING OF, & ACTIVITIES WITHIN SPACES
• QUALITIES OF LIGHT, COLOR, TEXTURE, VIEW, & ACOUSTICS

CONCEPTUAL

• Comprehension of the ordered or disordered relationships among a building's elements and systems, and responding to the meanings they evoke.

• IMAGES
• PATTERNS
• SIGNS
• SYMBOLS

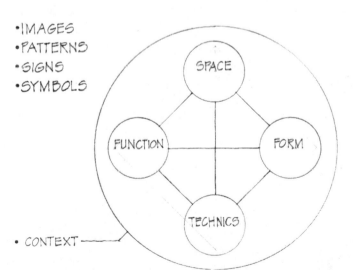

• CONTEXT

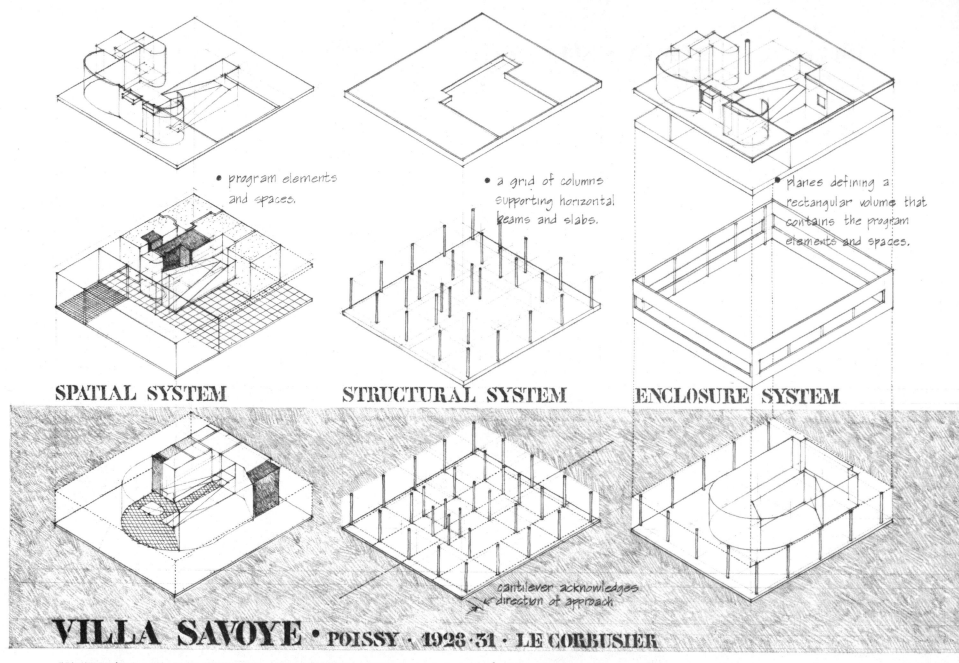

• program elements and spaces.

• a grid of columns supporting horizontal beams and slabs.

• planes defining a rectangular volume that contains the program elements and spaces.

SPATIAL SYSTEM **STRUCTURAL SYSTEM** **ENCLOSURE SYSTEM**

cantilever acknowledges direction of approach

VILLA SAVOYE · POISSY · 1928·31 · LE CORBUSIER

AN ANALYSIS OF THE INTERRELATIONSHIPS AMONG A BUILDING'S ELEMENTS AND SYSTEMS

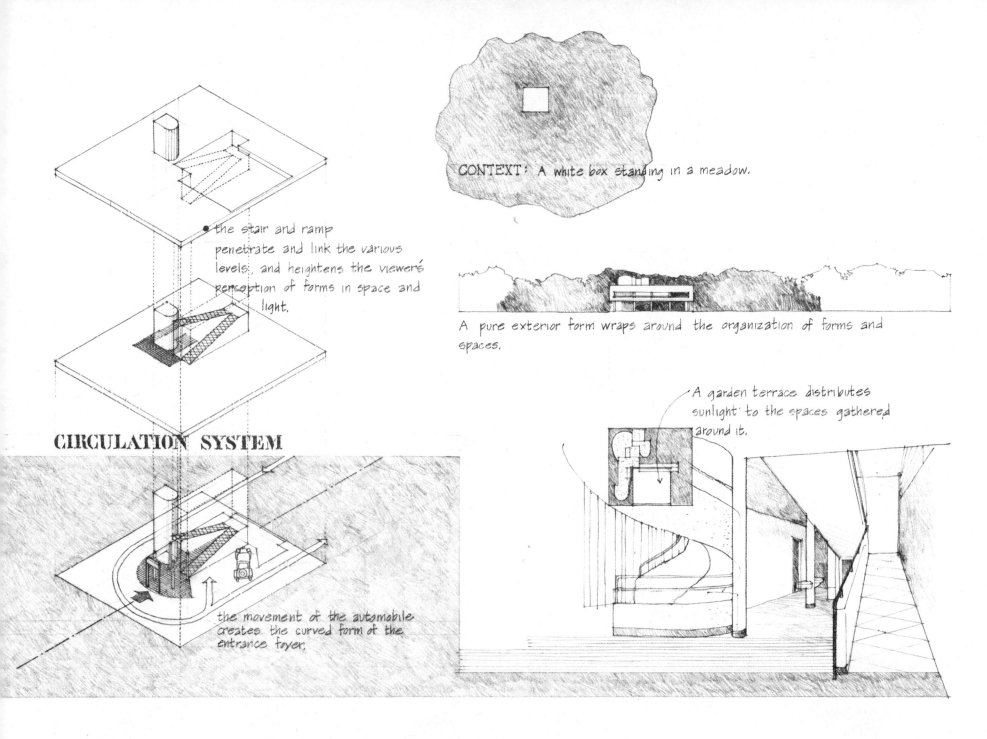

• the stair and ramp
penetrate and link the various
levels, and heightens the viewer's
perception of forms in space and
light.

CONTEXT: A white box standing in a meadow.

A pure exterior form wraps around the organization of forms and
spaces.

CIRCULATION SYSTEM

A garden terrace distributes
sunlight to the spaces gathered
around it.

the movement of the automobile
creates the curved form of the
entrance foyer.

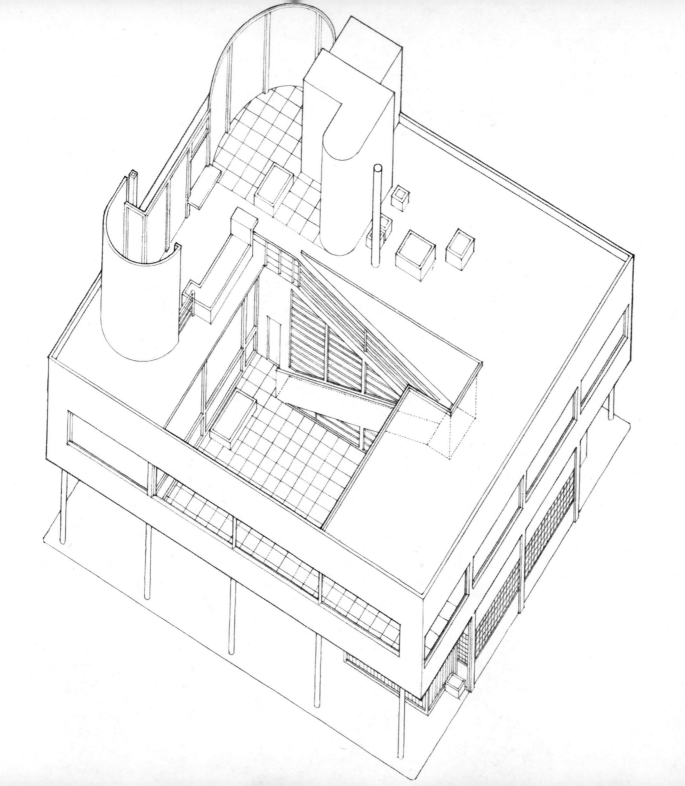

16

PRIMARY ELEMENTS 1

This chapter presents the primary elements of form: point, line, plane, and volume. Starting with the point as the prime generator of all form, each element is presented in the order of its growth from the point, first as a conceptual element, then as a visual element in the vocabulary of architectural design.

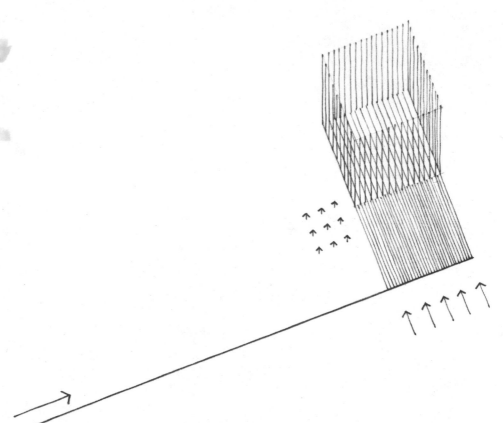

"All pictorial form begins with the point that sets itself in motion... The point moves... and the line comes into being - the first dimension. If the line shifts to form a plane, we obtain a two-dimensional element. In the movement from plane to spaces, the clash of planes gives rise to body (three-dimensional)... A summary of the kinetic energies which move the point into a line, the line into a plane, and the plane into a spatial dimension."

PAUL KLEE

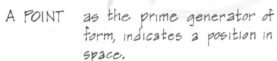

A POINT   as the prime generator of form, indicates a position in space.

LINE   A point extended becomes a with properties of:
- length
- direction
- position

1·D LINE

PLANE   A line extended becomes a with properties of:
- length & width
- shape
- surface
- orientation
- position

2·D PLANE

VOLUME   A plane extended becomes a with properties of:
- length, width, & depth
- form/space
- surface
- orientation
- position

3·D VOLUME

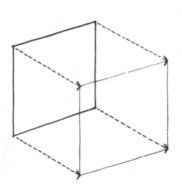

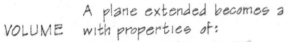

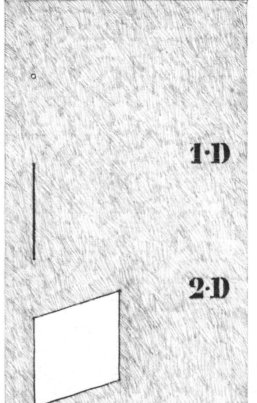

19

POINT

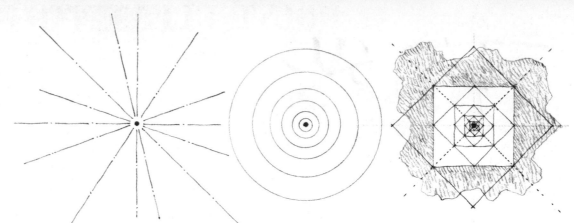

A point marks a position in space. Conceptually, it has no length, width, or depth, and is, therefore, static, directionless, and centralized.

As the prime element in the vocabulary of form, a point can serve to mark:

- the two ends of a line
- the intersection of two lines
- the meeting of lines at the corner of a plane or volume
- the center of a field.

Although a point is conceptually without shape or form, it begins to make its presence felt when placed within a visual field. At the center of its environment, a point is stable and at rest, organizing surrounding elements about itself and dominating its field.

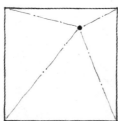
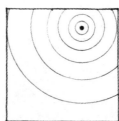

When the point is moved off-center, however, its field becomes more aggressive and begins to compete for visual supremacy. A visual tension is created between the point and its field.

POINT·ELEMENTS IN ARCHITECTURE

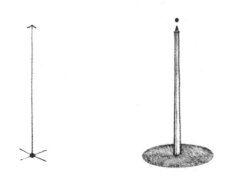

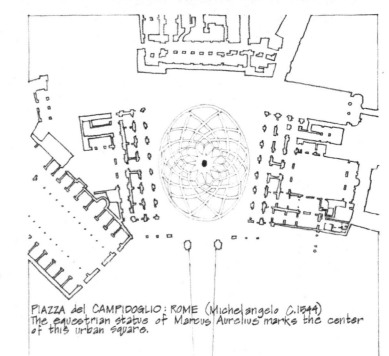

A point has no dimension. To visibly mark a position in space or on the ground plane, a point must be projected into a vertical linear element such as a column, obelisk, or tower. It should be noted that a columnar element is seen in plan as a point and therefore retains the visual characteristics of a point. Other point-generated forms that share the point's visual characteristics are:

PIAZZA del CAMPIDOGLIO: ROME (Michelangelo C.1544)
The equestrian statue of Marcus Aurelius marks the center of this urban square.

• the circle

GREEK TEMPLE: EPIDAUROS
c. 300 B.C.

• the cylinder

BAPTISTERY: PISA
Dioti Salvi 1153-1265

• the sphere

MONUMENT TO NEWTON
E.-L. Boulée C.1785

MONT S. MICHEL: FRANCE (Begun 1024)
The pyramidal composition culminates in a spire that serves to establish this fortified monastery as a specific place in the landscape.

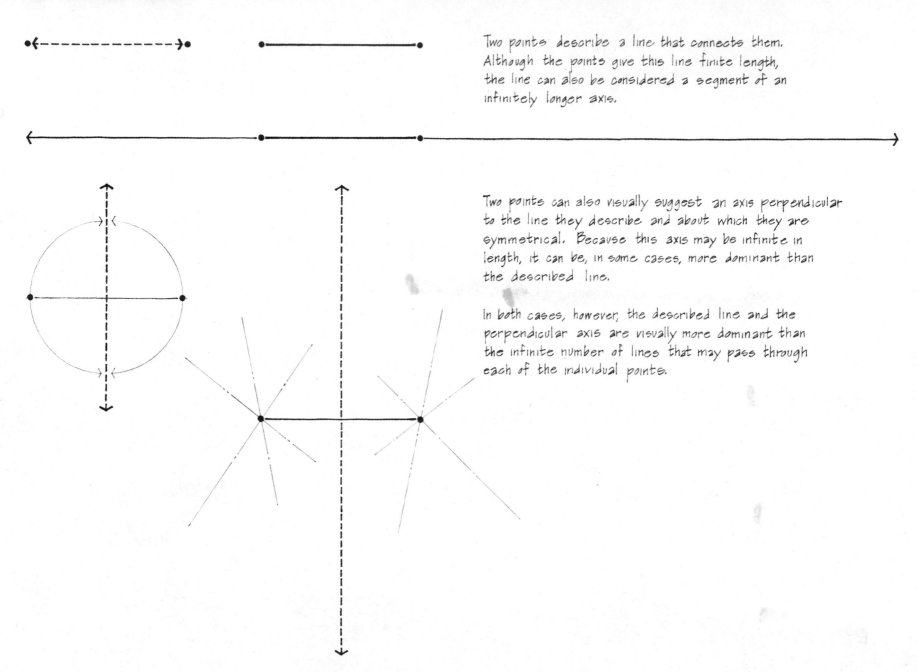

Two points describe a line that connects them. Although the points give this line finite length, the line can also be considered a segment of an infinitely longer axis.

Two points can also visually suggest an axis perpendicular to the line they describe and about which they are symmetrical. Because this axis may be infinite in length, it can be, in some cases, more dominant than the described line.

In both cases, however, the described line and the perpendicular axis are visually more dominant than the infinite number of lines that may pass through each of the individual points.

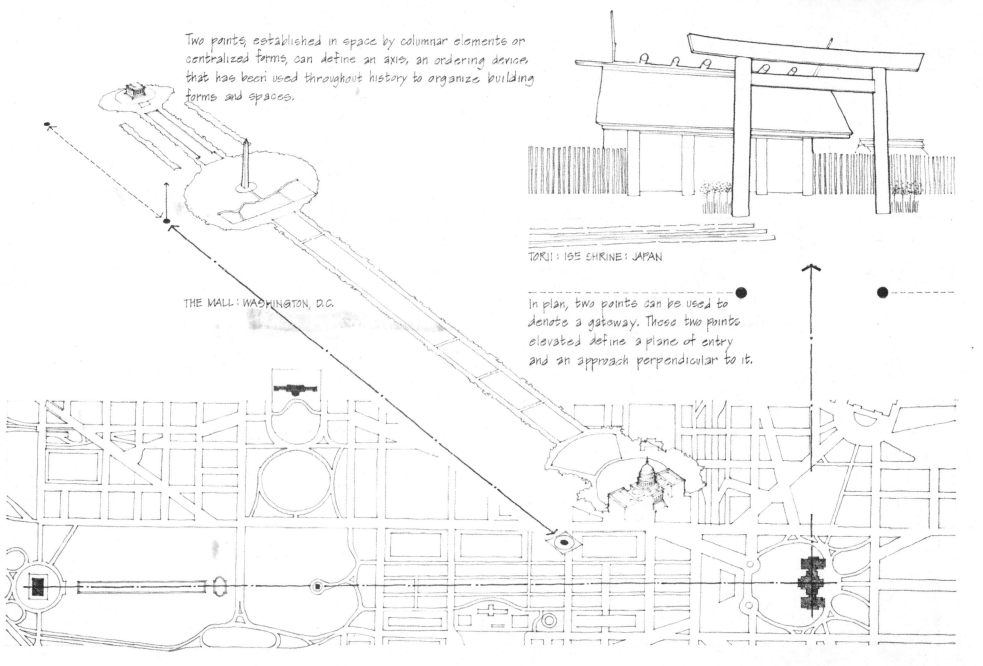

Two points, established in space by columnar elements or centralized forms, can define an axis, an ordering device, that has been used throughout history to organize building forms and spaces.

THE MALL: WASHINGTON, D.C.

TORII: ISE SHRINE: JAPAN

In plan, two points can be used to denote a gateway. These two points elevated define a plane of entry and an approach perpendicular to it.

LINE

A point extended becomes a line. Conceptually, a line has length, but no width or depth. Whereas a point is by nature static, a line, in describing the path of a point in motion, is capable of visually expressing direction, movement, and growth.

A line is an important element in the formation of any visual construction. It can serve to:

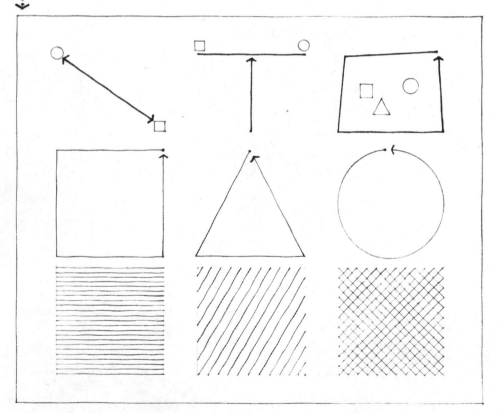

- join, link, support, surround, or intersect other visual elements

- describe the edges of, and give shape to, planes

- articulate the surfaces of planes.

Although a line conceptually has only one dimension, it must have some degree of thickness to become visible. It is seen as a line simply because its length dominates its width. The character of a line, whether taut or limp, bold or tentative, graceful or ragged, is determined by our perception of its length/width ratio, its contour, and its degree of continuity.

If continuous enough, the simple repetition of like or similar elements can also be seen as a line. This type of line has significant textural qualities.

The orientation or direction of a line can affect its role in a visual construction. While a vertical line can express a state of equilibrium with the forces of gravity, or the human condition, or mark a position in space, a horizontal line can represent stability, the ground plane, the horizon, or a body at rest.

An oblique line is a deviation from the perpendicular or horizontal. It can be seen as a vertical line falling or a horizontal line rising. In either case, whether it is falling toward a point on the ground plane or rising to a point in the sky, it is dynamic and visually active in its unbalanced state.

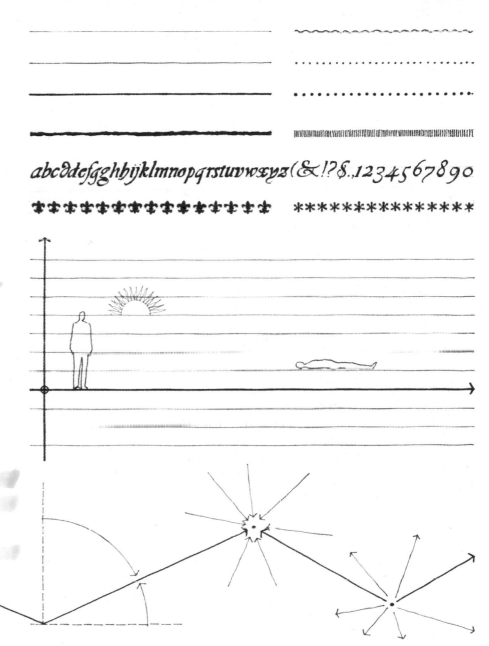

abcddefgghhijklmnopqrstuvwxyz(&!?§.,1234567890

25

LINEAR ELEMENTS IN ARCHITECTURE

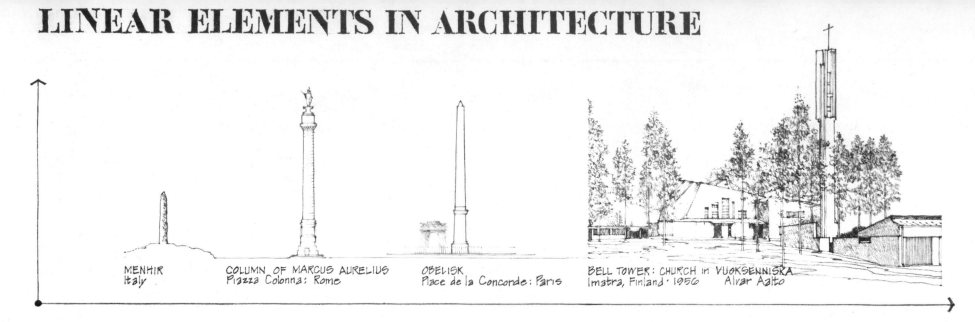

MENHIR
Italy

COLUMN OF MARCUS AURELIUS
Piazza Colonna: Rome

OBELISK
Place de la Concorde: Paris

BELL TOWER: CHURCH in VUOKSENNISKA
Imatra, Finland · 1956   Alvar Aalto

HAGIA SOPHIA: Constantinople (Istanbul) 532·7
Anthemius of Tralles & Isidorus of Miletus

Vertical linear elements, such as columns, obelisks, and towers, have been used throughout history to commemorate significant events and establish particular points in space.

Vertical linear elements can also be used to define transparent volumes of space. In the example illustrated to the left, the four minaret towers define a spatial field from which the dome of Hagia Sophia rises in splendor.

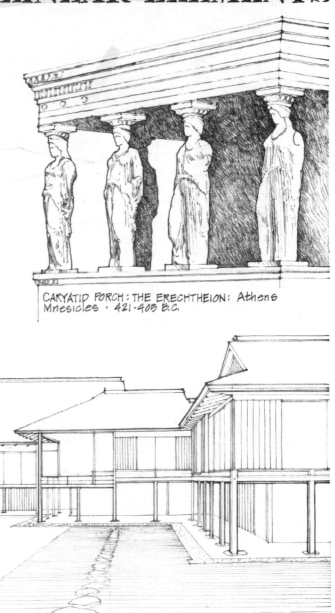

CARYATID PORCH: THE ERECHTHEION: Athens
Mnesicles · 421-405 B.C.

SALGINATOBEL BRIDGE
Switzerland   1929-30
Robert Maillart

IMPERIAL VILLA: KATSURA: Japan

In these three examples, linear elements are used to express movement across space, provide support for the overhead plane, and form a three-dimensional structural frame for architectural space.

LINEAR ELEMENTS

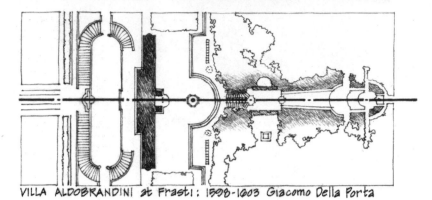

VILLA ALDOBRANDINI at Frasti: 1598-1603 Giacomo Della Porta

A line can be an imagined rather than a visible element in architecture. An example is the axis, a regulating line established by two points in space and about which elements can be symmetrically arranged.

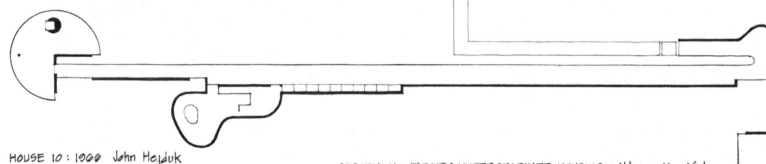

HOUSE 10: 1966 John Hejduk

Although architectural space exists in three dimensions, it can be linear in form to accommodate the path of movement through a building and link its spaces to one another.

Building forms also can be linear, particularly when they consist of repetitive spaces organized along a circulation path. As illustrated here, linear building forms have the ability to enclose exterior space as well as adapt to varying site conditions.

CORNELL UNIVERSITY UNDERGRADUATE HOUSING: Ithaca, New York
Richard Meier   1974

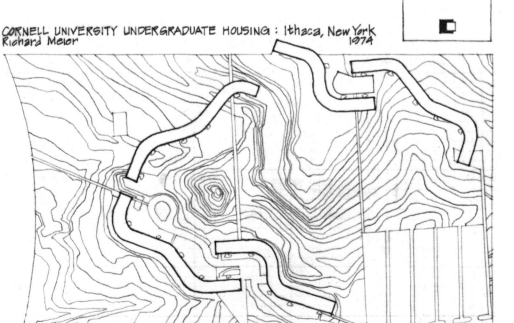

TOWN HALL: Säynätsalo, Finland 1950-52 Alvar Aalto

At a smaller scale, lines articulate the edges and surfaces of planes and volumes. These lines can be joints in or between building materials, frames around window or door openings, or a structural grid of columns and beams. How these linear elements affect a surface's texture will depend on their visual weight, direction, and spacing.

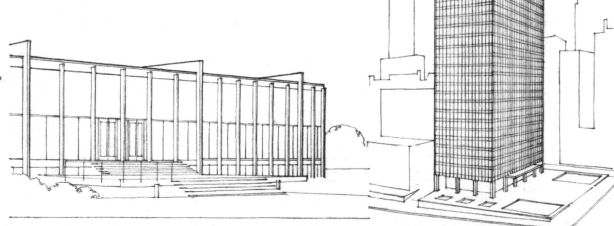

SCHOOL OF ARCHITECTURE AND DESIGN- CROWN HALL
Illinois Institute of Technology: Chicago, Illinois 1952
Mies van der Rohe

SEAGRAM BUILDING: New York 1958
Mies van der Rohe and
Philip Johnson

FROM LINE TO PLANE

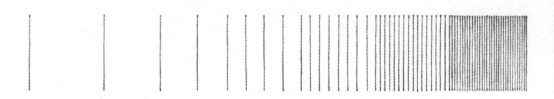

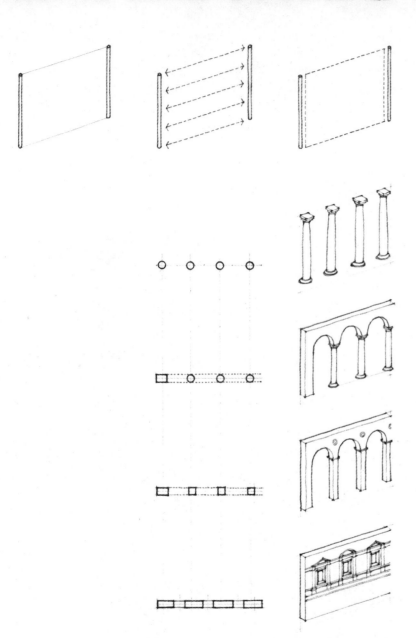

Two parallel lines have the ability to visually describe a plane. A transparent spatial membrane can be stretched between them to acknowledge their visual relationship. The closer these lines are to each other, the stronger will be the sense of plane they convey.

A series of parallel lines, through their repetitiveness, will reinforce our perception of the plane they describe.

As these lines extend themselves along the plane they describe, the implied plane becomes real, and the original voids between the lines become merely interruptions of the planar surface.

The diagrams illustrate the transformation of a row of round columns (lines), initially supporting a portion of a wall (plane), then becoming square piers (part of the wall plane), and finally remnants of the original columns occurring as a relief along the surface of the wall.

"The column is a certain strengthened part of a wall, carried up perpendicularly from the foundation to the top... A row of columns is indeed nothing but a wall, open and discontinued in several places."
ALBERTI

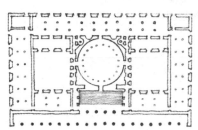

ALTES MUSEUM: Berlin 1823-30
K.F. Schinkel

A row of columns has often been used to define the front plane or facade of buildings, particularly public buildings that front on major public spaces. Colonnaded facades can be penetrated easily for entry, offer some degree of shelter from the elements, and form a semi-transparent screen - a "public face"- that unifies individual building forms behind it.

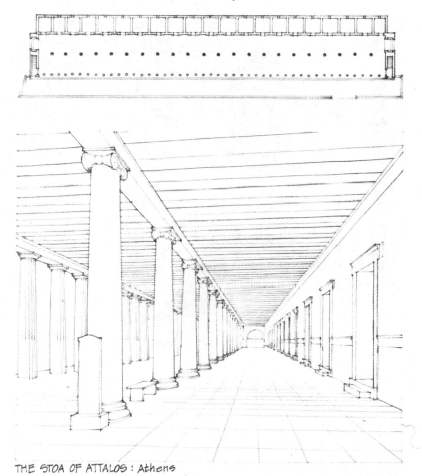

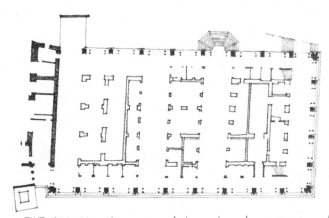

THE BASILICA: Vicenza - A two-story loggia or arcade was designed by Andrea Palladio in 1845 to wrap around an existing medieval structure. This addition not only buttressed the existing structure but also acted as a screen that disguised the irregularity of the original core and presented a uniform but elegant face to the Piazza dei Signori.

THE STOA OF ATTALOS: Athens

LINEAR ELEMENTS DEFINING PLANES

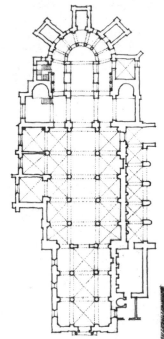

ST. PHILIBERT: Tournus, France
950-1120
◄ view of nave

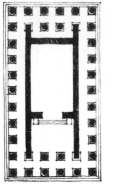

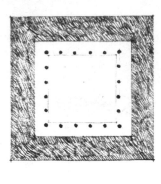

TEMPLE OF ATHENA POLIAS: Priene
Pythius   C. 334 B.C.

Two contrasting examples: Columns articulating the edges of a
building form in space as well as the edges of an exterior space
defined within a building form.

In addition to the structural role columns play
in supporting the overhead roof plane, they also
can articulate the edges of interior spatial
zones while allowing them to interlock easily
with adjacent spaces.

THE CLOISTER: Moissac Abbey, France

CARY HOUSE: Marin County, California
Joseph Esherick

Linear members spanning horizontally overhead can provide a moderate degree of definition and enclosure for outdoor spaces while allowing filtered sunlight and breezes to penetrate.

TRELLISED COURTYARD: Georgia O'Keefe Residence - New Mexico

Vertical and horizontal linear elements together can define a volume of space such as the solarium illustrated to the right. Note that the form of the volume is determined solely by the configuration of the linear elements.

SOLARIUM: CONDOMINIUM UNIT 1 - Sea Ranch
California
MLTW   1966

PLANE

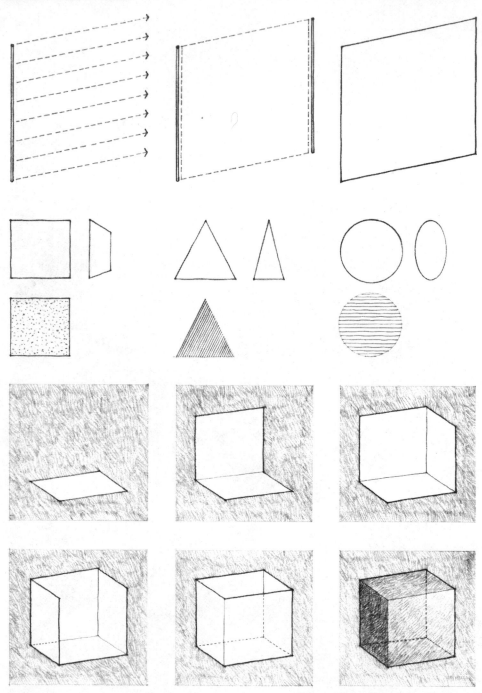

A line extended (in a direction other than its intrinsic direction) becomes a plane. Conceptually, a plane has length and width, but no depth.

Shape is a plane's primary identifying characteristic. It is determined by the contour of the line forming the edges of the plane. Since our perception of a plane's shape is distorted by perspective, we see the true shape of a plane only when we view it frontally.

The surface properties of a plane, its color and texture, will affect its visual weight and stability.

In the formation of a visual construction, a plane serves to define the limits or boundaries of a volume. Since architecture, as a visual art, deals specifically with the formation of three-dimensional volumes of form and space, the plane becomes a key element in the vocabulary of architectural design.

Planes in architecture define three-dimensional volumes of form and space. The properties of each plane (size, shape, color, texture) as well as their spatial relationship to one another will ultimately determine the visual properties of the form they define and the qualities of the space they enclose.

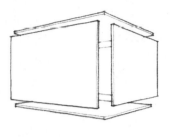
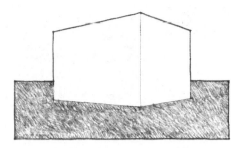

The generic types of planes that are manipulated in architectural design are:

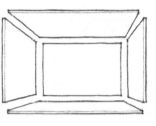
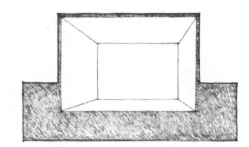

1. THE OVERHEAD PLANE

The overhead plane can be either the roof plane, a building's primary protection against the climatic elements, or the ceiling plane, the sheltering element in architectural space.

2. THE WALL PLANE

Vertical wall planes are visually the most active in defining and enclosing space.

3. THE BASE PLANE

The ground plane provides the physical support and the visual base for building forms. The floor plane supports our activities within buildings.

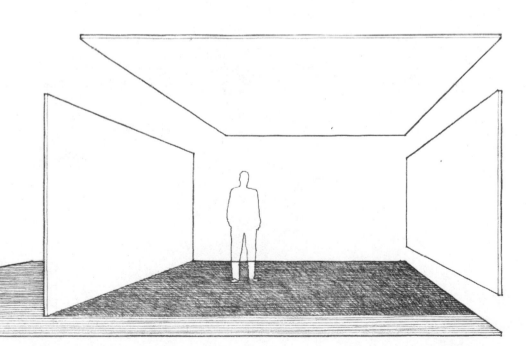

PLANAR ELEMENTS IN ARCHITECTURE

The ground plane ultimately supports all architectural construction. Along with the climatic and other geographical conditions of the site, the ground plane's topographical character should affect the form of the building that rises from it. The building can merge with the ground plane, sit on it, or be elevated above it.

The ground plane itself can be manipulated as well to receive a building form. It can be elevated to honor a sacred or significant place. It can be bermed to define outdoor spaces or buffer against undesirable elements. It can be carved or terraced to provide a suitable platform on which to build. It can be stepped to allow changes in topography to be easily traversed.

THE SPANISH STEPS (Scala di Spagna) Rome, 1721-25
Started by Alessandro Specchi to connect the Piazza di Spagna with SS. Trinita de'Monti. Completed by Francesco de Sanctis.

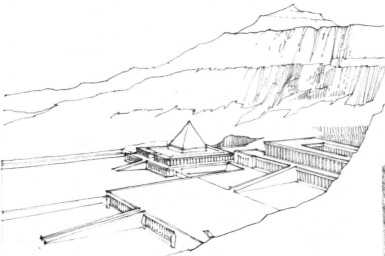

TEMPLE OF QUEEN HATSHEPSUT: Dêr el-Bahari, Thebes
Senmut   1511 - 1480 B.C.

MACHU PICCHU: Inca Town situated on a saddle between two mountains, 2000 ft. above the Urubamba River below. (C. 1500)

SITTING AREA, LAWRENCE HOUSE : Sea Ranch, California
MLTW/Moore-Turnbull   1966

Since the floor plane supports our activities within a building, it should, of course, be structurally sound and durable. It is also an important design element within a space. Its form, color, pattern, and texture will determine to what degree it will define the boundaries of a space and serve as a visual ground against which other elements in the space can be seen. The texture and density of the material underfoot will also affect how we walk across its surface.

Emperor's Seat
IMPERIAL PALACE
Kyoto, Japan

Like the ground plane, the floor plane can be manipulated. It can be stepped or terraced to break the scale of a space down to human dimensions and create platforms for sitting, viewing, or performing. It can be elevated to define an honorific or sacred place. It can be rendered as a neutral surface against which other elements in the space are seen.

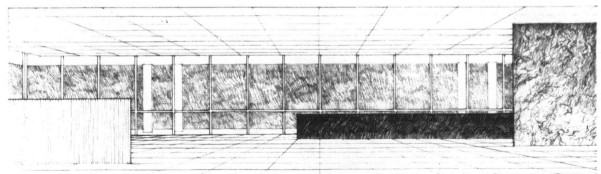

BACARDI OFFICE BUILDING : Santiago de Cuba 1958
Mie van der Rohe

PLANAR ELEMENTS

S. MARIA NOVELLA : Florence
Renaissance Facade by Alberti (1456-70)

The exterior wall planes of a building, along with the roof plane, control the penetration of climatic elements into the building's interior spaces. Openings in or between the exterior wall planes determine the degree to which the interior spaces will relate to outdoor spaces. The configuration of the exterior wall planes together with their openings will describe the building's overall form and massing.

As a design element, an exterior wall plane can be articulated as a building's "front face" or primary facade. In urban situations, these building facades serve as walls that define streets and public spaces such as marketplaces, piazzas, and squares.

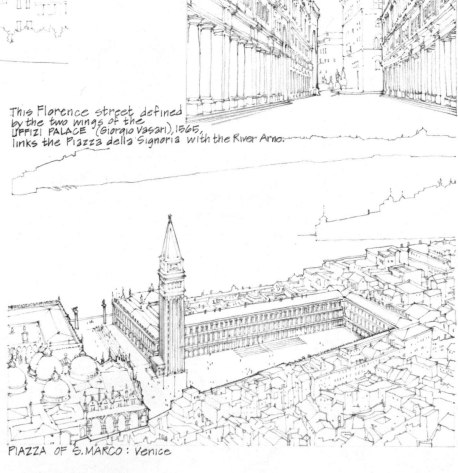

This Florence street defined by the two wings of the UFFIZI PALACE (Giorgio Vasari), 1565, links the Piazza della Signoria with the River Arno.

PIAZZA OF S. MARCO : Venice

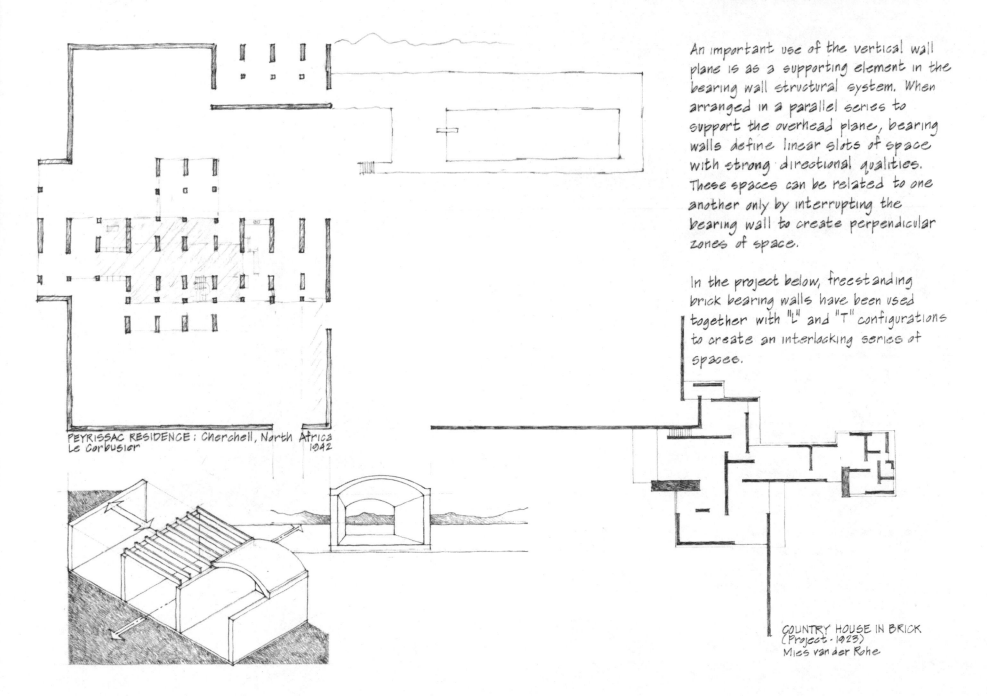

An important use of the vertical wall plane is as a supporting element in the bearing wall structural system. When arranged in a parallel series to support the overhead plane, bearing walls define linear slots of space with strong directional qualities. These spaces can be related to one another only by interrupting the bearing wall to create perpendicular zones of space.

In the project below, freestanding brick bearing walls have been used together with "L" and "T" configurations to create an interlocking series of spaces.

PEYRISSAC RESIDENCE; Cherchell, North Africa
Le Corbusier   1942

COUNTRY HOUSE IN BRICK
(Project - 1923)
Mies van der Rohe

PLANAR ELEMENTS

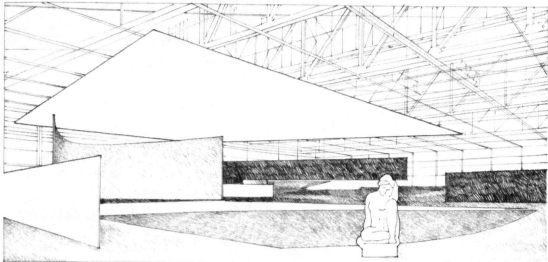

CONCERT HALL : Project, 1942   Mies van der Rohe

Interior wall planes define and enclose a building's spaces or "rooms."
Their visual properties, their relationship to one another, and the size and
distribution of openings within them will determine the quality of the
space they define and the degree to which the space will relate to
the spaces around it.

As a design element, a wall plane can merge with the floor or ceiling
plane, or be articulated as an isolated plane. It can be a neutral backdrop
for other elements in the space, or it can be a visually active element
within it. It can be opaque, or transparent, a source of light or view.

It is the surface of a wall that we see from within a room. It is this
thin layer of material that forms the vertical boundary of the space. The
actual thickness of a wall can be revealed only along its edges at door
and window openings.

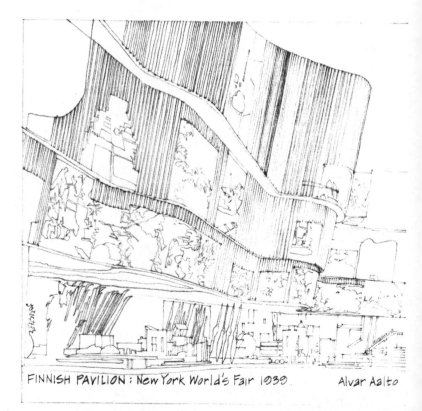

FINNISH PAVILION : New York World's Fair 1939   Alvar Aalto

40

While we have physical contact with floor and wall planes, the ceiling plane is usually more distant from us and is almost a purely visual event in a space. It can correspond to the form or be the under surface of the roof or floor plane above, and express its structure. It can also be a detached lining within a space.

As a detached lining, the ceiling plane can be manipulated to symbolize the vaulted sky plane. It can be raised or lowered to alter the scale of a space, or to define zones of space within a room. It can be formed to control the quality of light or acoustics within a space. It can be treated to have little or no impact on a space, or become the major unifying element for the space.

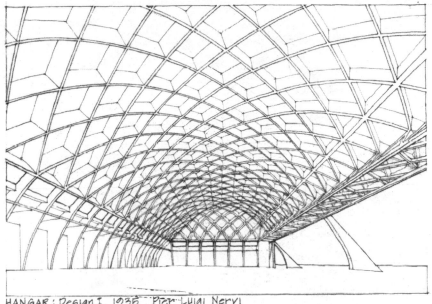

HANGAR: Design I, 1935 Pier Luigi Nervi

BRICK HOUSE: New Canaan, Connecticut, 1949
Philip Johnson

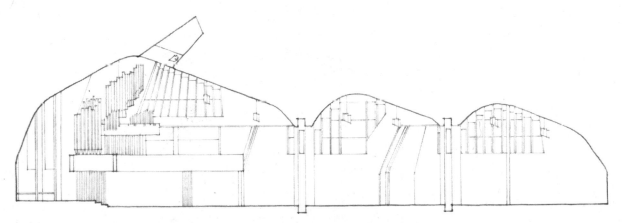

CHURCH IN VUOKSENNISKA: Imatra, Finland. 1956 Alvar Aalto

PLANAR ELEMENTS

DOLMEN of BISCEGLIE: near Bari, Italy

Dolmens are ancient megalithic stone structures that served as burial places for important men. In the type of dolmen illustrated here, the burial chamber consisted of three vertical stone slabs, across which a fourth slab spanned horizontally as a "roof."

After Edward Allen, Stone Shelters, © M.I.T. Press, 1969.

The roof plane is a building's prime sheltering element, protecting its interior from the climatic elements. Its form is determined by the geometry and materials of its structure, and the manner in which it spans across space and bears on its supports. As a visual design element, the roof plane is a building's "hat", and can have a significant impact on the building's form and silhouette.

The roof plane can be hidden from view by a building's walls, or it can merge with the walls to emphasize the building's volume and mass. Or it can be expressed as a horizontal or sloping plane.

The roof plane can hover over a building to shield openings in the walls below from sun or rain, or relate itself closely to the ground plane. It can be elevated above a building in warm climates to allow natural ventilation across and through a building's spaces.

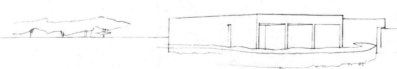

ROBIE HOUSE: Chicago, Illinois 1909   Frank Lloyd Wright

SHODHAN HOUSE: Ahmedabad, India 1956
Le Corbusier

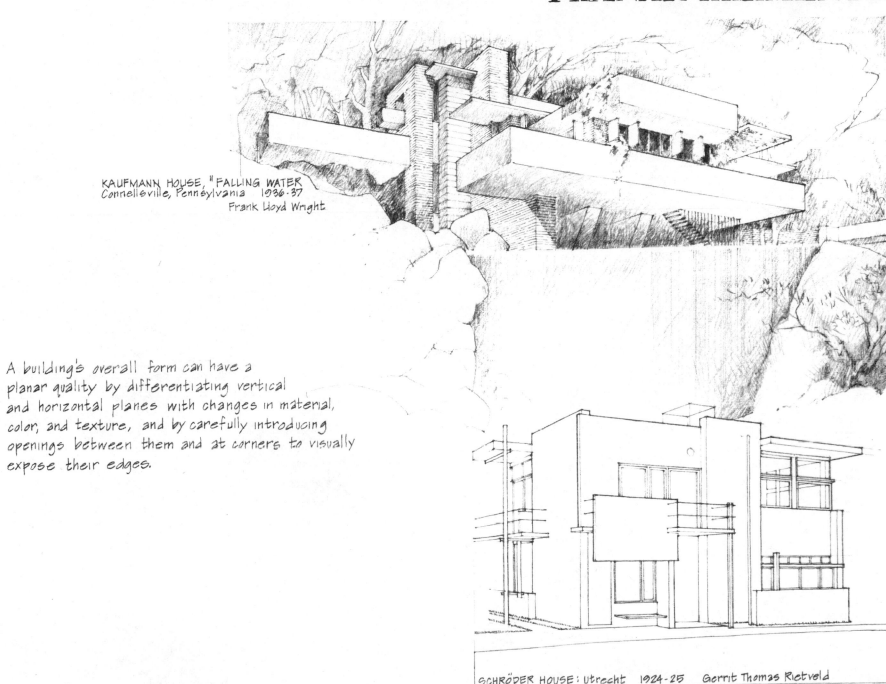

KAUFMANN HOUSE, "FALLING WATER
Connelleville, Pennsylvania 1936-37
Frank Lloyd Wright

A building's overall form can have a
planar quality by differentiating vertical
and horizontal planes with changes in material,
color, and texture, and by carefully introducing
openings between them and at corners to visually
expose their edges.

SCHRÖDER HOUSE: Utrecht 1924-25 Gerrit Thomas Rietveld

VOLUME

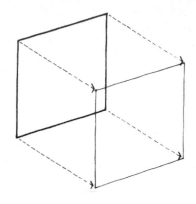

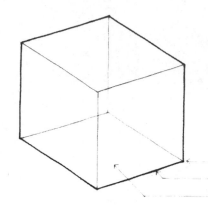

A plane extended (in a direction other than its intrinsic direction) becomes a volume. Conceptually, a volume has three dimensions: length, width, and depth.

All volumes can be analyzed and understood to consist of:

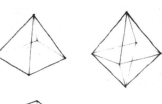

- points (vertices), where several planes come together;
- lines (edges), where two planes meet; and
- planes (surfaces), the limits or boundaries of a volume.

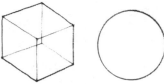

Form is the primary identifying characteristic of a volume. It is determined by the shapes and interrelationships of the planes that describe the boundaries of the volume.

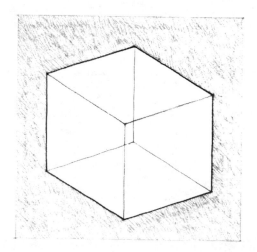

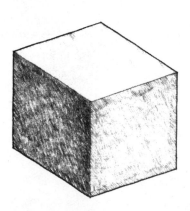

As the three-dimensional element in the vocabulary of architectural design, a volume can be either solid, space displaced by mass, or void, space contained or enclosed by planes.

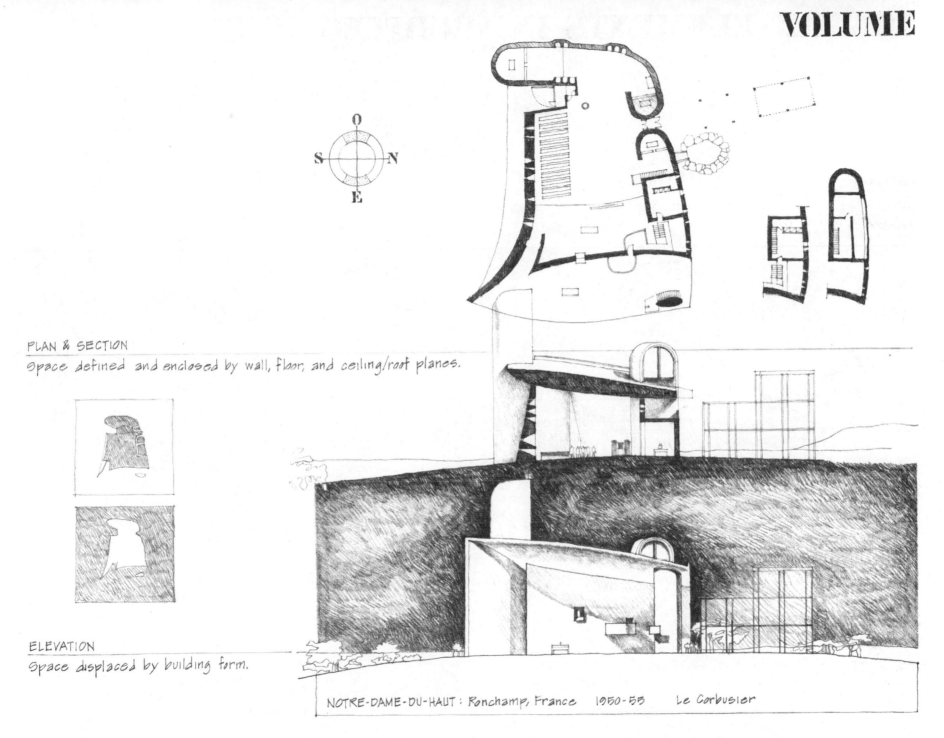

PLAN & SECTION
Space defined and enclosed by wall, floor, and ceiling/roof planes.

ELEVATION
Space displaced by building form.

NOTRE-DAME-DU-HAUT: Ronchamp, France   1950-55   Le Corbusier

VOLUME · ELEMENTS IN ARCHITECTURE

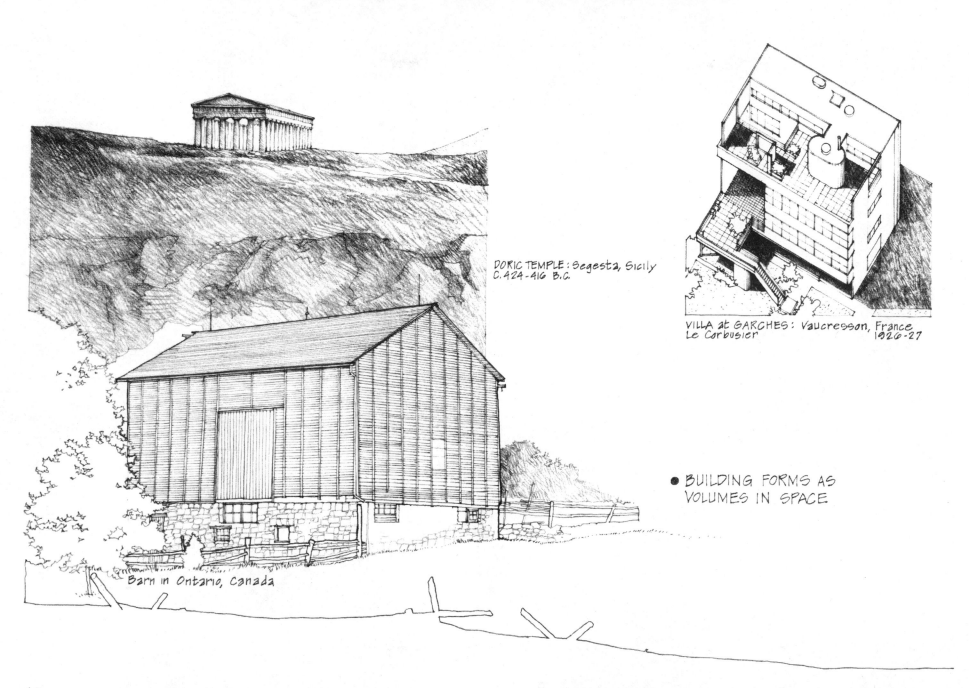

DORIC TEMPLE: Segesta, Sicily
C. 424-416 B.C.

VILLA at GARCHES: Vaucresson, France
Le Corbusier   1926-27

● BUILDING FORMS AS
VOLUMES IN SPACE

Barn in Ontario, Canada

● BUILDING FORMS DEFINING
   VOLUMES OF SPACE

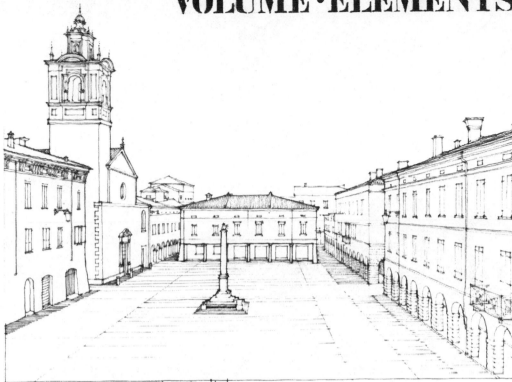

PIAZZA MAGGIORE: Sabbioneta, Italy

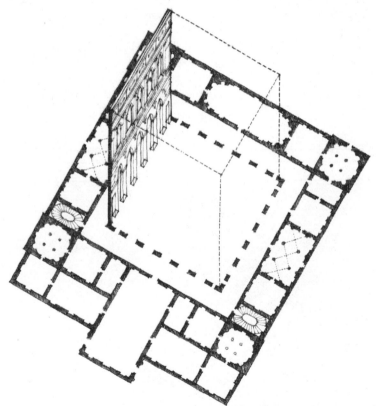

PALAZZO THIENE: Vicenza, Italy
Andrea Palladio   1545

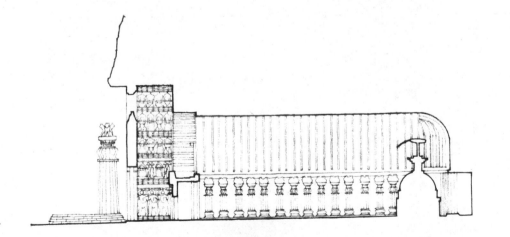

BUDDHIST CHAITYA-HALL at Karli

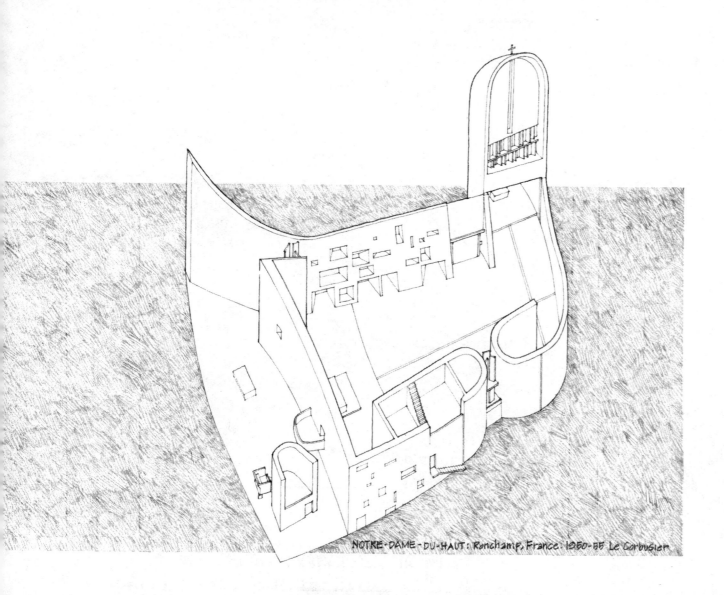

NOTRE-DAME-DU-HAUT: Ronchamp, France: 1950-55 Le Corbusier

2
FORM

VISUAL PROPERTIES OF FORM

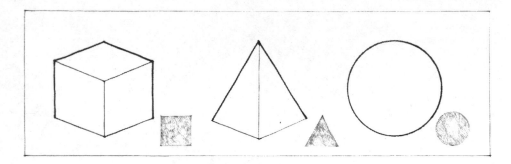

SHAPE : the principal identifying characteristic of form; shape results from the specific configuration of a form's surfaces and edges.

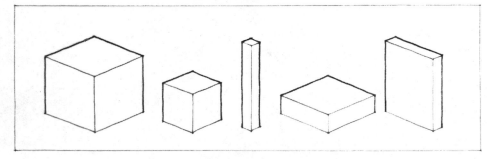

SIZE : the real dimensions of form, its length, width, and depth; while these dimensions determine the proportions of a form, its scale is determined by its size relative to other forms in its context.

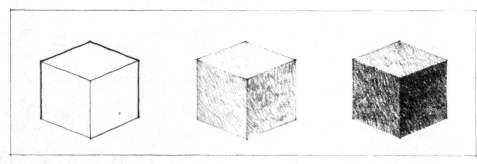

COLOR : the hue, intensity, and tonal value of a form's surface; color is the attribute that most clearly distinguishes a form from its environment. It also affects the visual weight of a form.

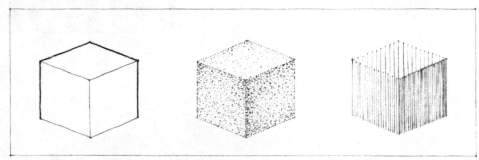

TEXTURE : the surface characteristics of a form; texture affects both the tactile and light-reflective qualities of a form's surfaces.

POSITION   : a form's location relative to its environment or visual field.

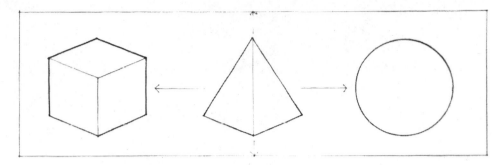

ORIENTATION   : a form's position relative to the ground plane, the compass points, or to the person viewing the form.

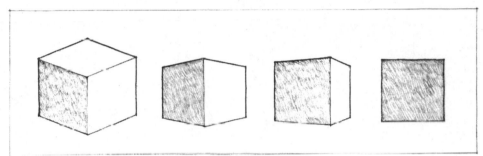

VISUAL INERTIA   : the degree of concentration and stability of a form; the visual inertia of a form depends on its geometry as well as its orientation relative to the ground plane and our line of sight.

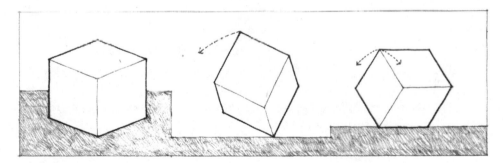

All of these visual properties of form are in reality affected by the conditions under which we view them:

- our perspective or angle of view
- our distance from the form
- lighting conditions
- the visual field surrounding the form.

SHAPE

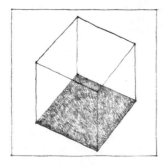

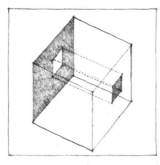

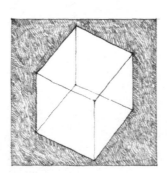

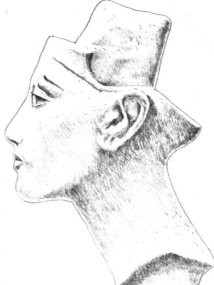

BUST OF QUEEN NEFERTITI

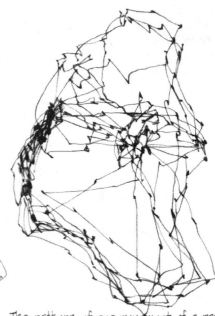

The pattern of eye movement of a person viewing the figure. (From research by Alfred L. Yarbus of the Institute for Problems of Information Transmission in Moscow.)

Shape refers to the edge contour of a plane or the silhouette of a volume. It is the primary means by which we recognize and identify the form of an object. Since it is seen as the line that separates a form from its background, our perception of a form's shape will depend on the degree of visual contrast between the form and its background.

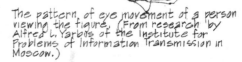

In architecture, we are concerned with the shapes of:

- planes (floors, walls, ceiling) that enclose space
- openings (windows and doors) within a spatial enclosure
- the silhouettes of building forms.

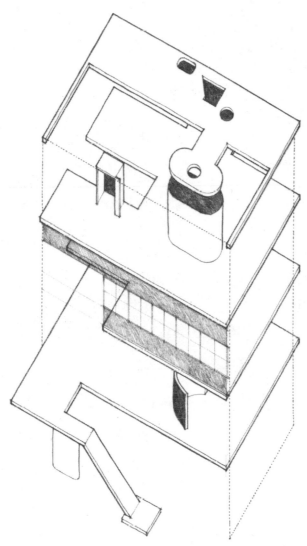

VILLA at GARCHES: Vaucresson, France 1926-27
Le Corbusier

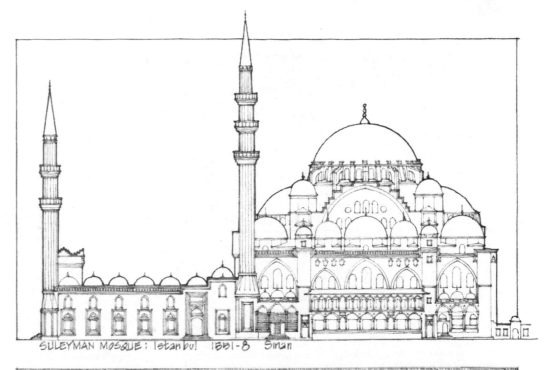

SULEYMAN MOSQUE: Istanbul 1551-8 Sinan

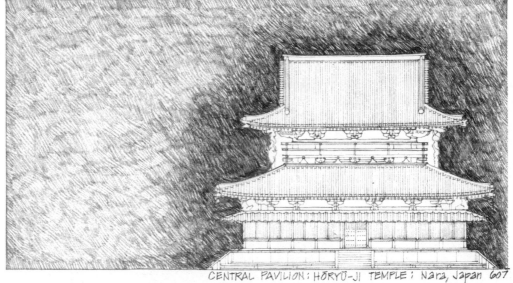

CENTRAL PAVILION: HŌRYŪ-JI TEMPLE: Nara, Japan 607

PRIMARY SHAPES

Given any composition of forms, we will tend to reduce the subject matter in our field of vision to the simplest and most regular shapes. The simpler and more regular a shape is, the easier it is to perceive and understand.

From geometry we know the regular shapes to be the circle, and the infinite series of regular (ie. having equal sides meeting at equal angles) polygons that can be inscribed within it. Of these, the most significant are the primary shapes: the circle, the triangle, and the square.

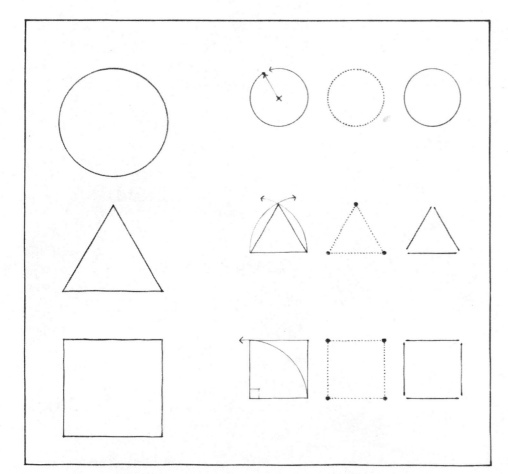

THE CIRCLE : a series of points arranged equally and balanced about a point.

THE TRIANGLE : a plane figure bounded by three sides, and having three angles.

THE SQUARE : a plane figure having four equal sides and four right angles.

The circle is a centralized, introverted figure that is normally stable and self-centering in its environment. Placing a circle in the center of a field will reinforce its natural centrality. Associating it with straight or angular forms, or placing an element along its circumference, can induce in it an apparent rotary motion.

PLAN OF AN IDEAL CITY, SFORZINDA: Filarete 1464

THE ROMAN THEATER ACCORDING TO VITRUVIUS

neutral	stable	unstable	equilibrium
stable	self-centered	dynamic	fixed in place

COMPOSITIONS OF CIRCLES AND CIRCULAR SEGMENTS

THE TRIANGLE

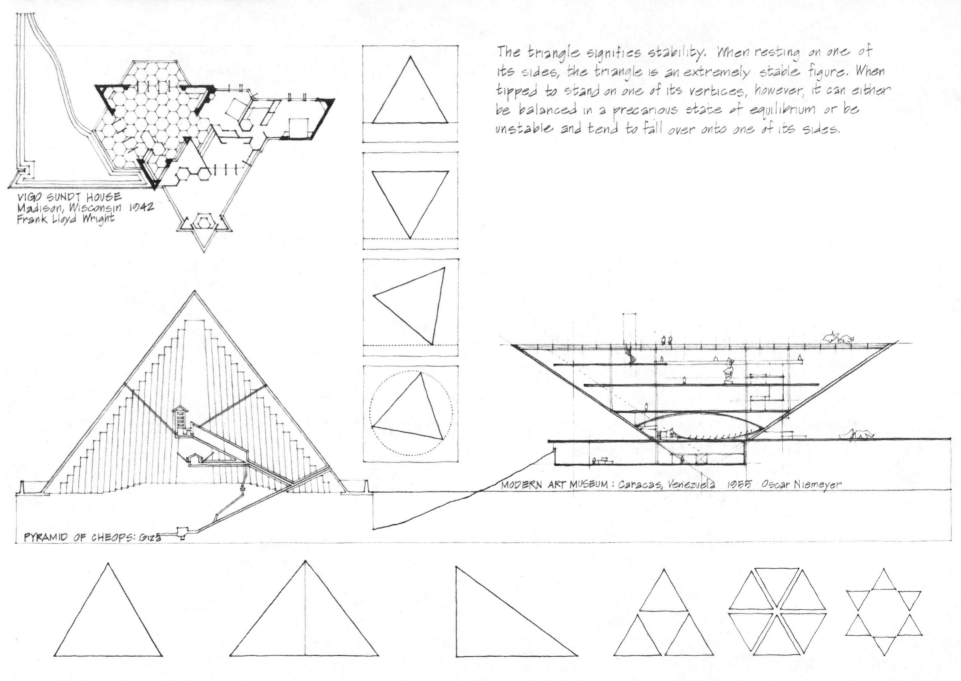

The triangle signifies stability. When resting on one of its sides, the triangle is an extremely stable figure. When tipped to stand on one of its vertices, however, it can either be balanced in a precarious state of equilibrium or be unstable and tend to fall over onto one of its sides.

VIGO SUNDT HOUSE
Madison, Wisconsin 1942
Frank Lloyd Wright

PYRAMID OF CHEOPS: Giza

MODERN ART MUSEUM: Caracas, Venezuela 1955 Oscar Niemeyer

The square represents the pure and the rational. It is a static and neutral figure having no preferred direction. All other rectangles can be considered variations of the square, deviations from the norm by the addition of height or width. Like the triangle, the square is stable when resting on one of its sides, and dynamic when standing on one of its corners

THE AGORA OF EPHESUS, Asia Minor

BATH HOUSE: TRENTON JEWISH COMMUNITY CENTER
Trenton, New Jersey 1954-59   Louis Kahn

COMPOSITIONS RESULTING FROM THE ROTATION AND MODIFICATION OF THE SQUARE

PLATONIC SOLIDS

The primary shapes can be extended or rotated to generate volumes whose forms are distinct, regular, and easily recognizable. These forms are referred to as the platonic solids. Circles generate spheres and cylinders; triangles generate cones and pyramids; squares generate cubes.

"... cubes, cones, spheres, cylinders, or pyramids are the great primary forms that light reveals to advantage; the image of these is distinct and tangible within us and without ambiguity. It is for this reason that these are beautiful forms, the most beautiful forms."

LE CORBUSIER

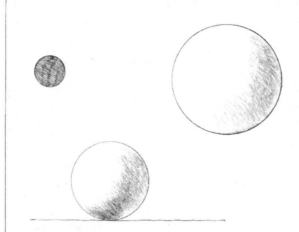

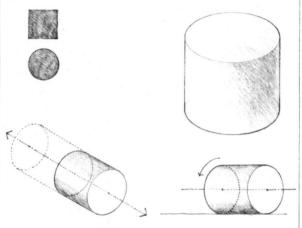

THE SPHERE

The sphere is a centralized and highly concentrated form. It is, like the circle from which it is generated, self-centering and normally stable in its environment. It can be inclined toward a rotary motion when placed on a sloping plane. From any viewpoint, it retains its circular shape.

THE CYLINDER

The cylinder is centralized about the axis defined by the centers of its two circular faces. It can be extended easily along this axis. The cylinder is a stable form if it rests on one of its circular faces; it becomes unstable when its central axis is inclined.

THE CONE

The cone is generated by rotating an equilateral triangle about its vertical axis. Like the cylinder, the cone is a highly stable form when resting on its circular base, and unstable when its vertical axis is tipped or overturned. It can also be stood on its apex in a precarious state of balance.

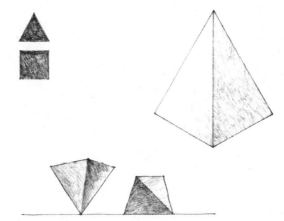

THE PYRAMID

The pyramid has properties similar to those of the cone. Because all of its surfaces are flat planes, however, the pyramid can rest in a stable manner on any of its faces. While the cone is a soft form, the pyramid is relatively hard and angular.

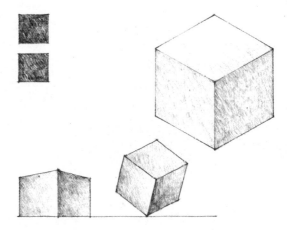

THE CUBE

The cube is a prismatic form that has six square faces of equal size, and twelve edges of equal length. Because of the equality of its dimensions, the cube is a static form that lacks apparent movement or direction. It is a stable form except when it stands on one of its edges or corners. Even though its angular profile is affected by our viewpoint, the cube remains a highly recognizable form.

PLATONIC SOLIDS

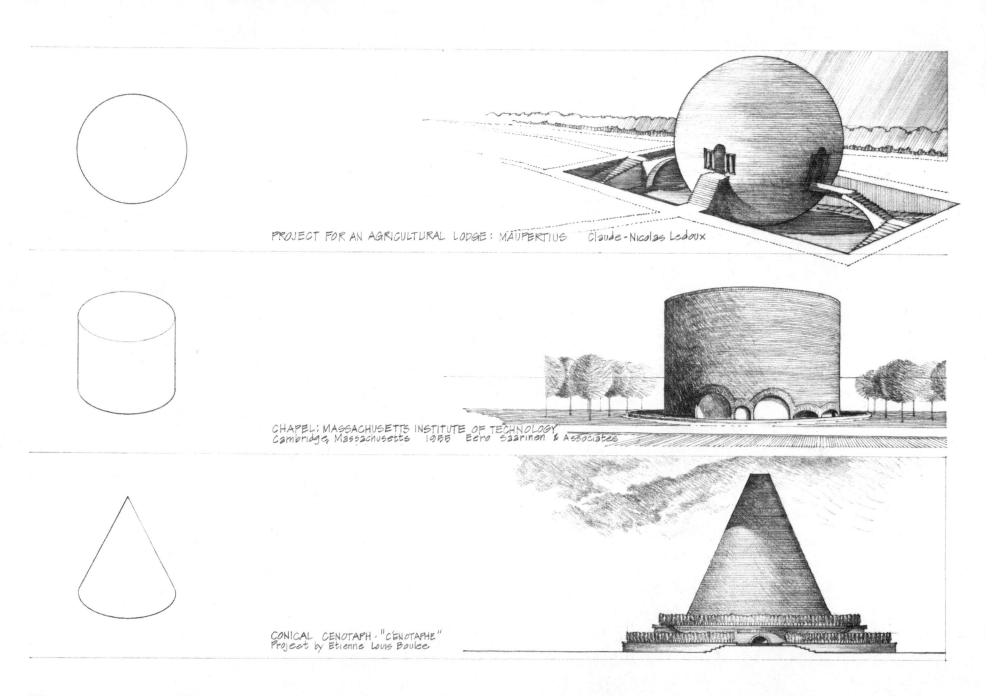

PROJECT FOR AN AGRICULTURAL LODGE: MAUPERTIUS   Claude-Nicolas Ledoux

CHAPEL: MASSACHUSETTS INSTITUTE OF TECHNOLOGY
Cambridge, Massachusetts   1955   Eero Saarinen & Associates

CONICAL CENOTAPH · "CÉNOTAPHE"
Project by Etienne Louis Boulee

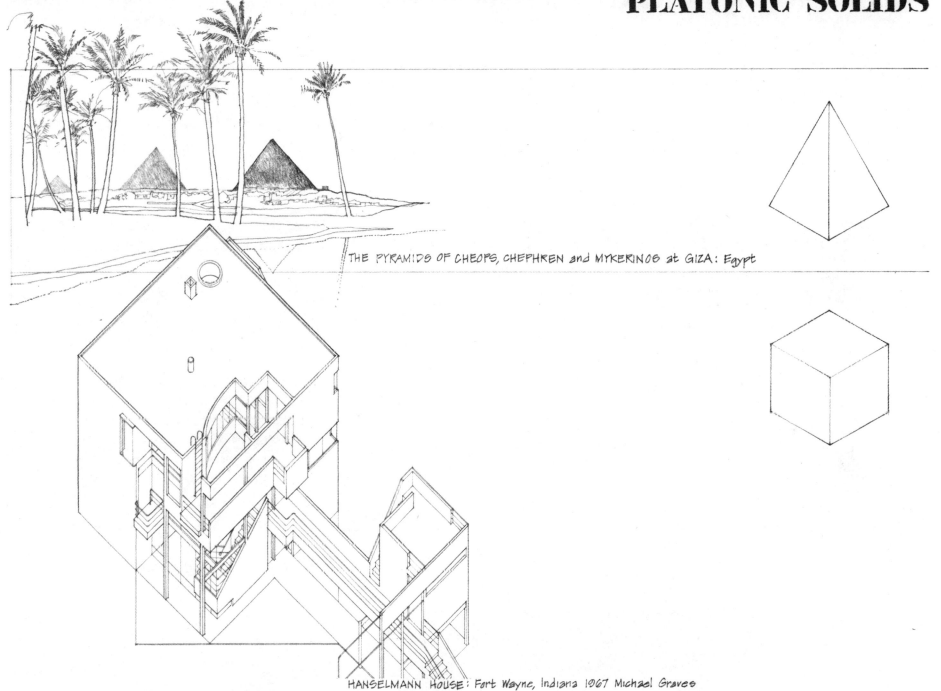

THE PYRAMIDS OF CHEOPS, CHEPHREN and MYKERINOS at GIZA: Egypt

HANSELMANN HOUSE: Fort Wayne, Indiana 1967 Michael Graves

REGULAR & IRREGULAR FORMS

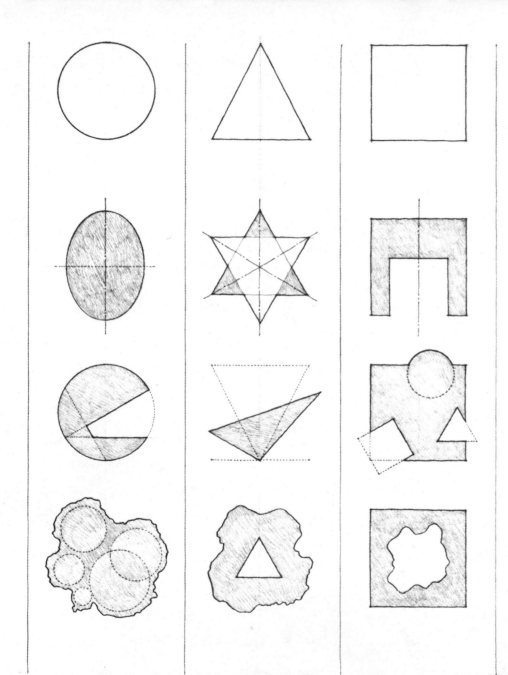

Regular forms refer to those whose parts are related to one another in a consistent and orderly manner. They are generally stable in nature and symmetrical about one or more axes. The platonic solids are prime examples of regular forms.

Forms can retain their regularity even when transformed dimensionally, or by the addition or subtraction of elements.

Irregular forms are those whose parts are dissimilar in nature and related to one another in an inconsistent manner. They are generally asymmetrical and more dynamic than regular forms. They can be regular forms from which irregular elements have been subtracted or an irregular composition of regular forms.

Since we deal with both solids and voids in architecture, regular forms can be contained within irregular forms. Similarly, irregular forms can be enclosed by regular forms.

REGULAR FORMS & IRREGULAR FORMS

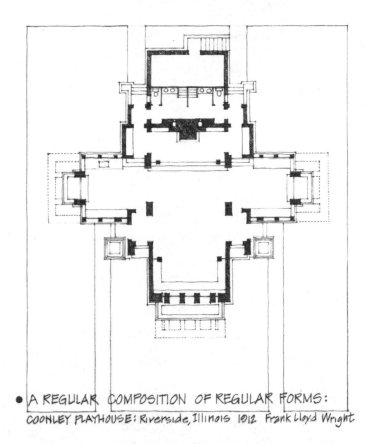

● A REGULAR COMPOSITION OF REGULAR FORMS:
COONLEY PLAYHOUSE: Riverside, Illinois 1912 Frank Lloyd Wright

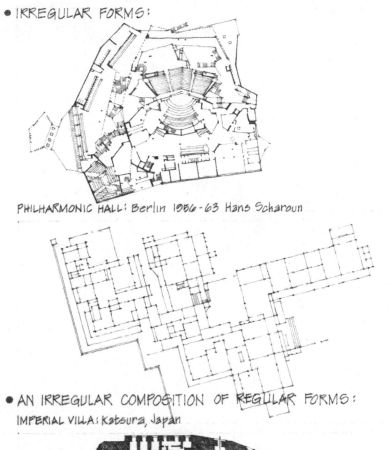

● IRREGULAR FORMS:

PHILHARMONIC HALL: Berlin 1956-63 Hans Scharoun

● AN IRREGULAR COMPOSITION OF REGULAR FORMS:

IMPERIAL VILLA: Katsura, Japan

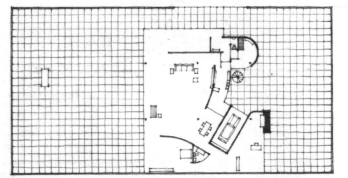

● IRREGULAR FORMS WITHIN A REGULAR FIELD:

COURT HOUSE PROJECT: 1934 Mies van der Rohe

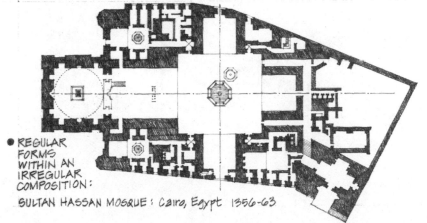

● REGULAR FORMS WITHIN AN IRREGULAR COMPOSITION:

SULTAN HASSAN MOSQUE: Cairo, Egypt 1356-63

THE TRANSFORMATION OF FORM

All other forms can be understood to be transformations of the platonic solids, variations that are generated by the manipulation of their dimensions, or by the subtraction or addition of elements.

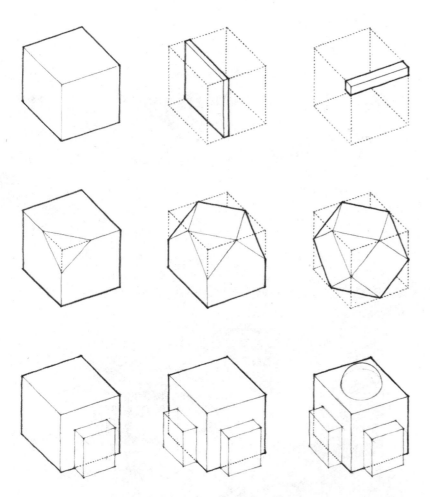

DIMENSIONAL TRANSFORMATIONS:

A form can be transformed by altering one or more of its dimensions and still retain its family identity. A cube, for example, can be transformed into other prismatic forms by altering its height, width, or length. It can be compressed into a planar form, or stretched into a linear one.

SUBTRACTIVE TRANSFORMATIONS:

A form can be transformed by subtracting a portion of its volume. Depending on the extent of the subtractive process, the form can retain its initial identity, or be transformed into a form of another family. For example, a cube can retain its identity as a cube even though a portion of it is removed, or be transformed slowly into a polyhedron approximating a sphere.

ADDITIVE TRANSFORMATIONS:

A form can be transformed by the addition of elements to its volume. The nature of the additive process will determine whether the identity of the initial form is retained or altered.

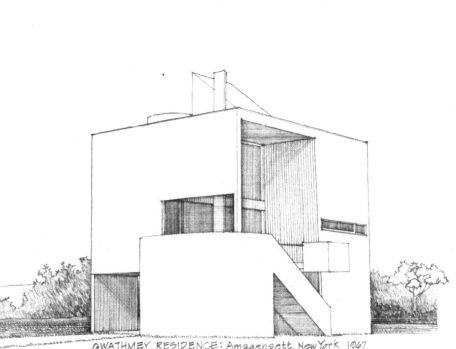

GWATHMEY RESIDENCE: Amagansett, New York 1967
Charles Gwathmey/Gwathmey Siegel

SUBTRACTIVE VOLUMES

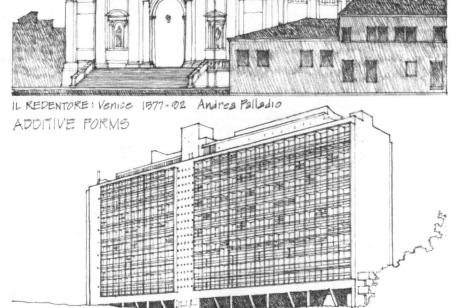

IL REDENTORE: Venice 1577-92 Andrea Palladio
ADDITIVE FORMS

UNITÉ D'HABITATION: Firminy-Vert, France 1965-68 Le Corbusier
CUBE DIMENSIONALLY TRANSFORMED INTO A VERTICAL SLAB

DIMENSIONAL TRANSFORMATION

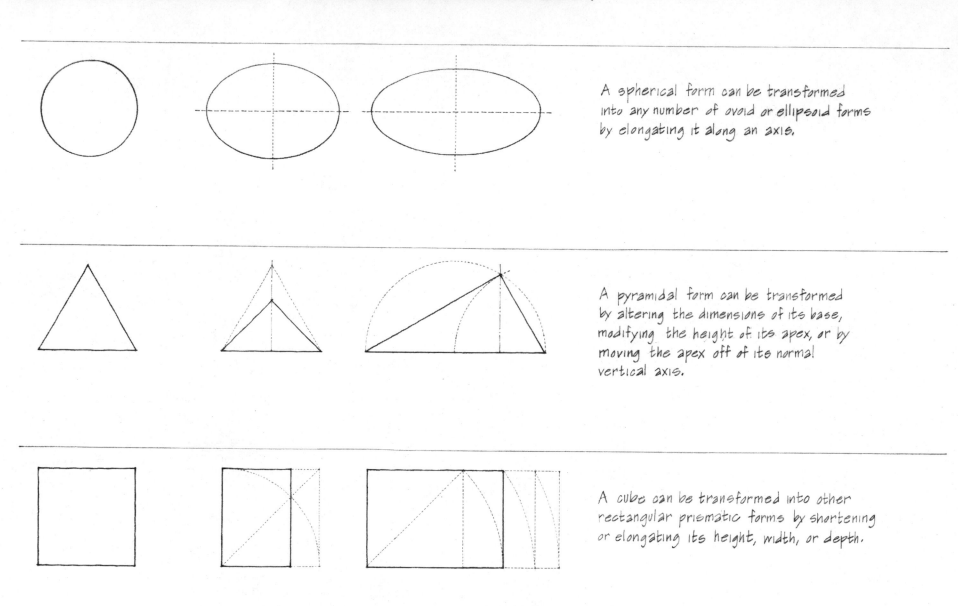

A spherical form can be transformed into any number of ovoid or ellipsoid forms by elongating it along an axis.

A pyramidal form can be transformed by altering the dimensions of its base, modifying the height of its apex, or by moving the apex off of its normal vertical axis.

A cube can be transformed into other rectangular prismatic forms by shortening or elongating its height, width, or depth.

DIMENSIONAL TRANSFORMATION

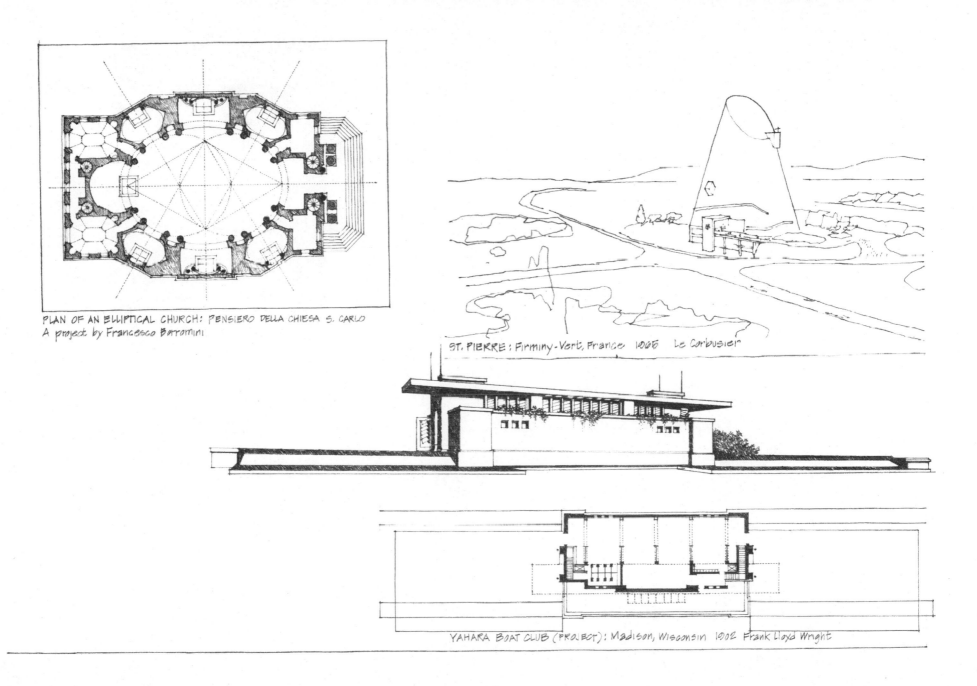

PLAN OF AN ELLIPTICAL CHURCH: PENSIERO DELLA CHIESA S. CARLO
A project by Francesco Borromini

ST. PIERRE: Firminy-Vert, France 1965 Le Corbusier

YAHARA BOAT CLUB (PROJECT): Madison, Wisconsin 1902 Frank Lloyd Wright

SUBTRACTIVE FORMS

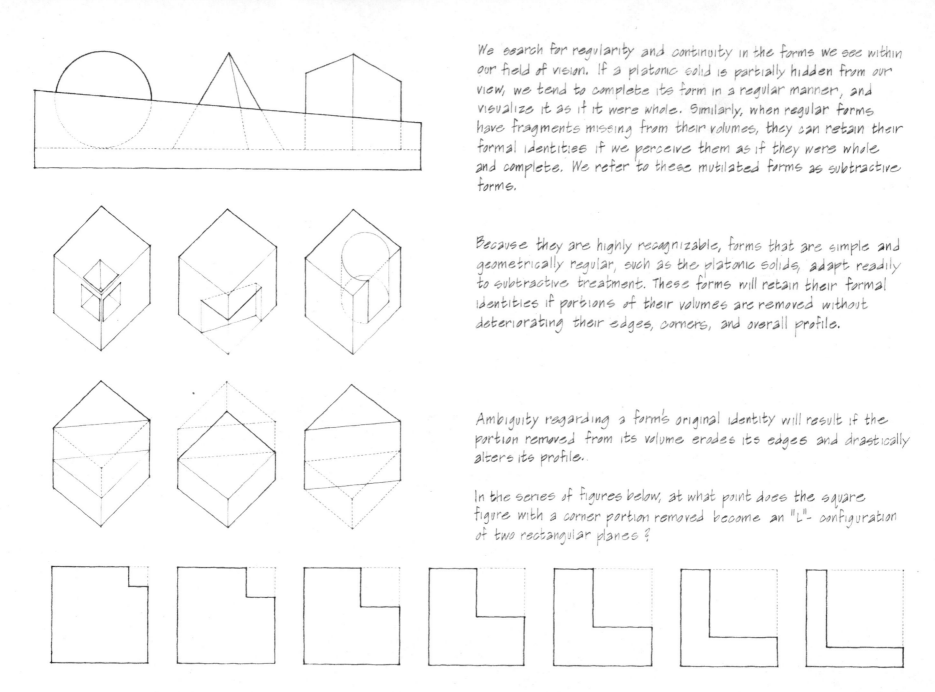

We search for regularity and continuity in the forms we see within our field of vision. If a platonic solid is partially hidden from our view, we tend to complete its form in a regular manner, and visualize it as if it were whole. Similarly, when regular forms have fragments missing from their volumes, they can retain their formal identities if we perceive them as if they were whole and complete. We refer to these mutilated forms as subtractive forms.

Because they are highly recognizable, forms that are simple and geometrically regular, such as the platonic solids, adapt readily to subtractive treatment. These forms will retain their formal identities if portions of their volumes are removed without deteriorating their edges, corners, and overall profile.

Ambiguity regarding a form's original identity will result if the portion removed from its volume erodes its edges and drastically alters its profile.

In the series of figures below, at what point does the square figure with a corner portion removed become an "L"- configuration of two rectangular planes?

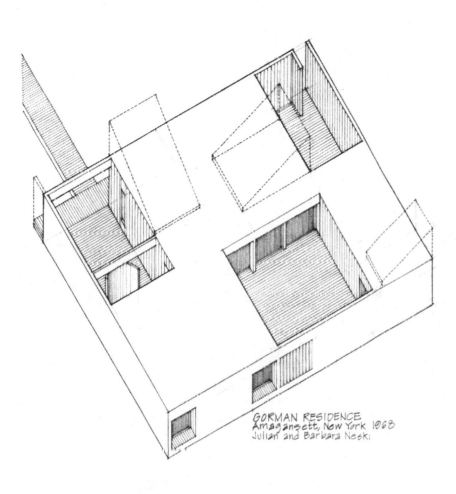

GORMAN RESIDENCE
Amagansett, New York 1968
Julian and Barbara Neski

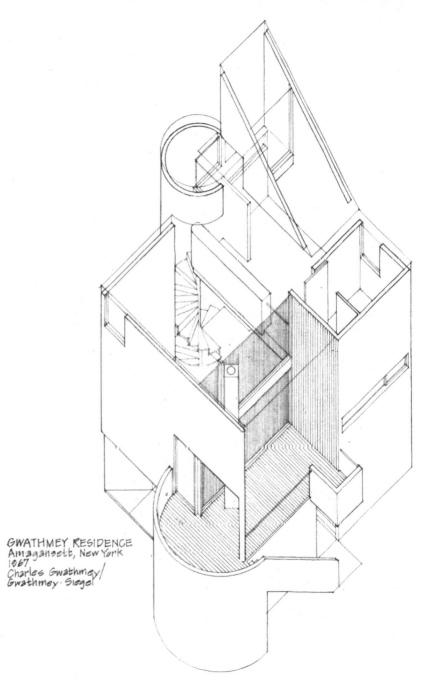

GWATHMEY RESIDENCE
Amagansett, New York
1967
Charles Gwathmey/
Gwathmey·Siegel

Volumes may be subtracted from a form to create recessed entrances, well-defined, private courtyard spaces, or window openings shaded by the vertical and horizontal surfaces of the recess.

SUBTRACTIVE FORMS

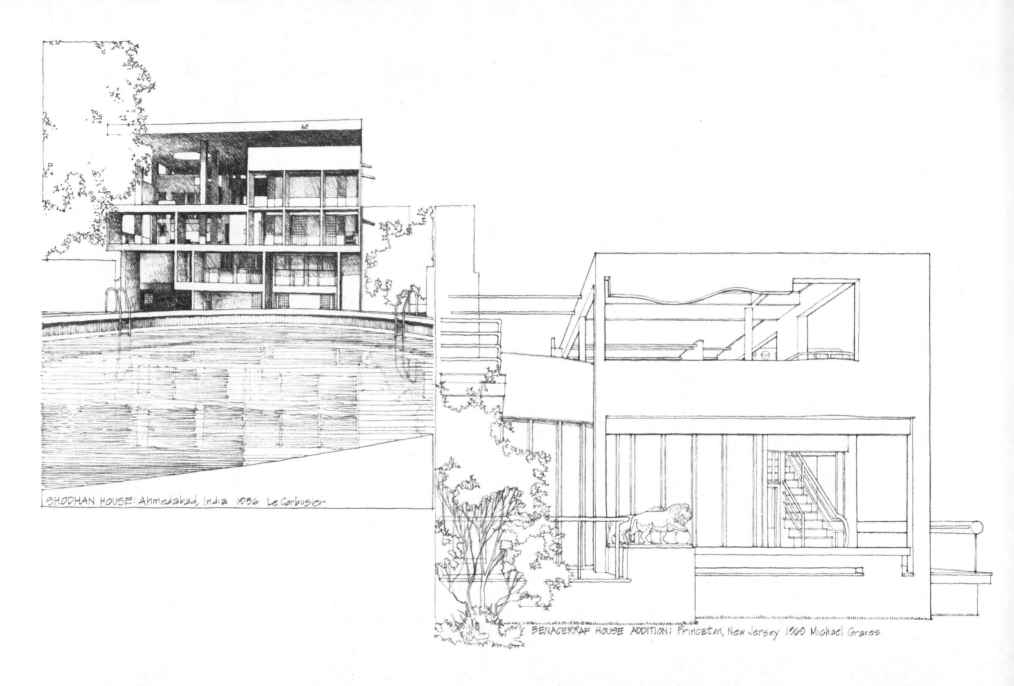

SHODHAN HOUSE: Ahmedabad, India 1956 Le Corbusier

BENACERRAF HOUSE ADDITION: Princeton, New Jersey 1969 Michael Graves

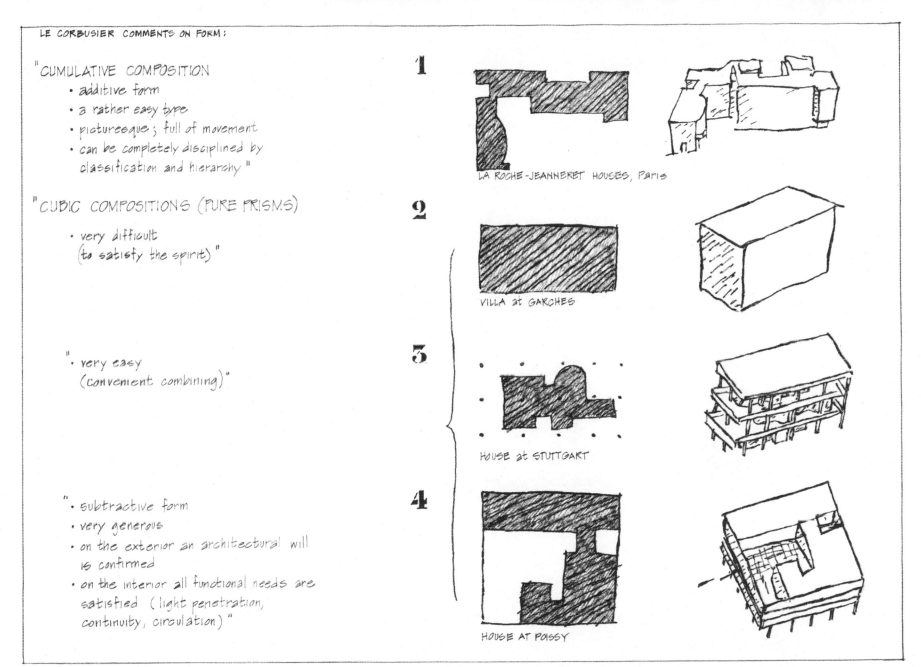

LE CORBUSIER COMMENTS ON FORM:

"CUMULATIVE COMPOSITION
- additive form
- a rather easy type
- picturesque; full of movement
- can be completely disciplined by
  classification and hierarchy "

"CUBIC COMPOSITIONS (PURE PRISMS)

- very difficult
  (to satisfy the spirit) "

" • very easy
  (convenient combining) "

" • subtractive form
- very generous
- on the exterior an architectural will
  is confirmed
- on the interior all functional needs are
  satisfied (light penetration,
  continuity, circulation) "

1 LA ROCHE-JEANNERET HOUSES, Paris

2 VILLA at GARCHES

3 HOUSE at STUTTGART

4 HOUSE AT POISSY

After a sketch, "Four House Forms," by Le Corbusier for the cover of volume two of the "Œuvre complète", published in 1935.

ADDITIVE FORMS

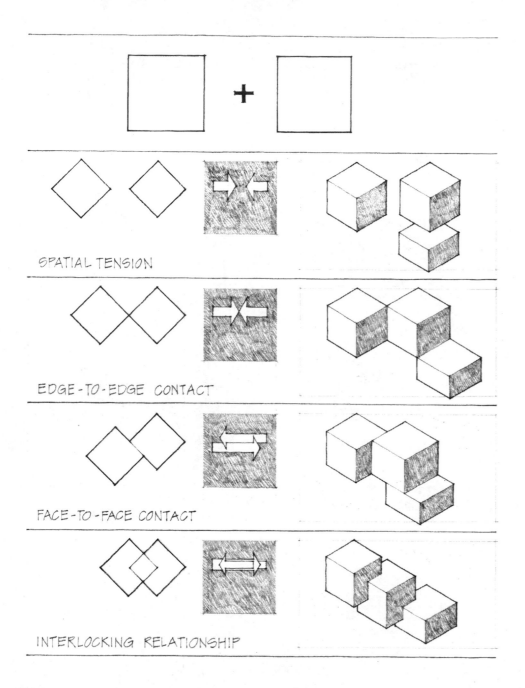

SPATIAL TENSION

EDGE-TO-EDGE CONTACT

FACE-TO-FACE CONTACT

INTERLOCKING RELATIONSHIP

While a subtractive form results from the removal of a portion of its original volume, an additive form is produced by the addition of another form to its volume.

The basic possibilities for two forms to group together are:

• by spatial tension; this type of relationship requires that the two forms be relatively close to each other, or share a common visual trait such as shape, material, or color.

• by edge-to-edge contact; in this type of relationship, two forms share a common edge, and can pivot about that edge.

• by face-to-face contact; this type of relationship requires the two forms to have flat, planar surfaces that are parallel to each other.

• by interlocking volumes; in this type of relationship, two forms interpenetrate each other's space. These forms need not share any visual traits.

Additive forms, resulting from the accretion of elements to one another, can be characterized generally by their ability to grow and merge with other forms. For us to perceive additive groupings as unified compositions of form, as figures in our visual field, the component forms must be related to one another in a coherent and close-knit manner.

The diagrams are intended to categorize additive forms according to the nature of the relationships that exist among the component forms as well as their overall configurations. This discussion of formal organizations should be compared with a similar discussion of spatial organizations in Chapter 4.

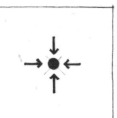

CENTRALIZED FORMS
consist of a number of secondary forms clustered about dominant, central parent-forms.

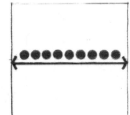

LINEAR FORMS
consist of forms arranged sequentially in a row.

RADIAL FORMS
are compositions of linear forms that extend outward from central forms in a radial manner.

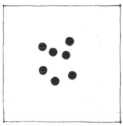

CLUSTERED FORMS
consist of forms that are grouped together by proximity or the sharing of a common visual trait.

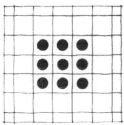

GRID-FORMS
are modular forms whose relationships are regulated by three-dimensional grids.

CENTRALIZED FORMS

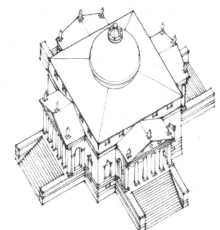

THE ROTONDA: VILLA CAPRA, Vicenza, Italy 1552-67 Andrea Palladio

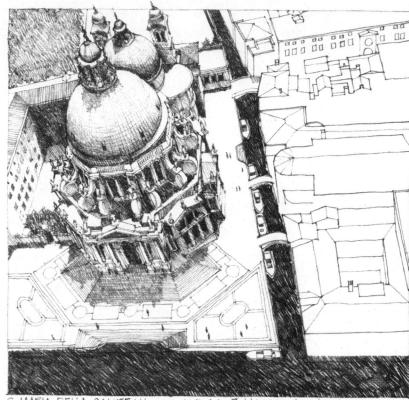

S. MARIA DELLA SALUTE: Venice 1631-82 Baldassare Longhena

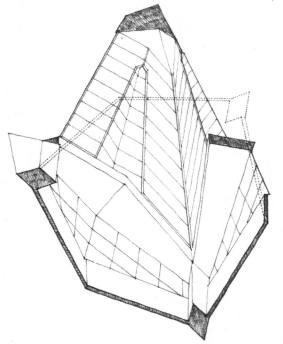

BETH SHOLOM SYNAGOGUE: Elkins Park, Pennsylvania 1959 Frank Lloyd Wright

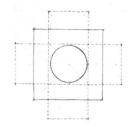 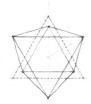 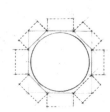

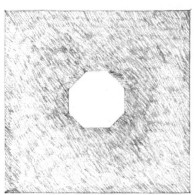

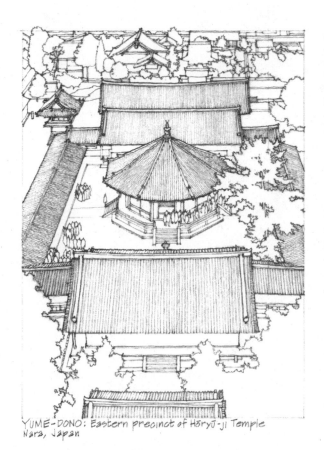

YUME-DONO: Eastern precinct of Hōryū-ji Temple
Nara, Japan

TEMPIETTO, S. PIETRO in Montorio, Rome   1502   Donato Bramante

Centralized forms require the visual dominance of a geometrically regular, centrally located form, such as the sphere, cylinder, or polyhedron. Because of their centrality, these forms share the self-centering properties of the point and circle. They are ideal as freestanding structures, isolated within their context, dominating a point in space, or occupying the center of a defined field. They can embody sacred or honorific places, or commemorate significant persons or events.

LINEAR FORMS

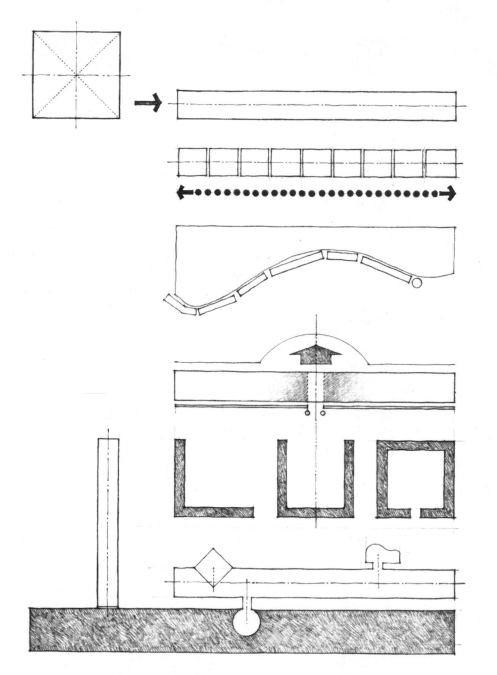

A linear form can result from a proportional change in a form's dimensions, or the arrangement of a series of forms along a line. In the latter case, the series of forms may be repetitive, or they may be dissimilar in nature and organized by a separate and distinct element such as a wall or path.

A linear form can be segmented or curvilinear to respond to conditions of its site such as topography, view, or vegetation.

A linear form can be used to front or define an edge of an exterior space, or define a plane of entry to the spaces behind it.

A linear form can be manipulated to enclose space.

A linear form can be oriented vertically as a tower element to fix a point in space.

A linear form can act as an organizing element to which a variety of forms can be attached.

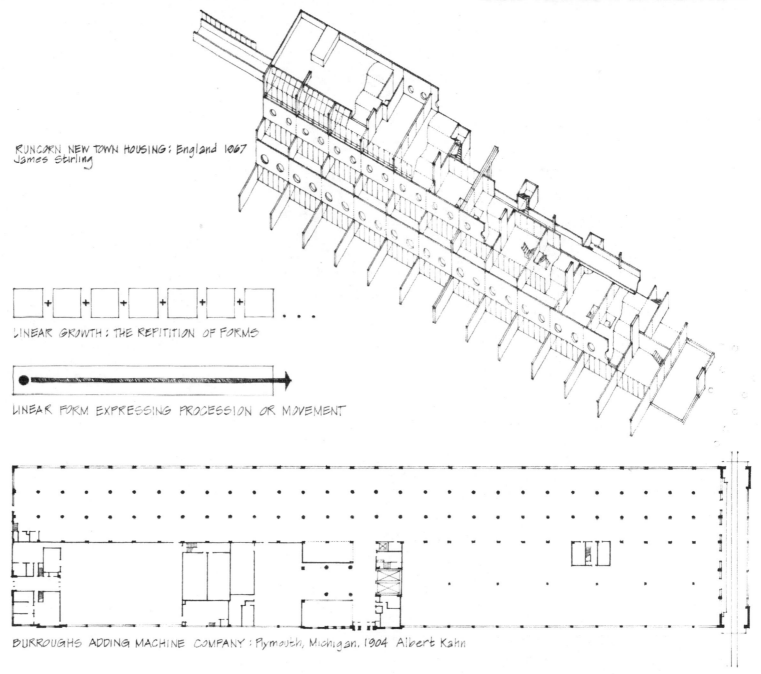

RUNCORN NEW TOWN HOUSING: England 1067
James Stirling

LINEAR GROWTH: THE REPITITION OF FORMS

LINEAR FORM EXPRESSING PROCESSION OR MOVEMENT

BURROUGHS ADDING MACHINE COMPANY: Plymouth, Michigan. 1904 Albert Kahn

LINEAR FORMS

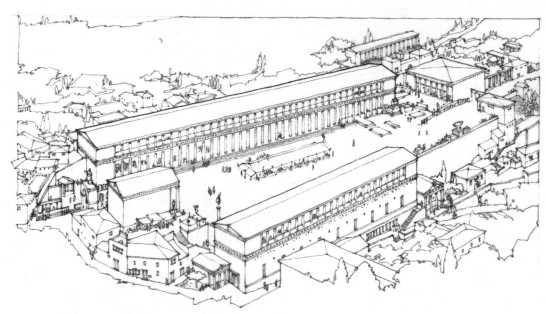

AGORA of ASSOS: Asia Minor   2nd Century, B.C.

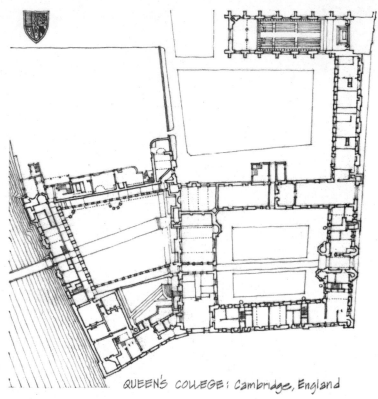

QUEEN'S COLLEGE: Cambridge, England

LINEAR FORMS FRONTING ON & DEFINING
EXTERIOR SPACE

18th centuries fronting a tree-lined canal in The Kampen, Holland.

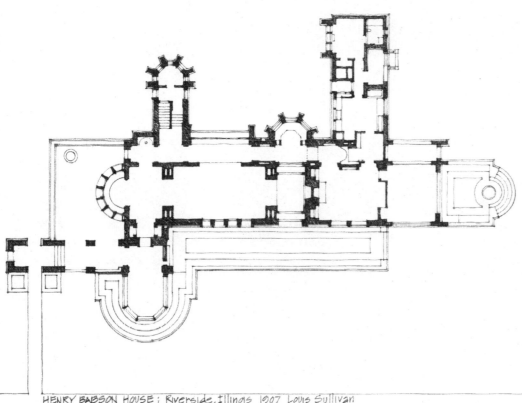

HENRY BABSON HOUSE: Riverside, Illinois 1907 Louis Sullivan

LINEAR ORGANIZATIONS OF SPACE

THE MILE-HIGH ILLINOIS: Skyscraper Project, Chicago, Illinois
Frank Lloyd Wright   1956

RADIAL FORMS

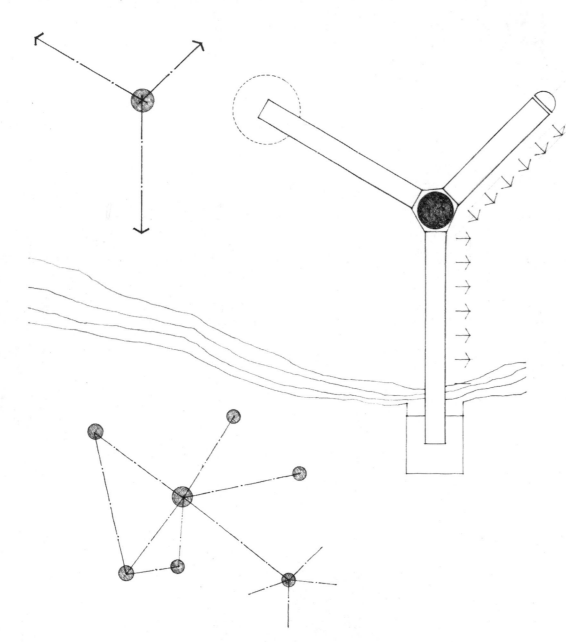

A radial form consists of linear forms that extend outward from a centrally located core element in a radiating manner. It combines the aspects of centrality and linearity into a single composition.

The core is either the symbolic or functional center of the organization. Its central position can be articulated with a visually dominant form, or it can merge with and become subservient to the radiating arms.

The radiating arms, having properties similar to those of linear forms, give a radial form its extroverted nature. They can reach out and relate or attach themselves to specific features of their site. They can expose their long surfaces to desirable conditions of sun, wind, view, or space.

Radial forms can grow into a network where several centers are linked by linear forms.

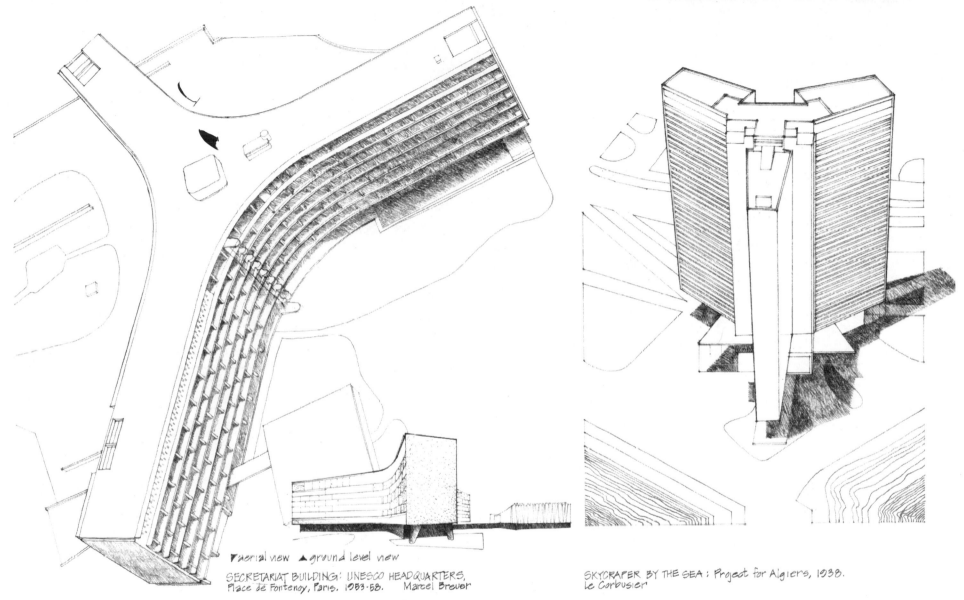

▼aerial view ▲ground level view
SECRETARIAT BUILDING: UNESCO HEADQUARTERS,
Place de Fontenoy, Paris. 1953-58.   Marcel Breuer

SKYSCRAPER BY THE SEA: Project for Algiers, 1938.
Le Corbusier

The organization of a radial form can best be seen and understood from an aerial view. When it is viewed from ground level, its central core element may not be clearly visible, and the radiating pattern of its linear arms may be obscured or distorted through perspective.

CLUSTERED FORMS

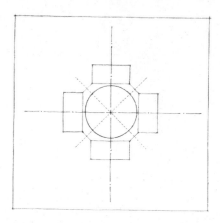

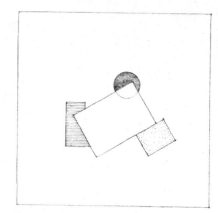

While a centralized organization has a strong geometrical basis for the ordering of its forms, a clustered organization groups its forms according to functional requirements of size, shape or proximity. Lacking the introverted nature and geometrical regularity of centralized forms, a clustered organization is flexible enough to incorporate forms of various shapes, sizes, and orientations into its structure.

Considering the flexibility of clustered organizations, their forms may be organized in the following ways:

- They can be attached as appendages to a larger parent form or space.

- They can be related by proximity alone to articulate and express their volumes as individual entities.

- They can interlock their volumes and merge into a single form that has a variety of faces.

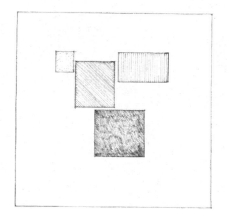

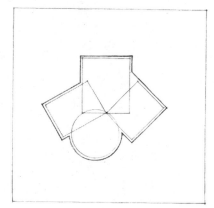

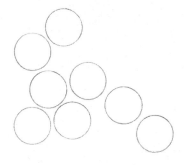

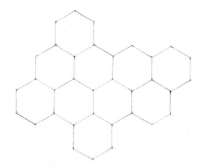

A clustered organization can also consist of forms that are generally equivalent in size, shape, and function. These forms are visually ordered into a coherent, non-hierarchical organization not only by their close proximity to one another, but also by the similarity of their visual properties.

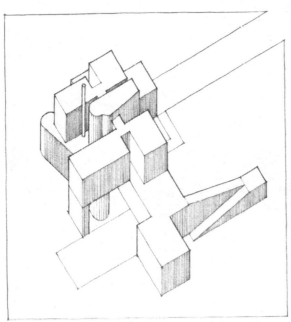

HOUSE STUDY: 1956 James Stirling & James Gowan
CLUSTERED FORMS ARTICULATED

G.N. BLACK HOUSE, "KRAGSYDE": Manchester-by-the-Sea, Massachusetts 1882-83
Peabody & Stearns
INTERLOCKING FORMS

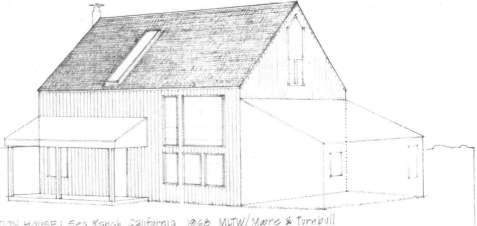

VACATION HOUSE: Sea Ranch, California 1968 MLTW/Moore & Turnbull
ADDITIVE ELEMENTS ATTACHED TO A PARENT FORM.

CLUSTERED FORMS

TRULLI VILLAGE: Alberobello, Italy

TAOS PUEBLO

Numerous examples of repetitive, clustered housing forms can be found in the vernacular architecture of various cultures. Even though each culture produced a unique type in response to differing technical, climatic, and socio-cultural factors, these clustered housing organizations generally maintained the individuality of each unit and a moderate degree of diversity within the context of a uniquely ordered whole.

HABITAT ISRAEL: Jerusalem 1969 Moshie Safdie

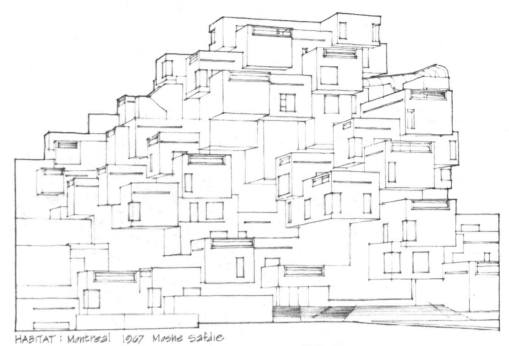

HABITAT: Montreal 1967 Moshe Safdie

Vernacular examples of clustered forms can be readily
transformed into modular, geometrically-ordered compositions
that are similar in nature to grid-organizations of forms.

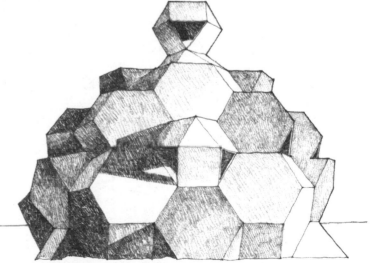

SYNAGOGUE IN THE NEGEV DESERT: Israel - Zvi Hecker

GRID FORMS

CONCEPTUAL DIAGRAM: GUNMA PREFECTURAL MUSEUM OF FINE ARTS
1974
Arata Isozaki

A grid can be defined as two or more intersecting sets of regularly spaced parallel lines. It generates a geometric pattern of regularly spaced points (where the grid lines intersect) and regularly shaped fields (defined by the grid lines).

The most common grid is based on the geometry of the square. Because of the equality of its dimensions and its bi-lateral symmetry, a square grid is essentially neutral, non-hierarchical, and non-directional. It can be used to break the scale of a surface down into measurable units and give it an even texture. It can be used to wrap several surfaces of a form and unify them with its repetitive and pervasive geometry.

The square grid, when projected into the third dimension, generates a spatial network of reference points and lines. Within this modular framework, any number of forms and spaces can be visually organized.

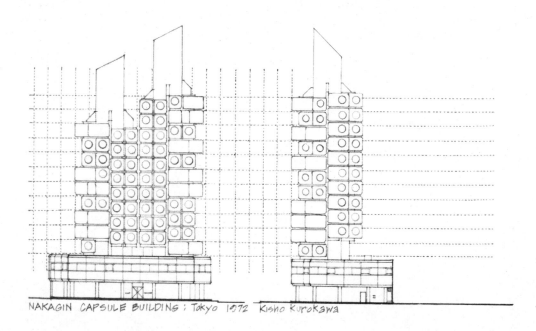

NAKAGIN CAPSULE BUILDING : Tokyo 1972 Kisho Kurokawa

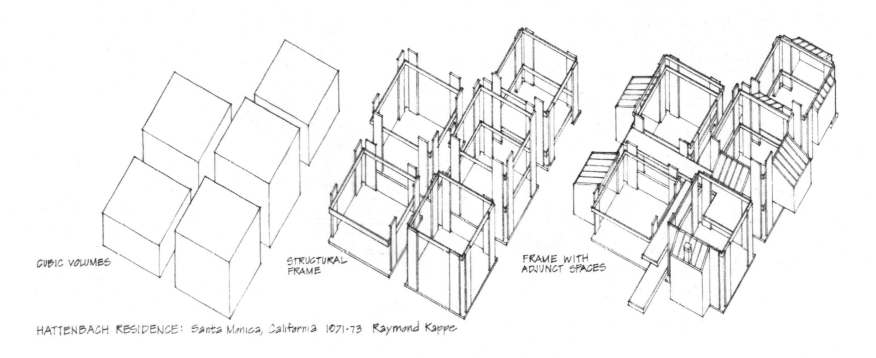

CUBIC VOLUMES   STRUCTURAL FRAME   FRAME WITH ADJUNCT SPACES

HATTENBACH RESIDENCE: Santa Monica, California 1071-73 Raymond Kappe

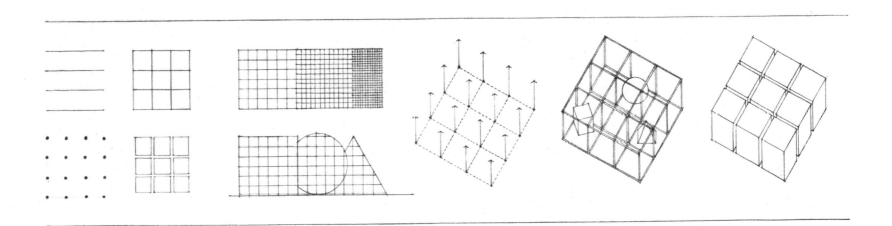

FORMAL COLLISIONS OF GEOMETRY

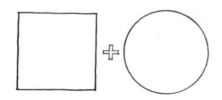

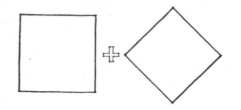

When two forms differing in geometry or orientation collide and interpenetrate each other's boundaries, each will vie for visual supremacy and dominance. In these situations, the following forms can evolve:

CIRCLE & SQUARE   ROTATED GRID

- The two forms can subvert their individual identities and merge to create a new composite form.

- One of the 2 forms can receive the other totally within its volume.

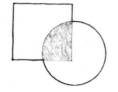
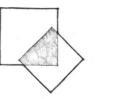

- The two forms can retain their individual identities and share the interlocking portions of their volumes.

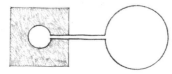
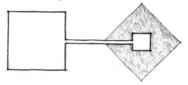

- The two forms can separate and be linked by a third element that recalls the geometry of one of the original forms.

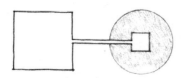
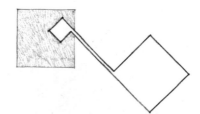

Forms differing in geometry or orientation may be incorporated into a single organization for any of the following reasons:

- To accommodate or accentuate the different requirements of interior space and exterior form; to express the functional or symbolic importance of a form or space within its context; to generate a composite form that incorporates the contrasting geometries into its centralized organization.

- To inflect a space toward a specific feature of the building site; to carve a well-defined volume of space from a building form; to express and articulate the various constructional/mechanical systems that exist within a building form.

- To reinforce a local condition of symmetry in a building form; to respond to contrasting geometries of a site's topography, vegetation, edges, or adjacent structures; to acknowledge an already existing path of movement through a building's site.

CIRCLES & SQUARES

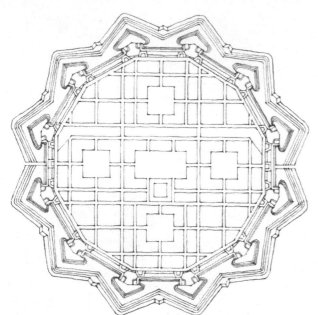

PLAN FOR AN IDEAL CITY by Vincenzo Scamozzi, 1615

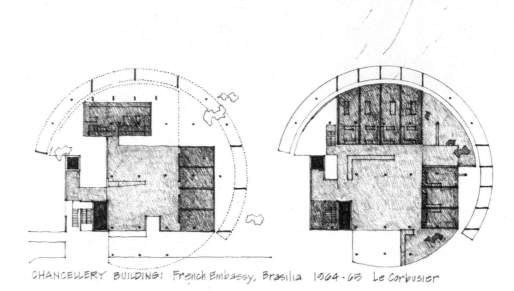

CHANCELLERY BUILDING: French Embassy, Brasilia 1064-65 Le Corbusier

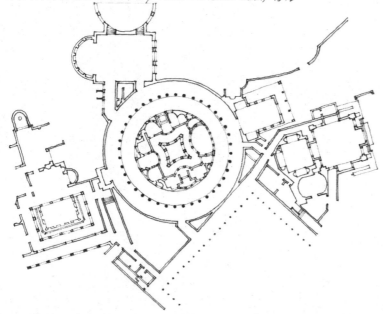

"TEATRO MARITTIMO" (THE ISLAND VILLA), HADRIAN'S VILLA: Tivoli AD 118-25

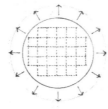

A circular form can be freestanding in its context to express its "ideal" shape and still incorporate a more functional, rectalinear geometry within its boundaries.

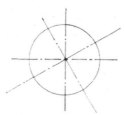

The centrality of a circular form enables it to act as a hub and unify forms of contrasting geometry or orientation about itself.

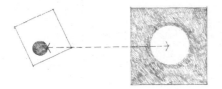

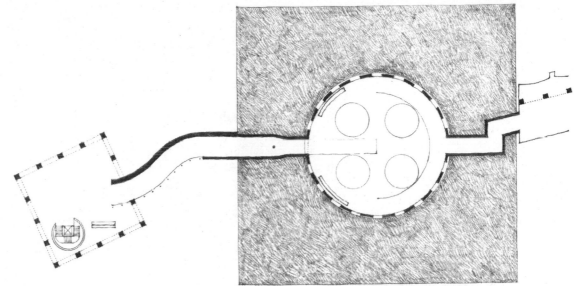

MUSEUM FOR NORTH RHINE - WESTPHALIA ; Dusseldorf, West Germany 1975
James Stirling & Michael Wilford

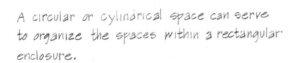

A circular or cylindrical space can serve to organize the spaces within a rectangular enclosure.

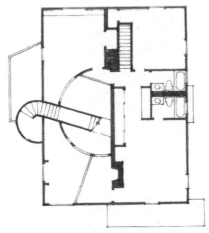

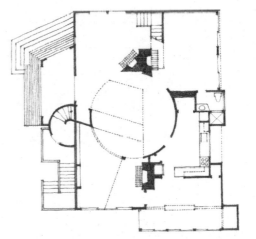

MURRAY HOUSE : Cambridge, Massachusetts 1960   MLTW/ Moore-Turnbull

ROTATED GRIDS

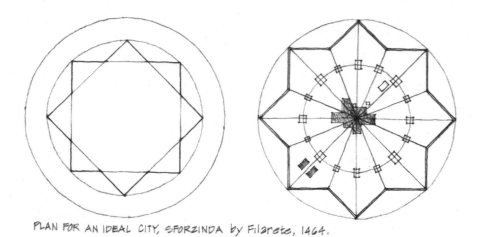

PLAN FOR AN IDEAL CITY, SFORZINDA by Filarete, 1464.

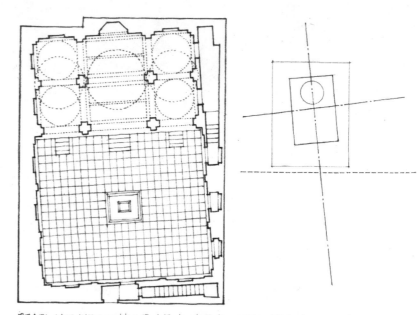

PEARL MOSQUE: in the Red Fort at Delhi 1658-1707 Aurangzib

The interior space of this mosque is oriented exactly with the cardinal points while its exterior conforms with the existing layout of the fort.

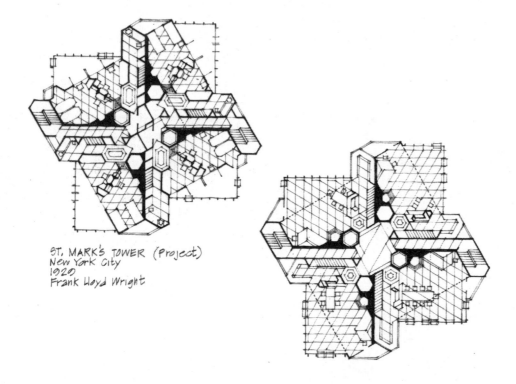

ST. MARK'S TOWER (Project)
New York City
1920
Frank Lloyd Wright

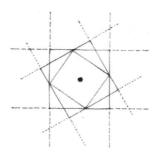

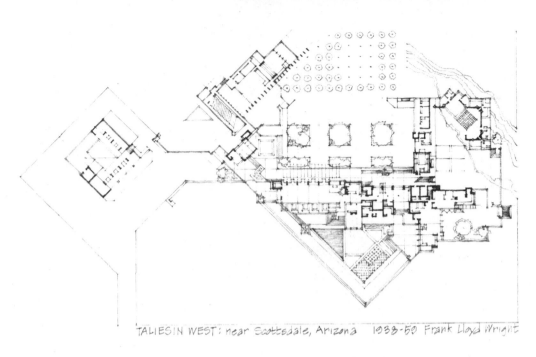

TALIESIN WEST: near Scottsdale, Arizona   1938-50 Frank Lloyd Wright

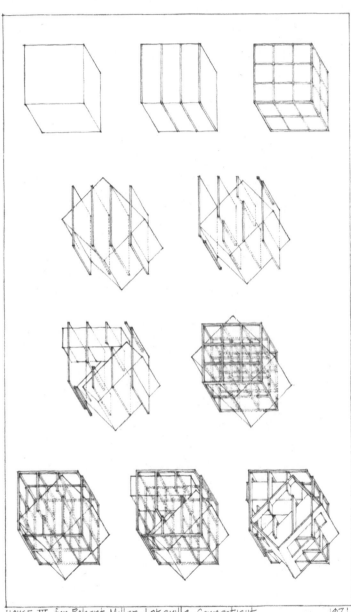

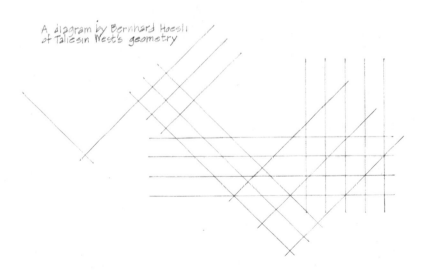

A diagram by Bernhard Hoesli
of Taliesin West's geometry

HOUSE III for Robert Miller, Lakeville Connecticut   1971
Design Development Drawings   Peter Eisenman

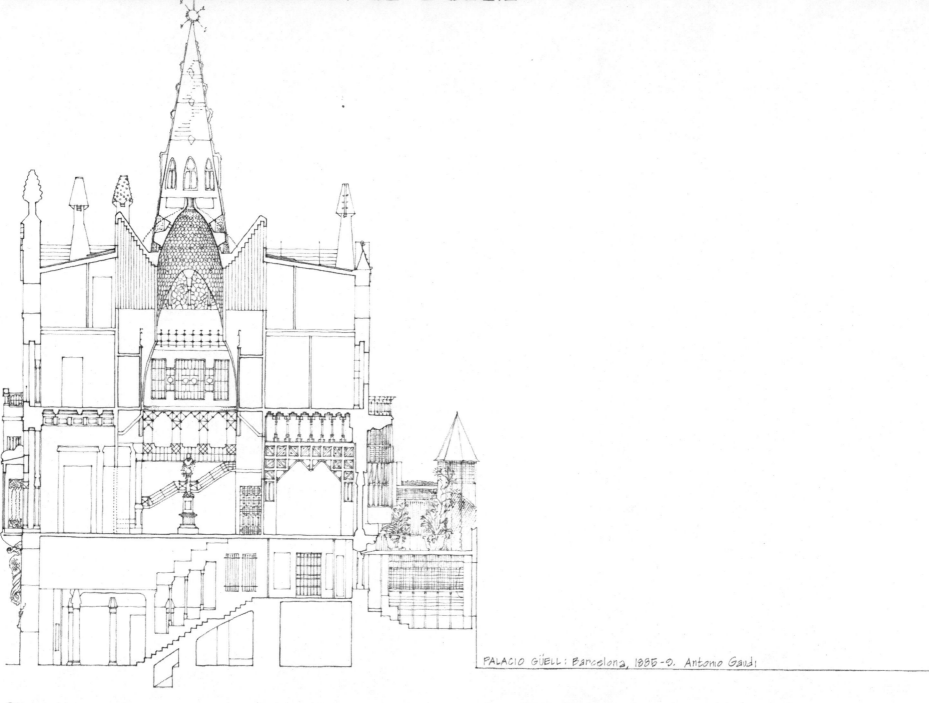

PALACIO GÜELL: Barcelona, 1885-9. Antonio Gaudi

Articulation refers to the manner in which the surfaces of a form come together to define its shape and volume. An articulated form clearly reveals the edges of its surfaces and the corners at which they meet. Its surfaces appear as planes with distinct shapes; their overall configuration is legible and easily perceived. Similarly, an articulated group of forms accentuates the joints between its constituent forms to visually express their individuality.

A form and its surface planes can be articulated by:
- differentiating adjacent surfaces with a change in material, color, texture, or pattern;
- developing the corner as a distinct linear element independent of the surfaces;
- removing the corner to physically separate adjacent planes;
- lighting the form to create sharp distinctions of light and dark at its corners.

In contrast to the above, the corners of a form can be rounded and smoothed over to emphasize the continuity of its surfaces. Or a material, color, texture, or pattern can be carried across a corner and the adjoining surfaces to de-emphasize the individuality of the surface planes and emphasize instead the volume of a form.

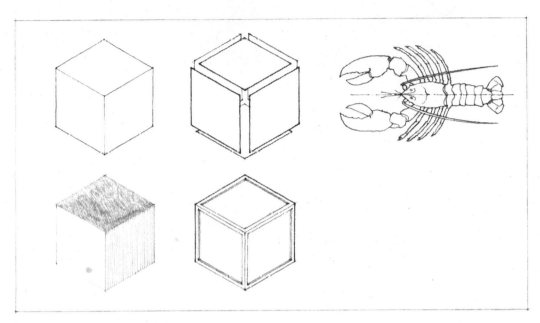

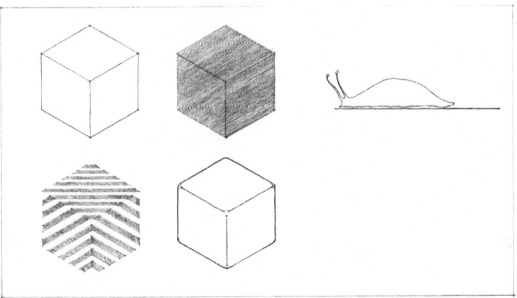

EDGES & CORNERS

Since the articulation of a form depends to a great degree on how its surfaces are defined and meet at corners, how corner conditions are resolved is important to a form's definition and clarity.

While a corner can be articulated by simply contrasting the surfaces of the adjoining planes, or obscured by layering it with an optical pattern, our perception of its existence is also affected by the laws of perspective and the quality of light that illuminates the form.

For a corner to be formally active in our visual field, there must be more than a slight deviation in the geometry of the adjoining planes. We search for regularity and continuity in the forms within our visual field, and we will tend, therefore, to regularize or smooth out slight irregularities in the forms we see. For example, a wall plane that is bent only slightly will appear to be a single, flat plane, perhaps with a surface imperfection. A corner would not be perceived.

At what point do these formal deviations become an acute angle? ... a right angle? ...

a segmented line? ... a straight line? ...

a circular segment? ... a change in a lines contour?

Corners define the meeting of two planes. If the two planes simply touch, and the corner remains unadorned, the appearance of the corner will depend on the visual treatment of the adjoining surfaces. This corner condition emphasizes the volume of a form.

A corner condition can be visually reinforced by introducing a separate and distinct element that is independent of the surfaces it joins. This element articulates the corner as a linear condition, defines the edges of the adjoining planes, and becomes a positive feature of the form.

If an opening is introduced at the corner, one of the planes will appear to bypass the other. This opening de-emphasizes the corner, weakens the definition of the volume within the form, and emphasizes the planar qualities of the surfaces.

If neither plane is extended to define the corner, a volume of space is created to replace the corner. This corner condition deteriorates the form's volume, allows the interior space to leak outward, and clearly reveals the surfaces as planes in space.

Rounding off the corner emphasizes the continuity of a form's surfaces, the compactness of its volume, and softness of its contour. The scale of the radius is important. If too small, it becomes visually insignificant; if large, it affects the interior space it encloses and the exterior form it describes.

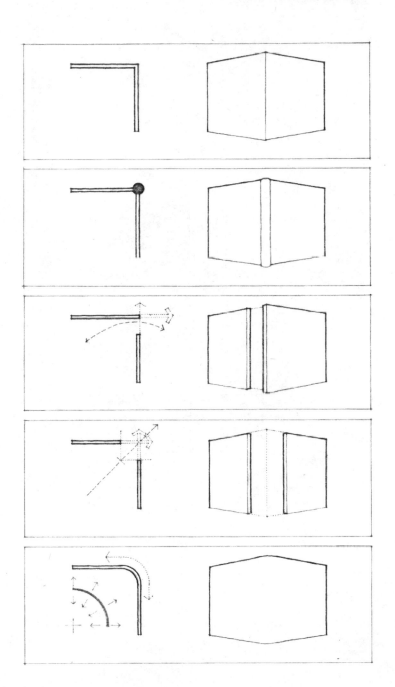

CORNERS

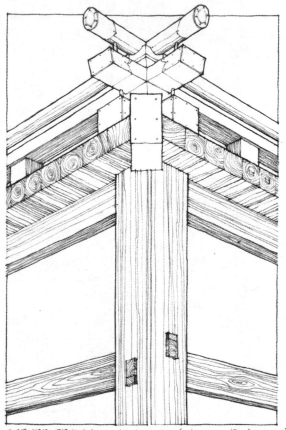

CORNER DETAIL: IZUMO SHRINE (Shimane Prefecture)

EVERSON MUSEUM: Syracuse, New York, 1968. I.M. PEI

THE CORNER CONDITION: DEFINING AND EXPRESSING THE MEETING OF ELEMENTS.

UNADORNED CORNERS EMPHASIZING THE VOLUME OF A FORM.

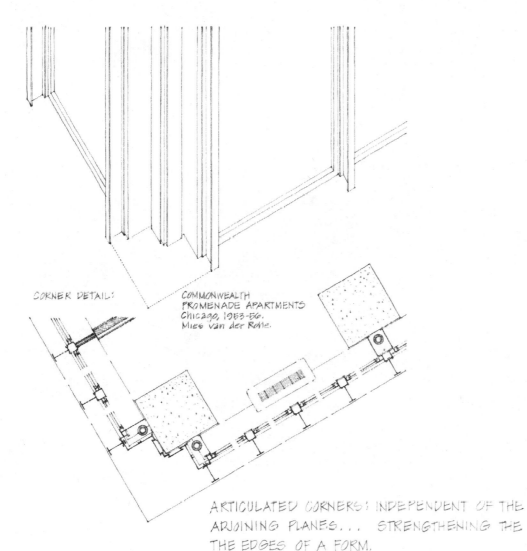

CORNER DETAIL:

COMMONWEALTH
PROMENADE APARTMENTS
Chicago, 1953-56.
Mies van der Rohe.

ARTICULATED CORNERS: INDEPENDENT OF THE
ADJOINING PLANES... STRENGTHENING THE
THE EDGES OF A FORM.

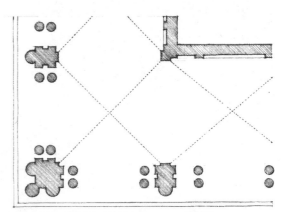

CORNER: THE BASILICA: Vicenza, 1549
Andrea Palladio

LABORATY TOWER: JOHNSON WAX BUILDING
Racine, Wisconsin   1950
Frank Lloyd Wright

EINSTEIN TOWER: Potsdam, 1910. Eric Mendelsohn

ROUNDED CORNERS EMPHASIZING CONTINUITY OF SURFACE, COMPACTNESS OF VOLUME, AND SOFTNESS OF FORM.

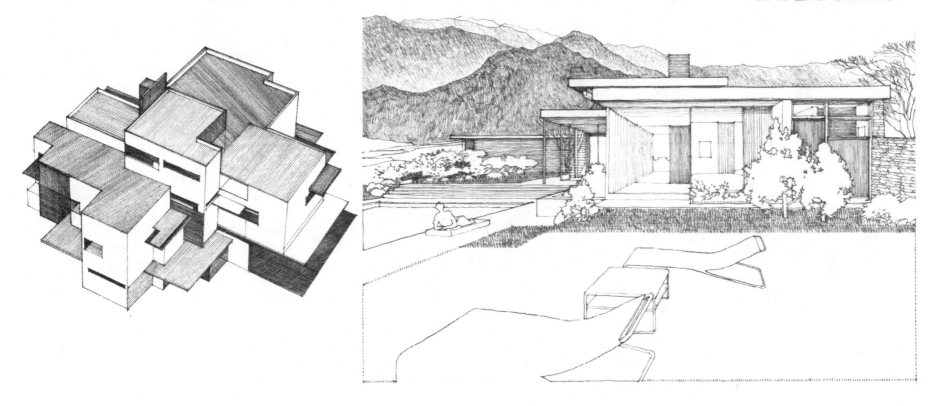

ARCHITECTURAL DESIGN STUDY: 1023
Van Doesburg and Van Esteren

KAUFMANN (DESERT) HOUSE: Palm Springs, California, 1046. Richard Neutra

OPENINGS AT CORNERS EMPHASIZING THE DEFINITION OF PLANES OVER VOLUME.

SURFACE ARTICULATION

Our perception of a plane's shape, size, scale, proportion, and visual weight is affected by its surface properties as well as its visual context.

A plane's shape can be articulated by contrasting the colors of its surface and the surrounding field. The visual weight of a plane can be increased or decreased by manipulating the tonal value of its surface color.

A frontal view reveals the true shape of a plane; oblique views distort it.

Elements of known size within a plane's visual field can aid our perception of its size and scale.

The texture of a plane's surface, together with its color, will affect its visual weight, scale, and light-reflective qualities.

The shape and proportion of a plane can be distorted or exaggerated by layering an optical pattern over its surface.

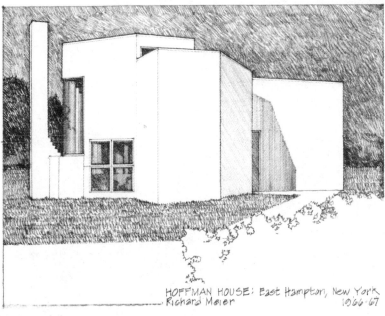

HOFFMAN HOUSE: East Hampton, New York
Richard Meier   1966-67

PALAZZO MEDICI - RICCARD: Florence   1444-60 Michelozzi

VINCENT STREET FLATS: London. 1928.
Sir Edwin Lutyens

EXAMPLES OF A SURFACE'S COLOR, TEXTURE, AND PATTERN AFFECTING THE VISUAL
WEIGHT OF A FORM, AND THE ARTICULATION OF ITS PLANES.

SURFACE ARTICULATION

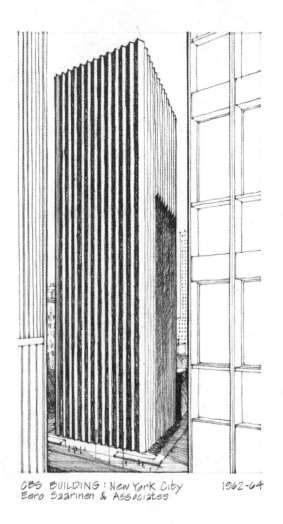

CBS BUILDING: New York City   1962-64
Eero Saarinen & Associates

FUKUOKA SOGO BANK: Saga Branch (Study), 1971. Arata Isozaki

EXAMPLES OF LINEAR PATTERNS REINFORCING THE HEIGHT
OR LENGTH OF A FORM, UNIFYING ITS SURFACES, AND
DEFINING ITS TEXTURAL QUALITY.

JOHN DEERE & COMPANY BUILDING: Moline, Illinois, 1961-64.   Eero Saarinen & Associates

SURFACE ARTICULATION

☐ EXAMPLES OF OPENINGS AND CAVITIES CREATING TEXTURE WITH SHADOW PATTERNS, AND INTERRUPTING THE CONTINUITY OF A FORM'S SURFACES.

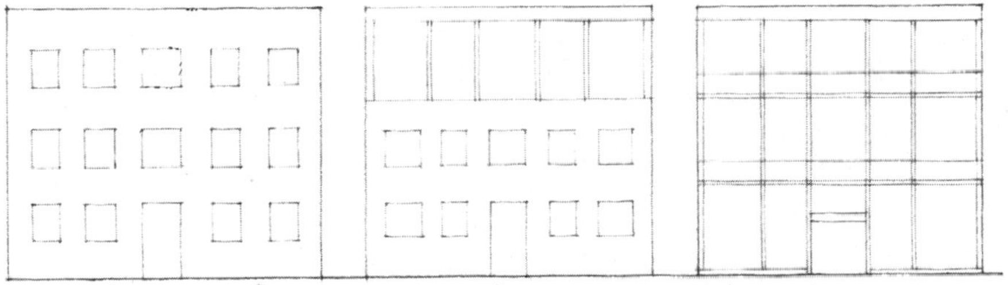

A transformation from a pattern of openings in a plane to an open facade articulated by a linear frame.

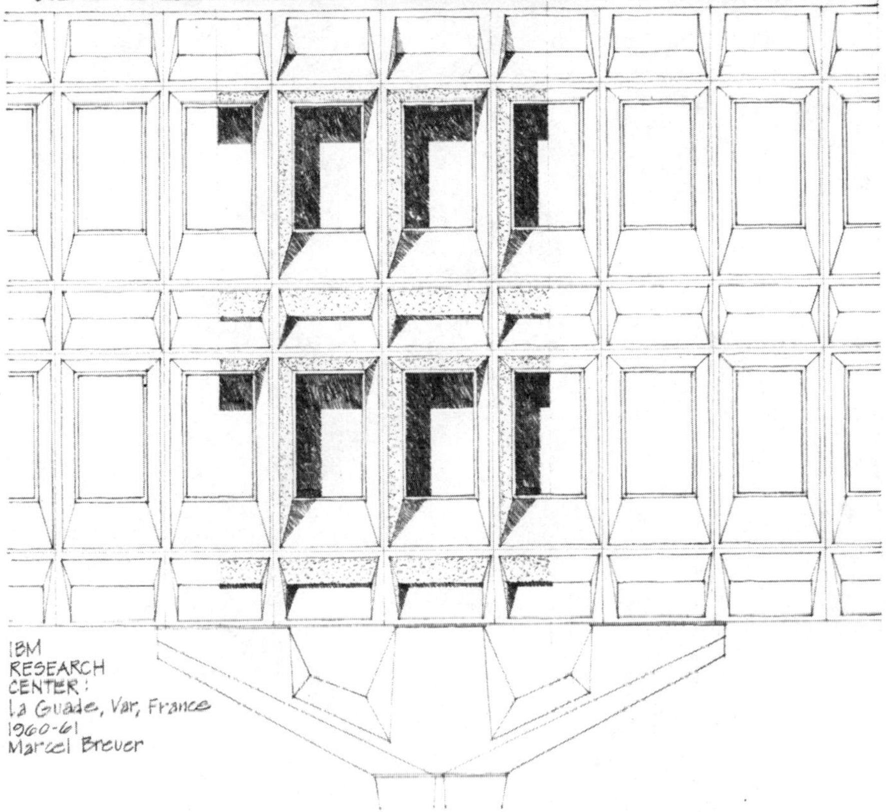

IBM RESEARCH CENTER: La Guade, Var, France 1960-61 Marcel Breuer

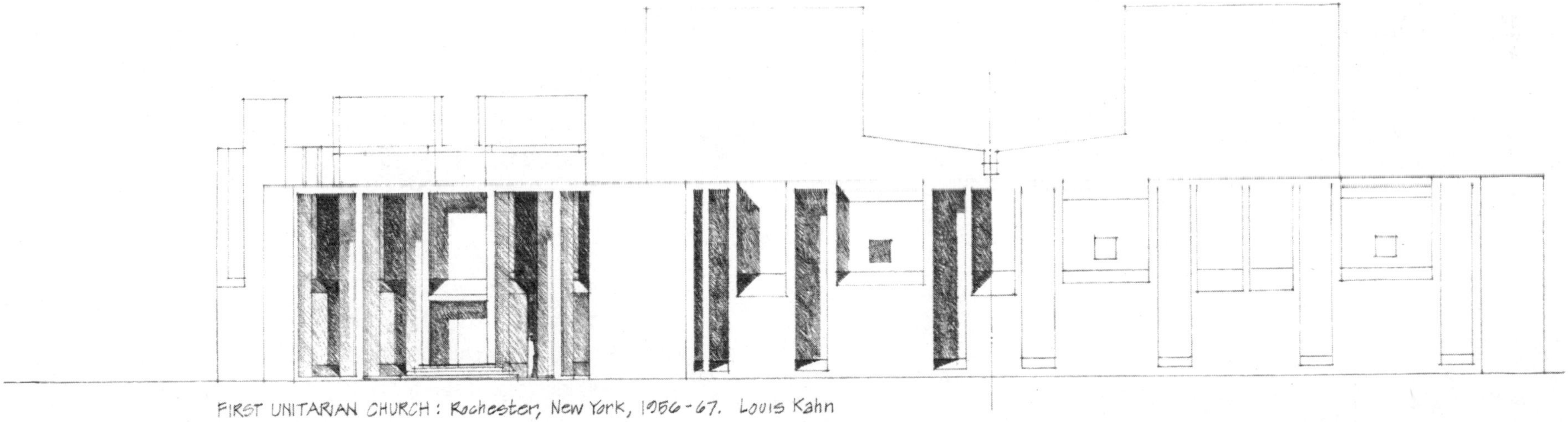

FIRST UNITARIAN CHURCH: Rochester, New York, 1956-67. Louis Kahn

"We put thirty spokes together and call it a wheel;
But it is on the space where there is nothing that
 the utility of the wheel depends.
We turn clay to make a vessel;
But it is on the space where there is nothing
 that the utility of the vessel depends.
We pierce doors and windows to make a house;
 and it is on these spaces where there is
 nothing that the utility of the house depends.
Therefore, just as we take advantage of what is,
 we should recognize the utility of what is not."

LAO TSE

3

FORM & SPACE

Space constantly encompasses our being.
Through the volume of space, we move, see forms
and objects, hear sounds, feel breezes, smell
the fragrances of a flower garden in bloom.
It is a material substance like wood or stone.
Yet it is inherently formless. Its visual form,
quality of light, dimensions and scale, depend
totally on its boundaries as defined by elements
of form. As space begins to be captured, enclosed,
molded, and organized by the elements of form,
architecture comes into being.

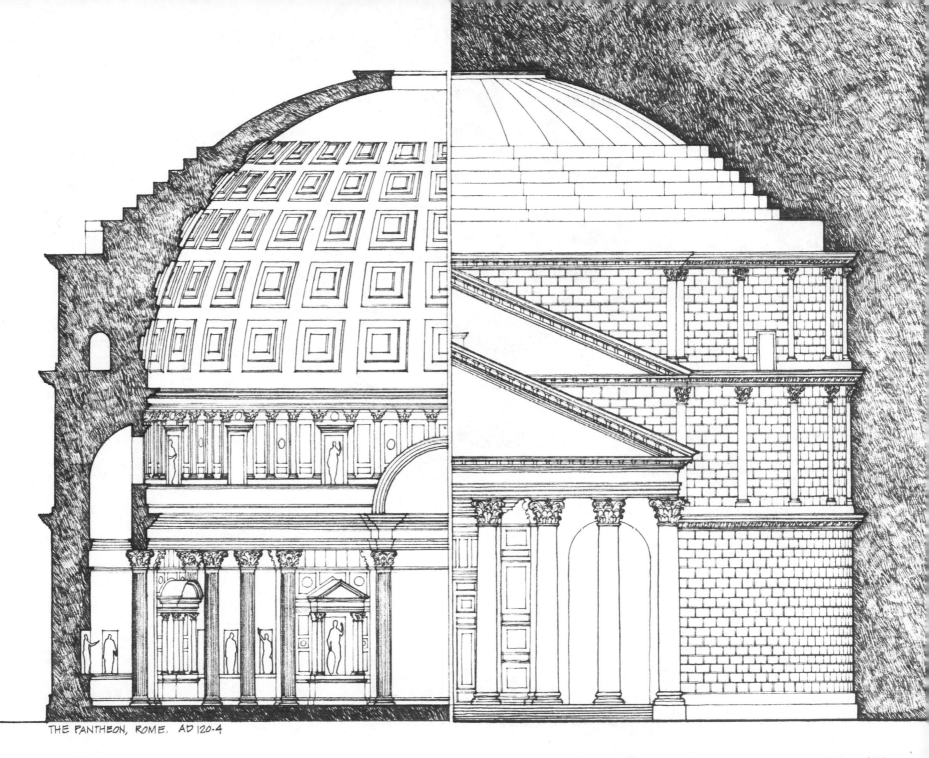

THE PANTHEON, ROME. AD 120-4

FORM & SPACE: THE UNITY OF OPPOSITES

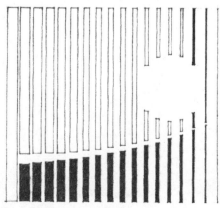

TWO FACES OR A VASE.........?

◄ WHITE·ON·BLACK OR BLACK·ON·WHITE.....?

Our visual field normally consists of heterogeneous elements, subject matter that differ in shape, size, color, etc. To better comprehend the structure of a visual field, we tend to organize the elements within it into two opposing groups: positive elements that are perceived as figures, and negative elements that provide a background for the figures.

Our perception and understanding of a composition depends on how we interpret the visual interaction between the positive and negative elements within its field. On this page, for example, letters are seen as dark figures against the white background of the paper's surface, and thus we are able to perceive their organization into words, sentences, and paragraphs. In the diagrams to the left, the letter "a" is seen as a figure, not only because we recognize it as a letter in our alphabet, but also because its profile is distinct, its value contrasts with that of its background, and its placement isolates it from its context. As it grows in size relative to its field, however, other elements within and around it begin to compete for our attention as figures. At times, the relationship between figures and their background is so ambiguous that we can visually switch their identities back and forth almost simultaneously.

In all cases, however, we should understand that figures, the positive elements that attract our attention, could not exist without a contrasting background. Figures and their background, therefore, are more than opposing elements. Together, they form an inseparable reality, a unity of opposites, just as the elements of form and space together form the reality of architecture.

TAJ MAHAL: Agra, India. 1630-53. Shah Jahan

A. Line defining the boundary between form and space.

B. Masonry form rendered as figure.

C. Space rendered as figure.

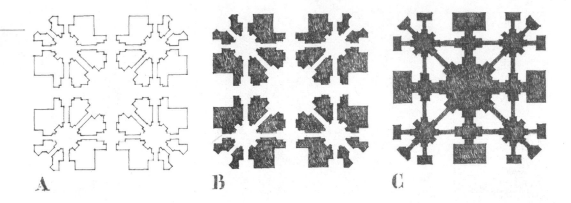

A　　　　**B**　　　　**C**

FRAGMENT OF A MAP OF ROME:

drawn by Giambattista Nolli in 1748

Depending on what we perceive to be positive elements, the figure/ground relationship of form and space can be inverted in different parts of this map of Rome. In portions of the map, buildings appear to be positive forms that define street space. In other portions, urban squares, courtyard spaces, and spaces within important public buildings read as extensions of the street space, and appear as positive elements seen against the background of the surrounding building mass.

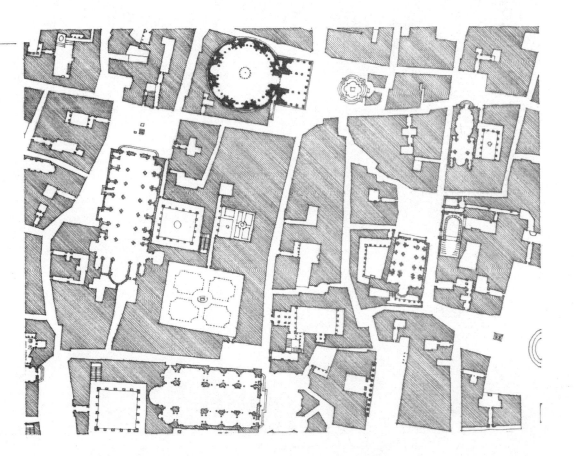

FORM & SPACE

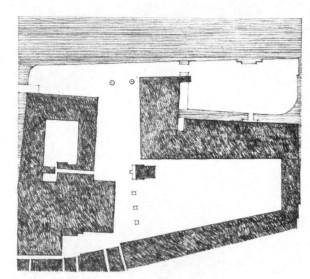

PIAZZA SAN MARCO, Venice

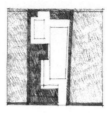 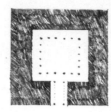  

A. Mexican House   B. Renaissance Palazzo   C. Johnson House Cambridge, Mass. 1942. Philip Johnson   D. Architect's Studio Helsinki 1955 Alvar Aalto

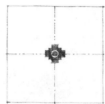 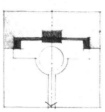 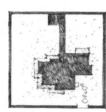 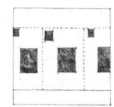

E. Villa Capra, Vicenza Palladio 1552   F. Renaissance Villa   G. Japanese House   H. American Suburban Houses

The symbiotic relationship of form and space in architecture can be examined and found to exist at several scales. At each level, we should be concerned not only with a building's form, but also its impact on the space around it. At an urban scale, we should consider whether a building should continue the existing fabric of a place, form a backdrop for other buildings, define an urban space, or whether it might be appropriate for it to stand free as an object in space.

At the scale of a building's site, there are various strategies for relating a building's form to the space around it. A building can:

A. form a wall along the edge of its site and define positive outdoor spaces;

B. surround and enclose a courtyard or atrium space within its volume;

C. merge its interior space with the private outdoor space of a walled site;

D. enclose a portion of its site as an outdoor room;

E. stand as a distinct form in space and dominate its site;

F. stretch out and present a broad face to a feature of its site;

G. stand free within its site and have the enclosed, private exterior space be an extension of its interior space;

H. stand as a positive form in negative space.

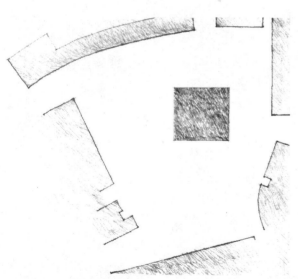

BOSTON CITY HALL : 1960. Kallmann, McKinnell & Knowles

At the scale of a building, we tend to read the configurations of walls as the positive elements of a plan drawing. The white space in between, however, should not be seen simply as background for the walls, but also as figures in the drawing that have shape and form.

The form and enclosure of each space in a building either determines, or is determined by, the form of of the spaces around it. In a building, such as the Theater in Seinäjoki, by Alvar Aalto, we can see several categories of spatial forms and analyze how they interact. Each category has an active or passive role in defining space.

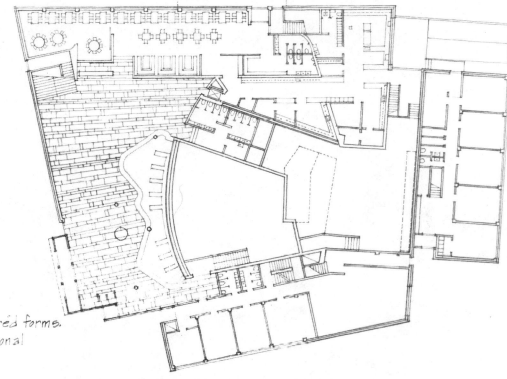

THEATER IN SEINÄJOKI: Finland   Designed 1968/69   Alvar Aalto

A. Some spaces, such as offices, have specific but similar functions and can be grouped into single, linear or clustered forms.

B. Some spaces, such as concert halls, have specific functional and technical requirements, and require specific forms that will affect the forms of the spaces around them.

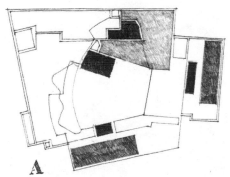

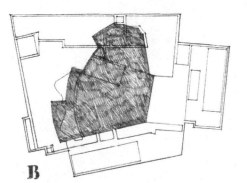

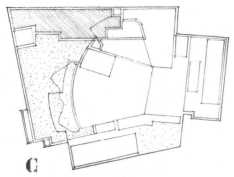

A

B

C

C. Some spaces, such as lobbies, are flexible in nature and can, therefore, be freely defined by the spaces or group of spaces around them.

FORM DEFINING SPACE

SQUARE IN GIRON, COLUMBIA

When we place a two-dimensional shape on a piece of paper, it will articulate and influence the white space around it. Similarly, any three-dimensional form will articulate the volume of space surrounding it and generate a field of influence or territory which it claims as its own. The following section of this chapter looks at horizontal and vertical elements of form, and presents examples of how their various configurations and orientation define specific types of space.

DEFINING SPACE WITH HORIZONTAL ELEMENTS

THE BASE PLANE

A simple field of space may be defined by a horizontal plane laying as a figure on a contrasting background. The following are ways in which this field can be visually reinforced.

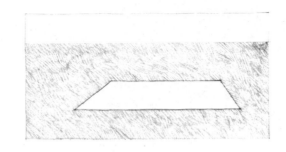 

THE BASE PLANE ELEVATED

A horizontal plane elevated above the ground plane establishes vertical surfaces along its edges that reinforce the visual separation between its field and the surrounding ground.

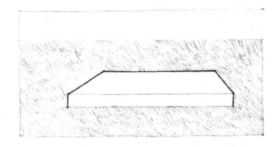 

THE BASE PLANE DEPRESSED

A horizontal plane depressed into the ground plane utilizes the vertical surfaces of the depression to define a volume of space.

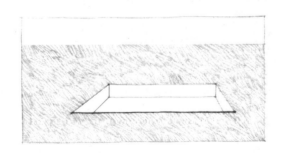 

THE OVERHEAD PLANE

A horizontal plane located overhead defines a volume of space between itself and the ground plane.

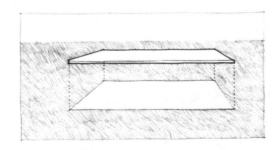 

THE BASE PLANE

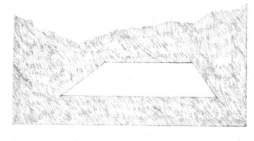

For a horizontal plane to be seen as a figure, there must be a perceptible change in color or texture between its surface and the plane upon which it lies.

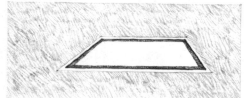

The stronger the edge definition of the horizontal plane is, the more articulate will be its field.

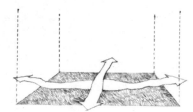

Although there is a continuous flow of space across an articulated field, it defines a territory, a zone of space, within its boundaries.

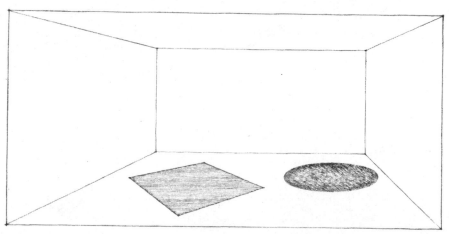

The articulation of the surface of the ground or floor plane is often used in architecture to define a zone of space within a larger spatial context. The examples on the facing page illustrate how this type of spatial definition has been used to differentiate between a path of movement and places of rest, define a field from which the form of a building rises out of the ground, or to articulate a functional zone within a one-room living environment.

STREET IN WOODSTOCK, Oxfordshire, England

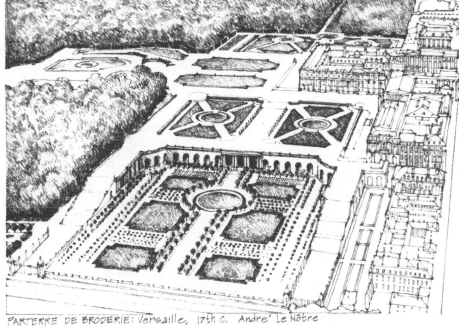

PARTERRE DE BRODERIE: Versaille, 17th c. André Le Nôtre

BUILDING-TO-SITE TRANSITION: IMPERIAL VILLA, Katsura

INTERIOR: GLASS HOUSE, New Canaan, Connecticut. 1949 Philip Johnson

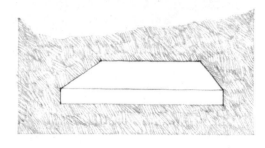

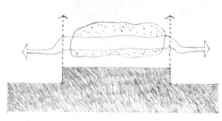

Elevating a portion of the base plane will create a field of space within a larger spatial context. The change in level along the edge of the elevated plane defines the boundaries of its field and interrupts the flow of space across its surface.

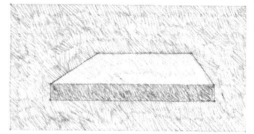

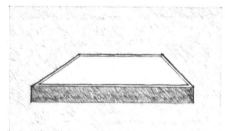

If the surface of the base plane continues up and across the elevated plane, then the field of the elevated plane will appear to be very much a part of the surrounding space. If, however, the edge condition is articulated by a change in form, color, or texture, then the field will become a plateau that is separate and distinct from its surroundings.

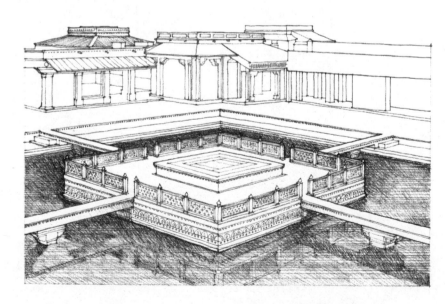

FATHEPUR SIKRI : Residence of the Great Mughul Akbar, India. 1569-74

◀ Platform in a square lake surrounded by the emperor's living and sleeping quarters.

The degree to which spatial and visual continuity is maintained between an elevated space and its surroundings depends on the scale of the level change.

1 • edge of the field is well-defined;
 • visual and spatial continuity is maintained;
 • physical access is easily accommodated.

2 • some visual continuity is maintained;
 • spatial continuity is interrupted;
 • physical access requires the use of stairs or ramps.

3 • visual and spatial continuity is interrupted;
 • the field of the elevated plane is isolated from the ground or floor plane;
 • the elevated plane is transformed into a sheltering element for the space below.

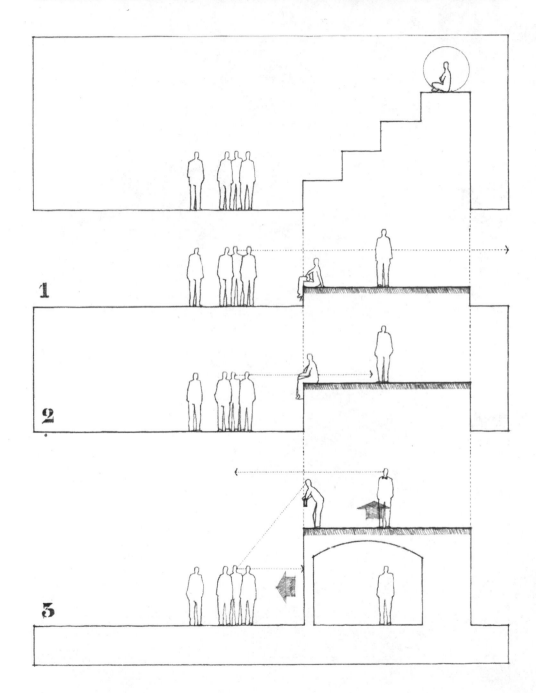

ELEVATED PLANES

THE ACROPOLIS, ATHENS

TEMPLE OF
JUPITER, ROME
509 B.C.

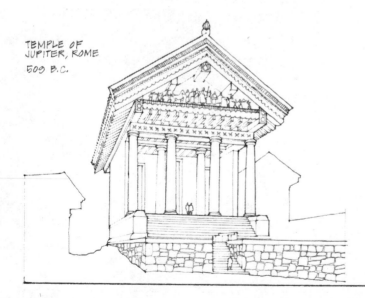

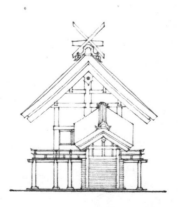

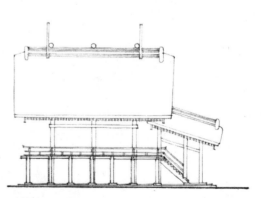

IZUMO SHRINE: Shimane Prefecture, Japan A.D. 550

The ground plane can be elevated to provide a platform
or podium that structurally and visually supports a
building's form. The elevated ground plane can be a
pre-existing site condition, or it can be artificially
constructed to deliberately raise a building above its
surrounding context or enhance its image in the
landscape. The examples on these two pages illustrate
how these techniques have been used to venerate
sacred and honorific buildings.

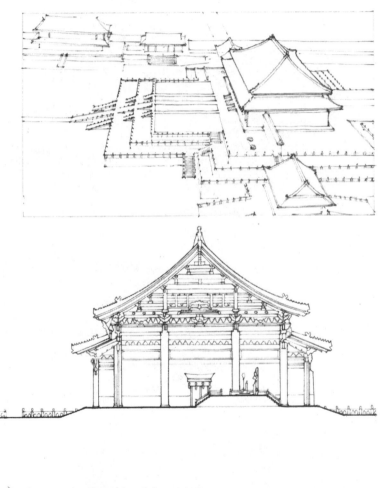

TAIHE DIAN (PAVILION OF SUPREME HARMONY): Peking, the Forbidden City. 1627

ELEVATED PLANES

FARNSWORTH HOUSE: Plano, Illinois.   1950
Mie van der Rohe

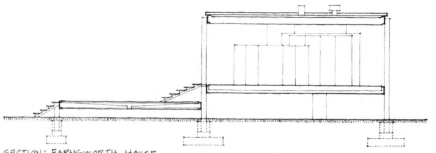

SECTION: FARNSWORTH HOUSE

In the Farnsworth House, an elevated floor plane has been used with an overhead roof plane to define a volume of space that hovers delicately above the surface of its site. The house was elevated above the flood plane of the site.

An elevated plane can define a transitional space between the exterior and interior of a building. Combined with a roof plane, it develops into the semi-private realm of a porch or veranda.

PRIVATE COURTYARD of the IMPERIAL PALACE; Peking, the Forbidden City. Begun 1406

EAST HARLEM PRE-SCHOOL: New York City. 1970 Hammel, Green & Abrahamson

HIGH ALTAR in the CHAPEL at the MONASTERY OF SAINTE-MARIE-DE-LA-TOURETTE: near Lyons, France. 1956-59   Le Corbusier

Within the interior spaces of a building, an elevated floor plane can define a space that serves as a retreat from the activity around it. It can be a platform for viewing the surrounding space. It can be used to articulate a sacred or singular space within a room.

THE BASE PLANE DEPRESSED

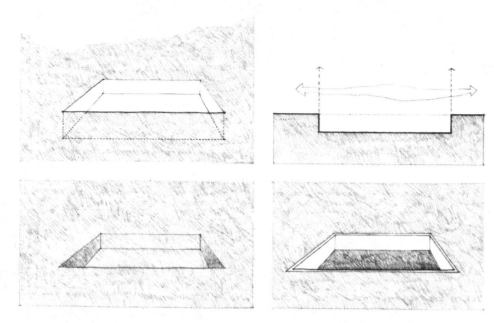

A field of space can be articulated by depressing a portion of the base plane. The boundaries of the field are defined by the vertical surfaces of the depression. These boundaries are not implied, as in the case of an elevated plane, but visible edges that begin to form the walls of the space.

The field of space can be further articulated by contrasting the surface treatments of the depressed area and the surrounding base plane.

A contrast in form, geometry, or orientation can also be used to visually reinforce the independence of the depressed field of space from its larger spatial context.

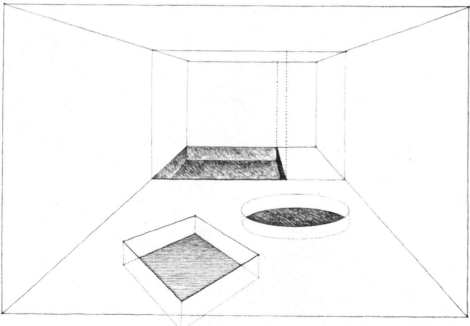

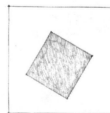

The degree of spatial continuity between the depressed field and the surrounding area depends on the scale of the level change.

1. The depressed field can be an interruption of the ground or floor plane and remain an integral part of the surrounding space.

2. Increasing the depth of the depressed field weakens its visual relationship with the surrounding space, and strengthens its definition as a distinct volume of space.

3. Once the original base plane is above our eye-level, the depressed field becomes, in effect, a separate and distinct room in itself.

Creating a gradual transition from one level to the other would help to promote the spatial continuity between the depressed field and the surrounding space.

Whereas the act of stepping up to an elevated space might express the extroverted nature or significance of the space, the lowering of a space below its surroundings might allude to its introverted nature or its sheltering and protective qualities.

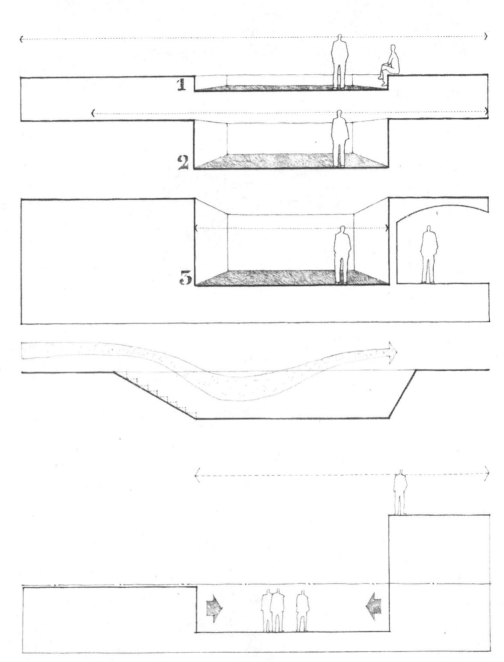

DEPRESSED PLANES

OUTDOOR THEATER COMPLEX: Built by the Inca tribe of the Maras between Machu Picchu and Cuzco in Peru.

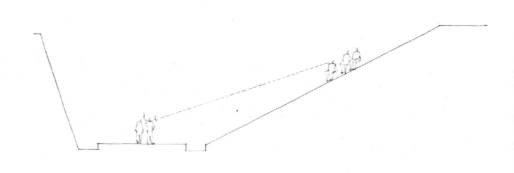

Depressed areas in the natural topography of a site can serve as stages for outdoor arenas and amphitheaters. The sight-lines and acoustical quality of these spaces benefit by the change in level.

THEATER at EPIDAUROS: C. 350 B.C.   Polycleitos

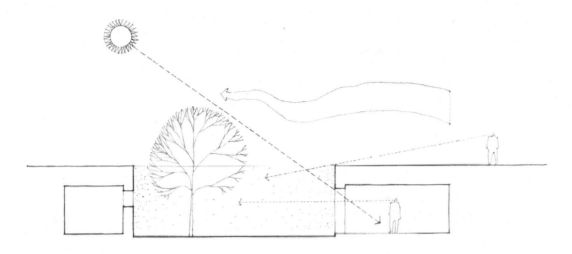

LOWER PLAZA: ROCKEFELLER CENTER. New York City
1930—   Wallace K. Harrison et. al.

Rockefeller Center's Lower Plaza, an outdoor cafe
in the summertime and a skating rink in the winter,
can be viewed from the upper plaza while shops
open onto it at the lower level.

UNDERGROUND VILLAGE near Loyang, China

The ground plane can be depressed to define sheltered outdoor spaces
for underground buildings. A sunken courtyard, protected from surface-level
wind, noise, etc. by the mass surrounding it, can be a source of air, light, and
view for the underground spaces opening onto it.

DEPRESSED PLANES

LIBRARY with "sunken" reading space: Wolfsburg Cultural Center
Essen, Germany   1962
Alvar Aalto

In these examples, Alvar Aalto has defined reading areas
within a library space by depressing their floor planes
below the main level of the library. He then uses the vertical
surfaces in the reading area for additional book storage.

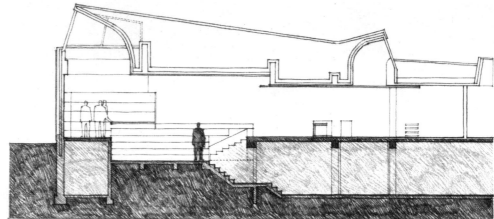

PARTIAL SECTION through the Library in Rovaniemi.

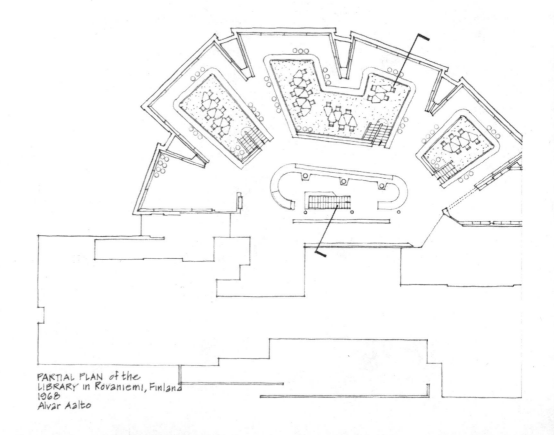

PARTIAL PLAN of the
LIBRARY in Rovaniemi, Finland
1968
Alvar Aalto

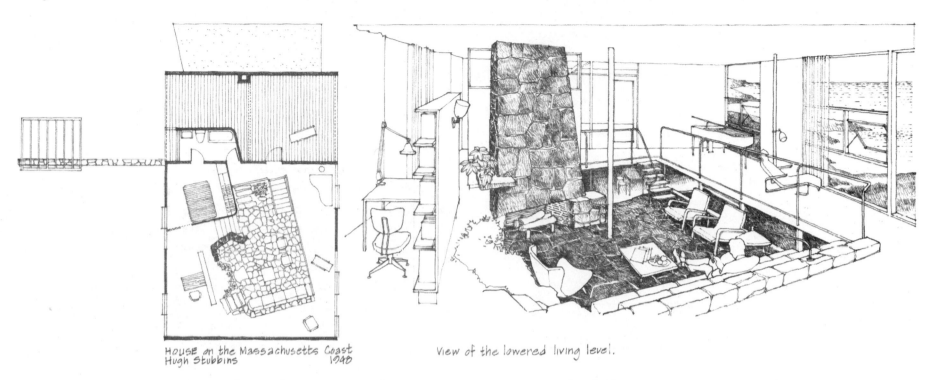

HOUSE on the Massachusetts Coast
Hugh Stubbins   1948

View of the lowered living level.

An area within a large room can be sunken to reduce the scale of the
room and define a more intimate space within it. The sunken area can
also serve as a transitional space between two levels of a building.

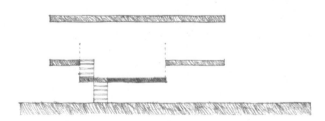

THE OVERHEAD PLANE

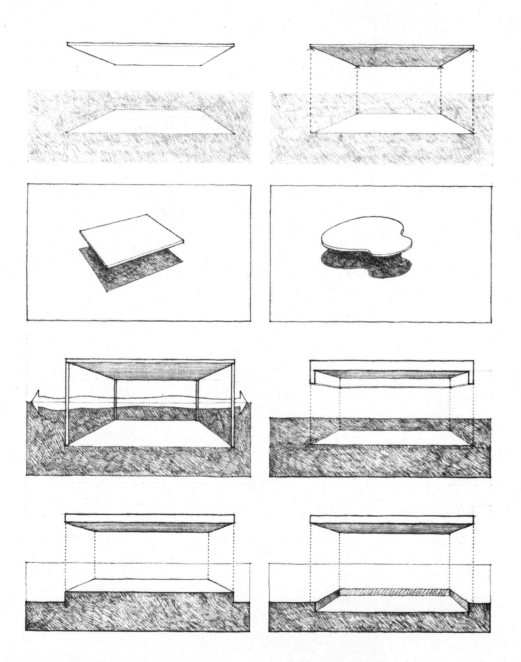

Similar to the manner in which a shade tree offers a sense of enclosure beneath its umbrella structure, an overhead plane defines a field of space between itself and the ground plane. Since the edges of this field are established by the edges of the overhead plane, the form of the space is determined by the plane's shape, size, and height above the ground plane.

While the previous manipulations of the ground or floor plane defined fields of space whose upper limits were established by their context, an overhead plane has the ability to define a discrete volume of space.

If vertical linear elements, such as posts or columns, are used to support the overhead plane, they will aid in visually establishing the limits of the defined space without disrupting the flow of space through the field.

Similarly, if the edges of the overhead plane are turned downward, or if the base plane beneath it is articulated by a change in level, the boundaries of the defined volume of space will be visually reinforced.

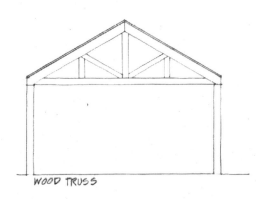

WOOD TRUSS

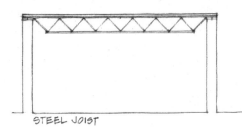

STEEL JOIST

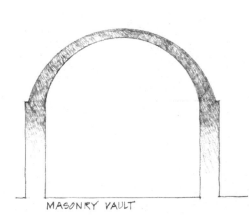

MASONRY VAULT

The major overhead element of a building is its roof plane. It not only shelters the building's interior spaces from sun, rain, snow, etc., but can affect as well the building's overall form and the form of its spaces. The form of the roof plane, in turn, is determined by the material, proportion, and geometry of the structural system that transfers its loads across space to its supports.

MOVING THE ROOF OF A HOUSE IN GUINEA

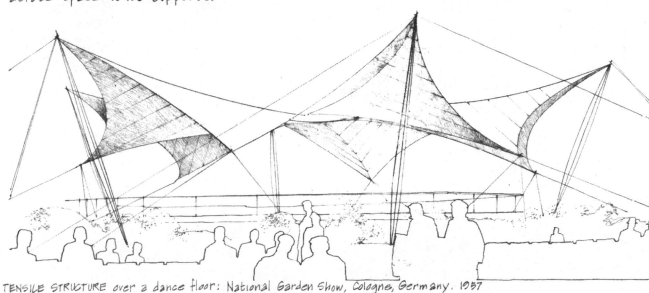

TENSILE STRUCTURE over a dance floor: National Garden Show, Cologne, Germany. 1957

OVERHEAD PLANES

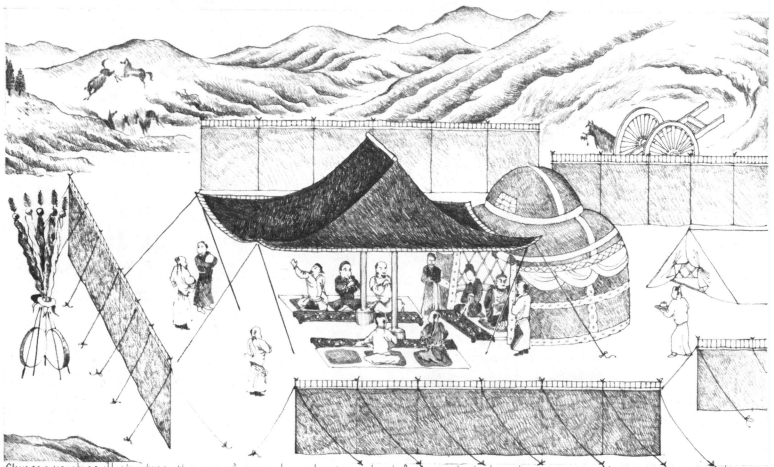

Chinese painting illustrating the use of a pavilion structure to define a shaded resting place within an encampment.

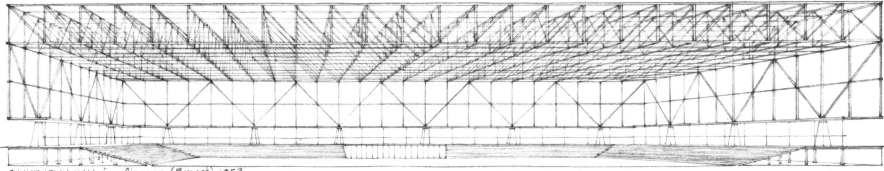

CONVENTION HALL for Chicago (Project) 1953
Mies van der Rohe

The roof plane can be visually
expressed as a planar element,
and be articulated by the pattern
of its structural system.

GLASS HOUSE: New Canaan, Connecticut. 1949
Philip Johnson

The roof plane can be the major space-defining element of a
building's form, and visually organize forms and spaces beneath
its shape.

CENTRE LE CORBUSIER: Zurich. 1963-67 Le Corbusier

OVERHEAD PLANES

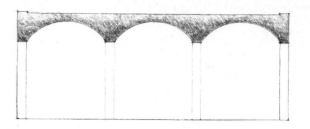

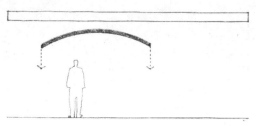

The ceiling plane of an interior space can reflect the form of the structural system supporting the overhead floor or roof plane. Since it need not resist weathering forces, nor carry major loads, however, the ceiling plane can also be detached from the floor or roof plane above and become a visually active element in a space.

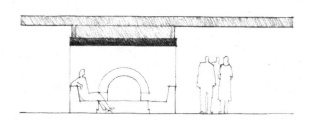

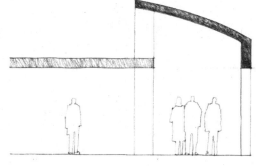

The ceiling plane, as in the case of the base plane, can be manipulated to define and articulate zones of space within a room. It can be lowered or elevated to alter the scale of a space, define a path of movement through it, or allow natural overhead light to enter it.

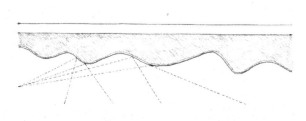

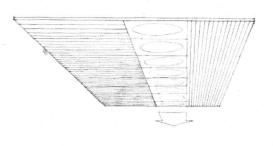

The form, color, texture, and pattern of the ceiling plane can also be manipulated to improve the acoustical qualities of a space, or give it a directional quality or orientation.

SIDE CHAPELS in the MONASTERY of Sainte-Marie-de-la-Tourette:
Le Corbusier   near Lyons, France, 1956-59

Well-defined "negative" areas within an overhead plane, such
as skylights, can be seen as "positive" shapes that articulate
the space below their openings.

INTERIOR OF CHURCH: Parish Center, Wolfsburg, Germany   1960-62
Alvar Aalto

135

VERTICAL ELEMENTS

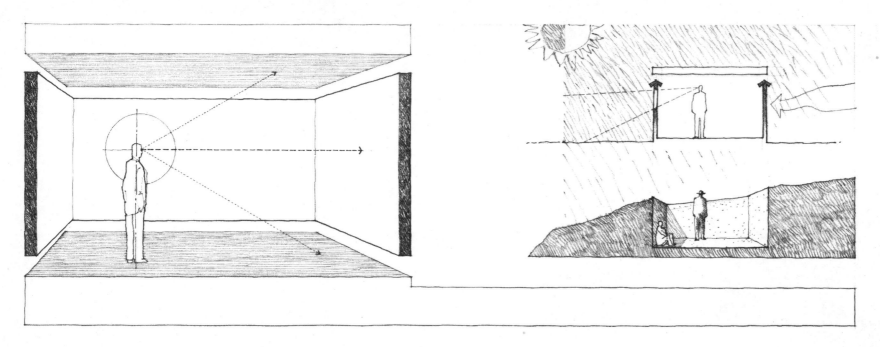

In the previous section of this chapter, horizontal planes defined fields of space whose vertical edges were implied. In the following section, vertical elements of form are used to visually establish the vertical boundaries of a space.

Vertical forms are generally more active in our visual field than horizontal planes, and are, therefore, instrumental in defining a volume of space and providing a strong sense of enclosure for those within it.

Vertical elements of form also serve as supports for a building's floor and roof planes. They control the visual and spatial continuity between a building's interior and the exterior environment. They aid in filtering the flow of air, light, noise, etc., through a building's interior spaces.

DEFINING SPACE WITH VERTICAL ELEMENTS

1. Linear vertical elements can define the vertical edges of a volume of space.

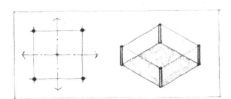 

2. A vertical plane will articulate the space that it fronts.

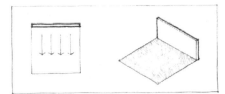 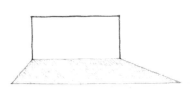

3. An "L"-shaped configuration of planes generates a field of space from its corner outward along a diagonal.

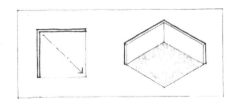 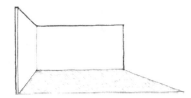

4. Parallel planes define a volume of space between them that is axially oriented toward the open ends of the configuration.

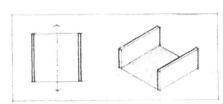 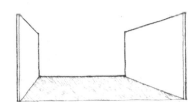

5. A "U"-shaped configuration of planes defines a volume of space that is oriented toward the open end of the configuration.

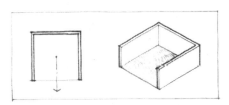 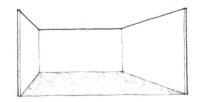

6. Four planes enclose an introverted space, and articulate the field of space around the enclosure.

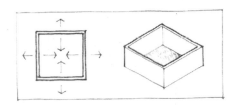 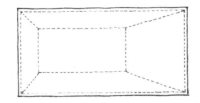

VERTICAL LINEAR ELEMENTS

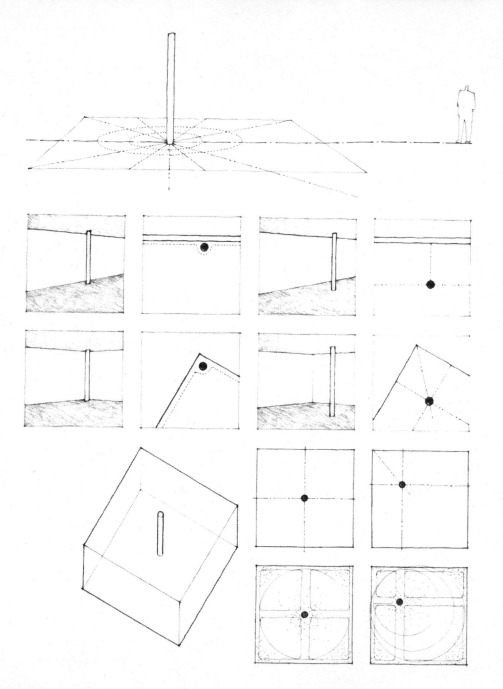

A vertical linear element, such as a column, establishes a point on the ground plane and makes it visible in space. Standing alone, a column is non-directional except for the path that would lead us to it. Any number of axes can be made to pass through it.

When located within a defined volume of space, a column will articulate the space around it and interact with the enclosure of the space. A column can attach itself to a wall and articulate its surface. It can reinforce the corner of a space and de-emphasize the meeting of its wall planes. Standing free within a space, a column can define zones of space within a room.

When centered within a room, a column will assert itself as the center of the space and define equal zones of space between itself and the surrounding wall planes. When offset, the column will define hierarchical zones of space that are differentiated by size, form, and location.

No volume of space can be established without the definition of its corners and edges. Linear elements serve this purpose in defining spaces that require visual and spatial continuity with their surroundings.

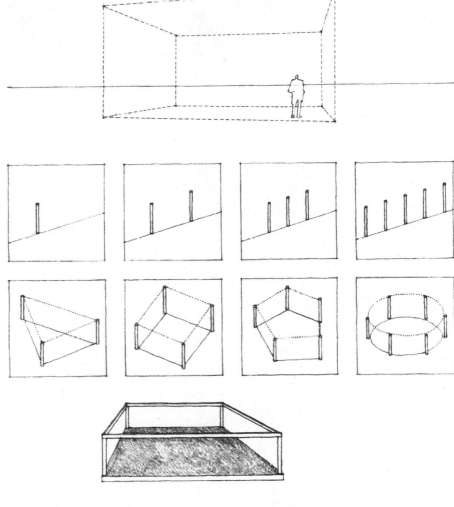

Two columns define a plane, a transparent spatial membrane that is created by the visual tension between them. Three or more columns can be arranged to define the corners of a volume of space. This space does not require a larger spatial context for its definition, but relates freely to it.

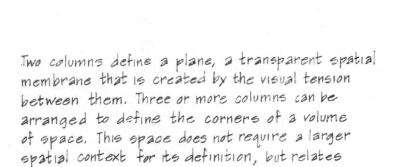

The edges of the volume of space can be visually reinforced by articulating its base plane and establishing its upper limits with beams spanning between the columns or with an overhead plane. The edge definition of the volume can also be strengthened by the repetition of column elements along its perimeter.

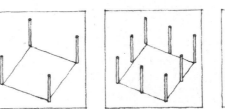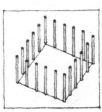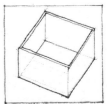

VERTICAL LINEAR ELEMENTS

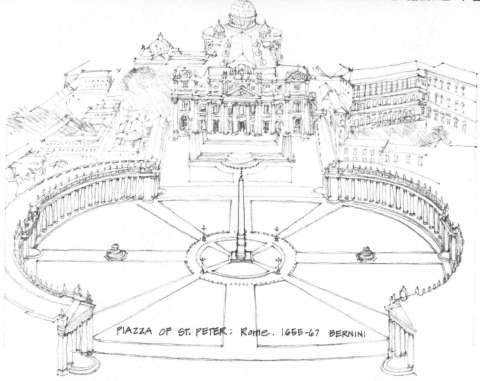

PIAZZA OF ST. PETER; Rome. 1655-67 BERNINI

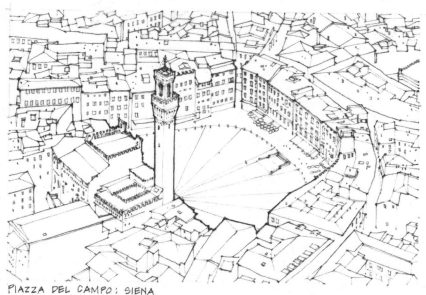

PIAZZA DEL CAMPO; SIENA

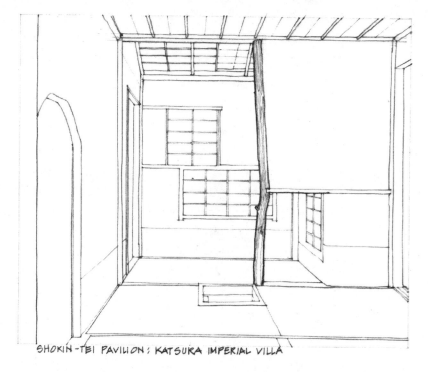

SHOKIN-TEI PAVILION; KATSURA IMPERIAL VILLA

Vertical elements can be used to terminate an axis, mark the center of an urban space, or provide a focus for an urban space along its edge.

In the example above, a rough, irregular post ("naka-bashira") is used as a symbolic element within a Japanese tea room.

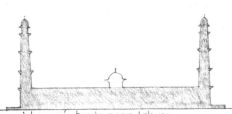
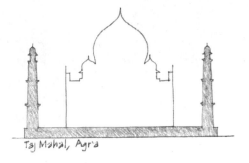

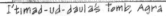
I'timad-ud-daula's Tomb, Agra   Jahangir's tomb, near Lahore   Taj Mahal, Agra

(from an analysis of Islamic Indian Architecture by Andreas Volwahsen)

In these examples, various forms of minaret towers are used to mark the corners of a platform and establish a field of space, a visual frame, for the Mogul mauseleum structures.

TAJ MAHAL, the Tomb of Mumtaz Mahal; Agra, India. 1632-54 Emperor Shah Jahan

COLUMNS IN SPACE

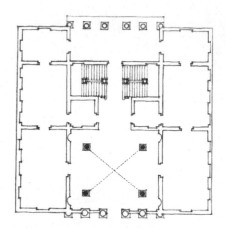

PALAZZO ANTONINI: Udine. 1556
Andrea Palladio

Four columns can be used to define a space within a room or articulate its corners. A number of Roman houses had an atrium space whose roof structure was supported by four columns (what Vitruvius termed a "tetrastyle" atrium).

During the Renaissance, Palladio incorporated the "tetrastyle" theme in the vestibules and halls of a number of villas and palazzos. The four columns not only supported the vaulted ceiling and floor above but also adjusted the room's dimensions to Palladian proportions.

TETRASTYLE ATRIUM: HOUSE OF THE SILVER WEDDING
Pompeii, 2d. Century B.C.

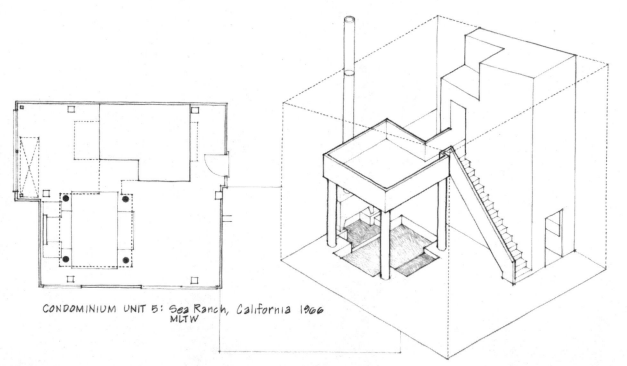

CONDOMINIUM UNIT 5: Sea Ranch, California 1966
MLTW

In the Sea Ranch condominium units, four posts, along with a sunken floor and an overhead plane, define an intimate alcove space within a larger room.

A row of columns, or colonnade, can define the edges of a volume of space while permitting visual and spatial continuity to exist between the space and its surroundings. It can also be attached to or support a wall plane and articulate its surface form, rhythm, and proportion.

A grid of columns within a large room not only supports the floor or roof plane above but also articulates its volume of space without interfering with the room's overall form and definition. It can diminish the scale of the room, help make its dimensions comprehensible, and define zones of space within it.

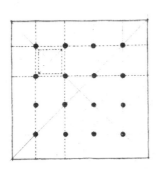

CLOISTER ▲ and "Salle des Chevaliers" ▼ in the Merveille (1203-28) of Mont. S. Michel, France

COLUMNS IN SPACE

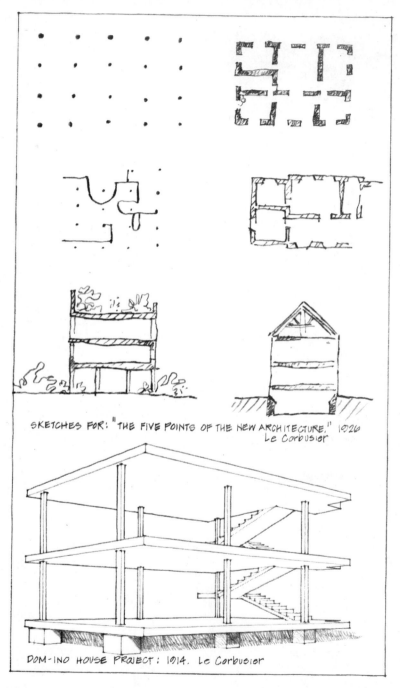

SKETCHES FOR: "THE FIVE POINTS OF THE NEW ARCHITECTURE." 1926
Le Corbusier

DOM-INO HOUSE PROJECT: 1914. Le Corbusier

In 1926, Le Corbusier stated what he believed to be the "Five Points of the New Architecture." His observations were, to a great extent, the result of the development of reinforced concrete construction that began in the late-nineteenth century. This type of construction, in particular, the use of concrete columns to support floor and roof slabs, afforded new possibilities for the definition and enclosure of a building's spaces.

Concrete slabs could cantilever beyond their column supports and enable the "free facade" of the building to be "light membranes" of "screen walls and windows." Within the building, a "free plan" was possible since the enclosure and layout of interior spaces were not determined or restricted by the pattern of heavy load-bearing walls. Interior spaces could be defined with non-load-bearing partitions, and their layout could respond freely to their programmatic requirements.

On the facing page, two contrasting examples of the use of a column-grid are illustrated:

1. A column-grid establishes a fixed, neutral (except for the circulation elements), field of space in which interior spaces are freely formed and distributed.

2. A grid of columns or posts corresponds closely to the layout of the interior spaces; there is a close "fit" between structure and space.

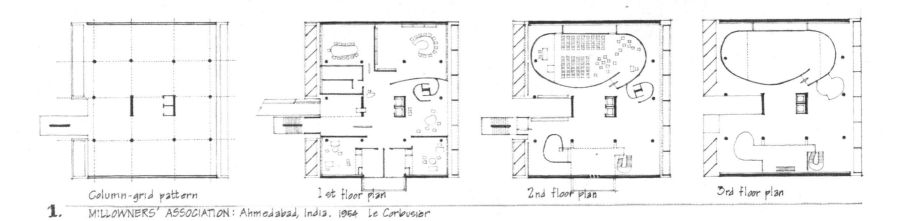

Column-grid pattern · 1st floor plan · 2nd floor plan · 3rd floor plan

1. MILLOWNERS' ASSOCIATION: Ahmedabad, India. 1954 Le Corbusier

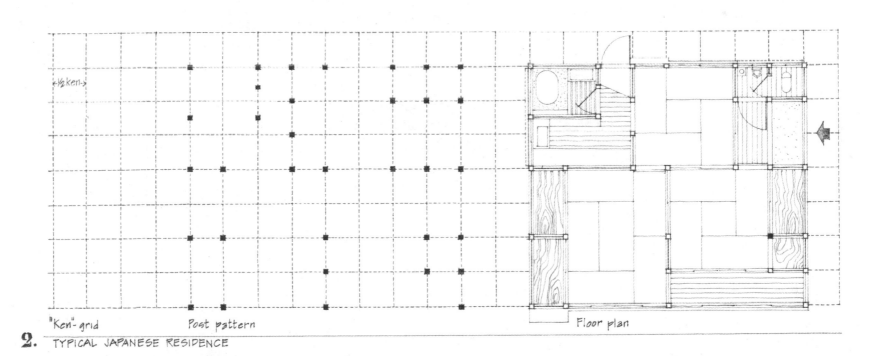

"Ken"-grid   Post pattern   Floor plan

2. TYPICAL JAPANESE RESIDENCE

SINGLE VERTICAL PLANE

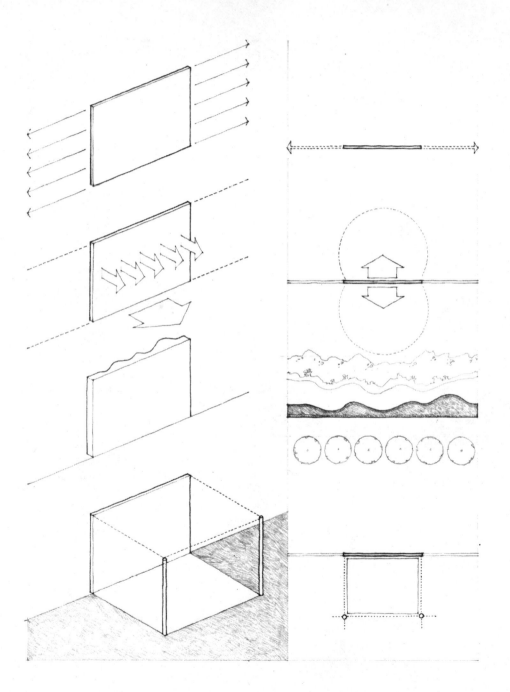

A single vertical plane, standing alone in space, has visual qualities uniquely different from those of a freestanding column.

It can appear to be merely a fragment of an infinitely larger or longer plane, slicing through and dividing a volume of space.

A plane has frontal qualities. Its two surfaces or "faces" front on and establish the edges of two separate volumes of space.

The two faces of a plane can be equivalent and front similar spaces. Or they can be differentiated in form, color, or texture, to respond to, or articulate, different spatial conditions. A plane, therefore, can have two "fronts", or a "front" and a "back".

The field of space a plane fronts on is not well-defined. A plane can establish only one of its edges. To define a volume of space, a plane must interact with other elements of form.

The height of a plane, relative to our height and eye-level, is the critical factor that affects the plane's ability to visually describe space. When two-feet high, a plane can define the edge of a field but provides little or no sense of enclosure for the field. When waist-level high, it begins to provide a sense of enclosure while allowing for visual continuity with surrounding spaces. When it approaches our eye-level in height, it begins to divide one space from another. Above our height, a plane interrupts visual and spatial continuity between two fields and provides a strong sense of enclosure.

The color, texture, and pattern of a plane's surfaces will affect our perception of its visual weight, proportion, and dimensions.

When related to a defined volume of space, a plane can be articulated to be the primary face of the space and give it a specific orientation. It can be articluated to be the front of the space and define a plane of entry into it. It can be a freestanding element within a space to divide it into two separate but related areas or serve as its focus or visual feature.

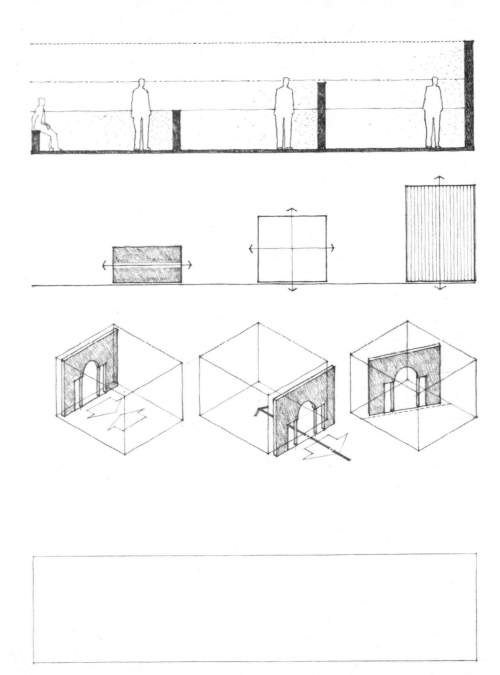

VERTICAL PLANES

S. AGOSTINO: Rome. 1479-83 Giacomo da Pietrasanta

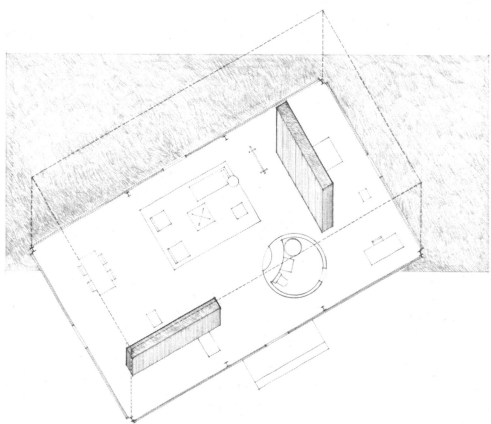

GLASS HOUSE: New Canaan, Connecticut. 1949. Philip Johnson

These examples illustrate the use of vertical planes to define a front facade of a building, a gateway, and zones within a space.

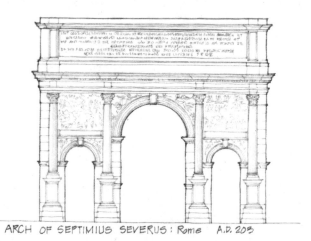

ARCH OF SEPTIMIUS SEVERUS: Rome   A.D. 203

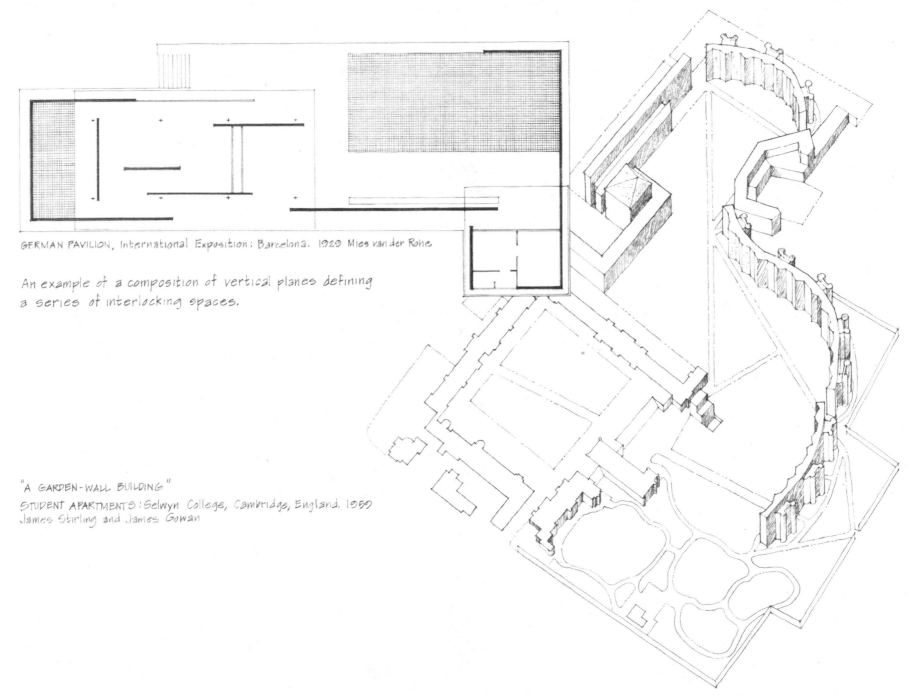

GERMAN PAVILION, International Exposition: Barcelona. 1929 Mies van der Rohe

An example of a composition of vertical planes defining
a series of interlocking spaces.

"A GARDEN-WALL BUILDING"

STUDENT APARTMENTS: Selwyn College, Cambridge, England. 1959
James Stirling and James Gowan

L·SHAPED CONFIGURATION OF PLANES

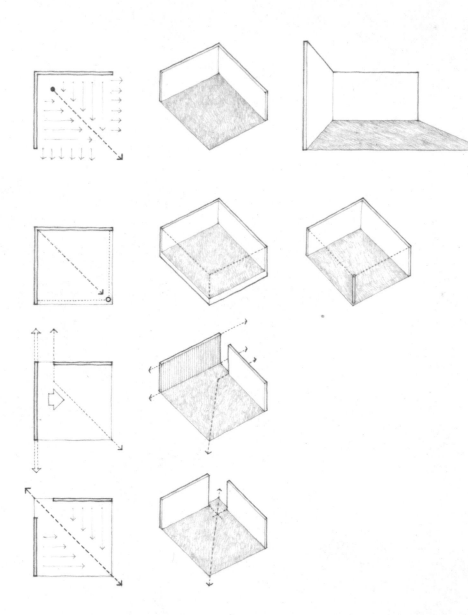

An "L"- configuration of vertical planes defines a field of space along a diagonal from its corner outward. While this field is strongly defined and enclosed by the corner of the configuration, it dissipates rapidly as it moves away from the corner. While the field is an introverted one at its inside corner, it becomes extroverted along its outer edges.

While two edges of the field are defined by the two planes of the configuration, its other edges will remain ambiguous unless further articulated by additional vertical elements, manipulations of the base plane, or an overhead plane.

If a void is introduced at the corner of the configuration, the definition of the field will be weakened. The two planes will be isolated from each other, and one will appear to slide by and visually dominate the other.

If neither plane extends to the corner, the field will become more dynamic in nature and organize itself along the diagonal of the configuration.

A building form can have an "L"- configuration and be subject
to the following readings. One of the arms of the configuration
can be a linear form that incorporates the corner within its
boundaries, while the other arm is seen as an appendage to it.
Or the corner can be articulated as an independent element
that joins two linear forms together.

A building can have an "L"- configuration to establish a corner
of its site, enclose a field of outdoor space to which its
interior spaces relate, or to shelter a portion of outdoor space
from undesirable conditions around it.

"L"- configurations of planes are stable and self-supporting,
and can stand alone in space. Because they are open-ended,
they are flexible space-defining elements. They can be used
in combination with one another or with other elements of
form to define a rich variety of spaces.

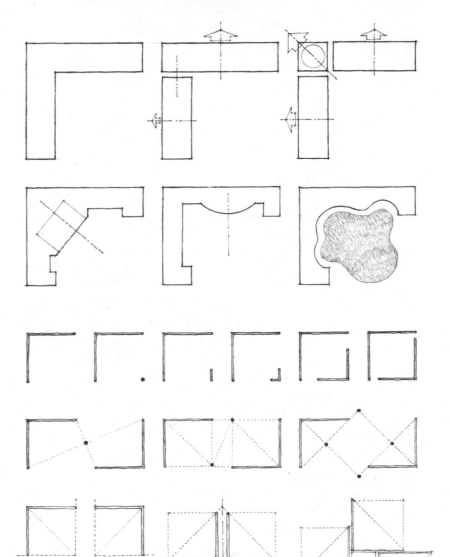

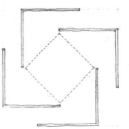

L·SHAPED PLANES

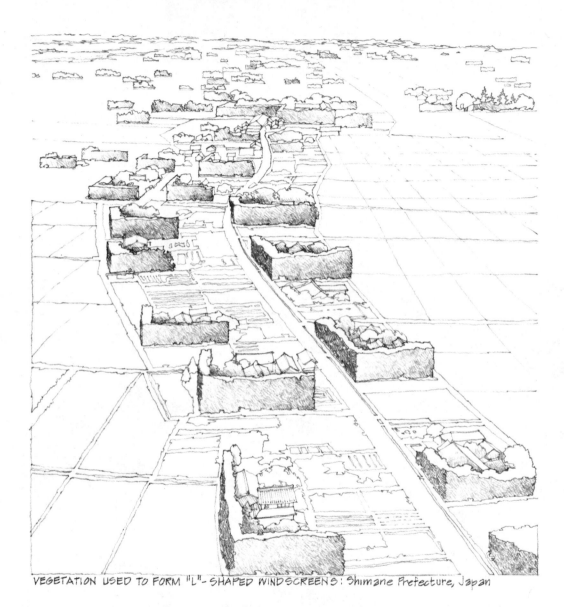

VEGETATION USED TO FORM "L"-SHAPED WINDSCREENS: Shimane Prefecture, Japan

The sheltering aspect of an "L"-shaped configuration is expressed well in this example where Japanese farmers coaxed pine trees to grow into thick, high, "L"-shaped hedges to shield their houses and land from winter winds and snowstorms.

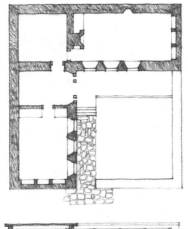

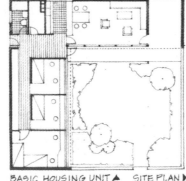

BASIC HOUSING UNIT ▲   SITE PLAN ▶

KINGÖ HOUSING ESTATE
near Elsinore, Denmark
1958-63
Jørn Utzon

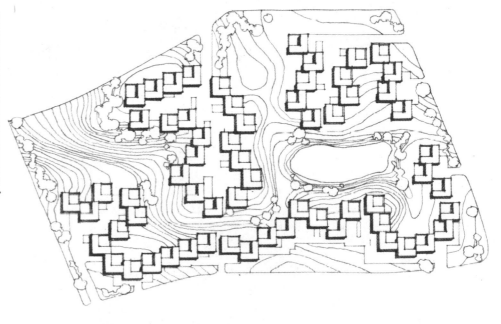

HOUSE IN KONYA, TURKEY

A common theme among examples of residential architecture is the "L"- configuration of rooms around an outdoor living space. Typically, one wing contains the group living spaces while the other contains private, individual spaces. The utility and service spaces usually occupy a corner position, or is strung along the backside of one of the wings.

The advantage of this type of layout is its provision of a private outdoor space, sheltered by the building form, and to which interior spaces can be directly related. In the Kingö Housing Estate, a fairly high degree of concentration is achieved with this type of unit, each with its own private outdoor space.

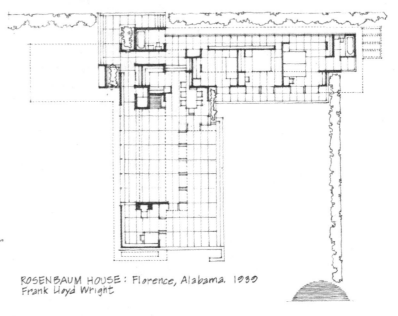

ROSENBAUM HOUSE: Florence, Alabama. 1939
Frank Lloyd Wright

L·SHAPED PLANES

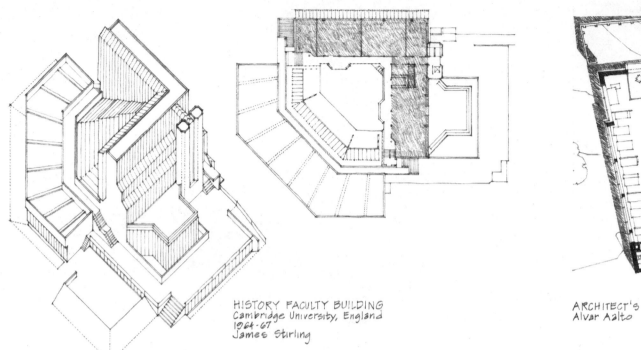

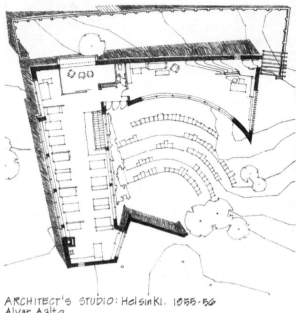

HISTORY FACULTY BUILDING
Cambridge University, England
1964-67
James Stirling

ARCHITECT's STUDIO: Helsinki. 1955-56
Alvar Aalto

Similar to the residential examples on the preceding page, these buildings use their "L"-shaped forms as sheltering or enclosing elements. The History Faculty Building at Cambridge uses a seven-story, "L"-shaped block to functionally and symbolically enclose a large, roof-lit library, the most important space in the building.

The outdoor space enclosed by the architect's studio in Helsinki is used as an amphitheater for lectures and social occasions. It is not a passive space whose form is determined by the building that encloses it. Rather, it asserts its positive form and pressures the form of its enclosure.

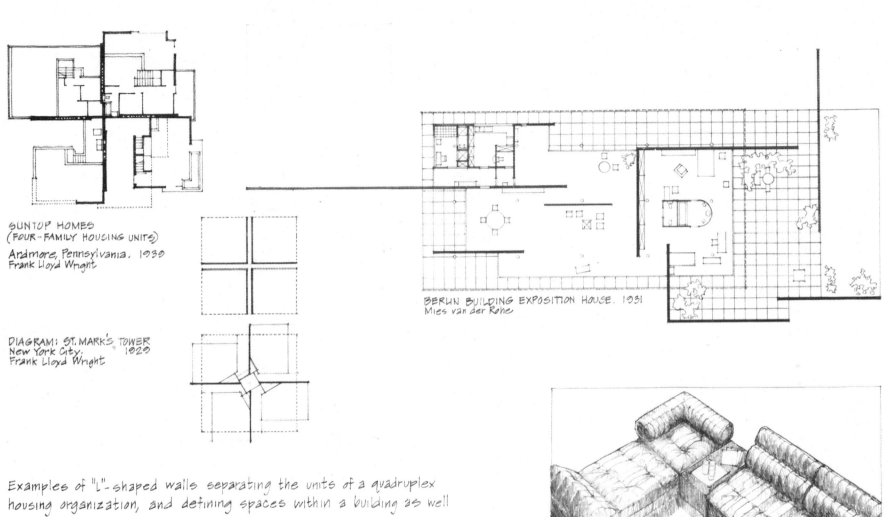

SUNTOP HOMES
(FOUR-FAMILY HOUSING UNITS)

Ardmore, Pennsylvania. 1939
Frank Lloyd Wright

DIAGRAM: ST. MARK'S TOWER
New York City.   1929
Frank Lloyd Wright

BERLIN BUILDING EXPOSITION HOUSE. 1931
Mies van der Rohe

Examples of "L"-shaped walls separating the units of a quadruplex
housing organization, and defining spaces within a building as well
as within a room.

PARALLEL VERTICAL PLANES

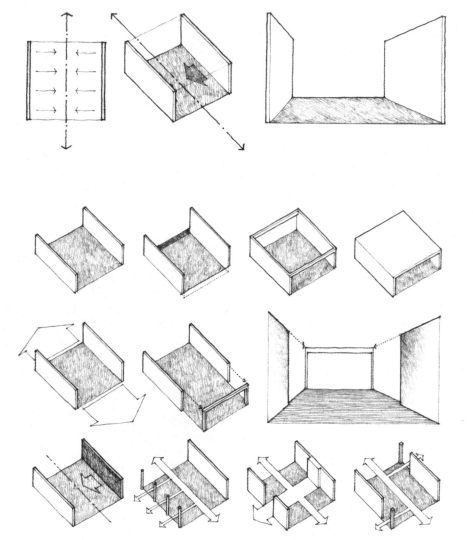

A set of parallel vertical planes defines a field of space between them. The open ends of the field, established by the vertical edges of the planes, give the space a strong directional quality. Its primary orientation is along the axis about which the planes are symmetrical. Since the parallel planes do not meet to form a corner and enclose a portion of the field, the space is extroverted in nature.

The definition of the spatial field along the open ends of the configuration can be visually reinforced by manipulating the base plane or adding overhead elements to the composition.

The spatial field can be visually expanded by extending the base plane beyond the open ends of the configuration. This expanded field can, in turn, be terminated by a vertical plane whose width and height is equal to that of the field.

If one of the parallel planes is differentiated from the other by a change in form, color, or texture, a secondary axis, perpendicular to the flow of the space, will be established within the field. Openings in one or both of the planes will also introduce secondary axes to the field and modulate the directional quality of the space.

Various elements in architecture can be seen as parallel planes that define a field of space. They can be the interior walls of a building, the exterior walls or facades of two adjacent buildings, a colonnade of columns, two rows of trees or hedges, or a natural topographical form in the landscape.

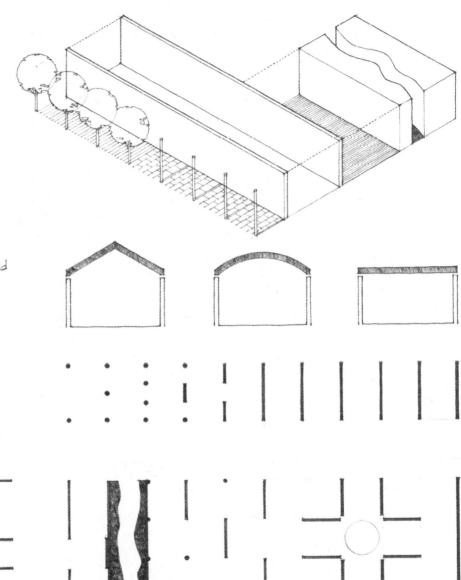

The image of parallel vertical planes is often associated with the bearing-wall structural system, wherein a floor or roof structure spans across two or more parallel, load-bearing walls.

Sets of parallel wall planes can be transformed into a wide variety of configurations. Their spatial fields can be related to one another through the open ends of their configurations or through openings in the planes themselves.

PARALLEL PLANES

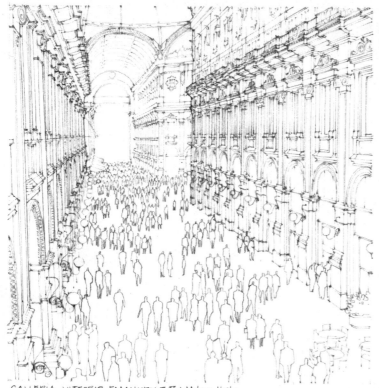

GALLERIA VITTORIO EMANUELLE II: Milan, Italy.

STREET IN ALBEROBELLO: Italy

After Edward Allen, Stone Shelters,
© M.I.T. Press 1969.

CHAMP DE MARS, PARIS

The directional quality and flow of the space defined by parallel planes is manifested in the circulation spaces of towns and cities, in their streets and boulevards. These linear spaces can be defined by the facades of the buildings fronting them, as well as by more permeable planes such as arcades or rows of trees.

The paths of movement within a building, its halls, galleries and corridors, also express the natural flow of the space defined by parallel planes.

The parallel planes that define a circulation space can be solid and opaque to provide privacy for the spaces along the circulation path. The planes can also be established by a row of columns so that the circulation path, open on one or both of its sides, becomes part of the spaces it passes through.

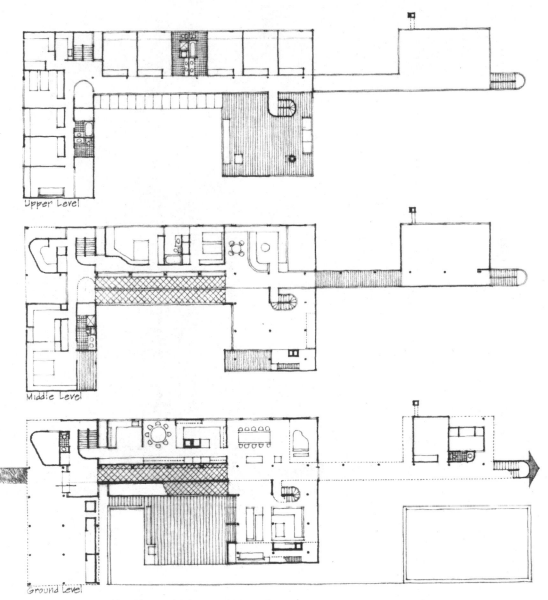

Upper Level

Middle Level

Ground Level

HOUSE IN OLD WESTBURY: New York. 1969-71. Richard Meier

PARALLEL PLANES

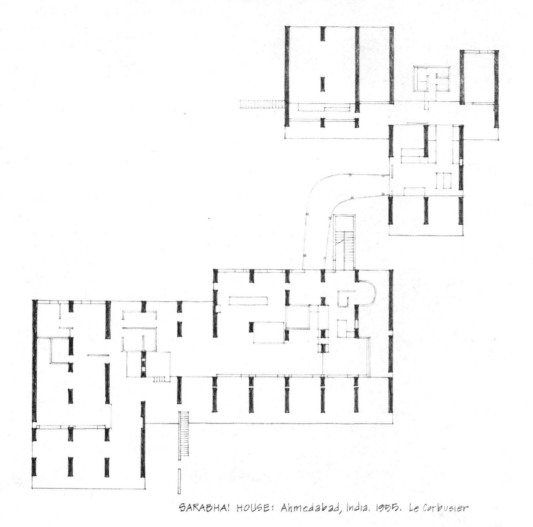

SARABHAI HOUSE: Ahmedabad, India. 1955. Le Corbusier

The parallel walls of a bearing-wall structural system can be the generating force behind a building's form and organization. Their repetitive pattern can be modified by varying their length, and by introducing voids within the planes to accommodate the dimensional requirements of large spaces. These voids can also define circulation paths and establish visual relationships perpendicular to the wall planes.

The slots of space defined by parallel wall planes can also be modulated by altering the spacing and configuration of the planes.

ARNHEIM PAVILION: The Netherlands. 1966
Aldo van Eyck

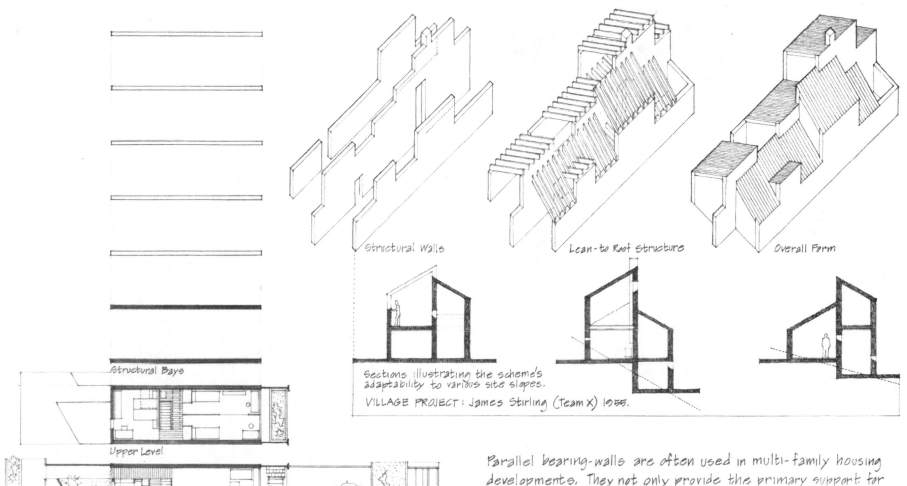

Structural Walls   Lean-to Roof Structure   Overall Form

Structural Bays

Upper Level

Entry Level

Ground Level

SIEDLUNG HALEN: near Bern, Switzerland. 1961. Atelier 5

Sections illustrating the scheme's
adaptability to various site slopes.
VILLAGE PROJECT: James Stirling (Team X) 1955.

Parallel bearing-walls are often used in multi-family housing
developments. They not only provide the primary support for
the floors and roofs of each housing unit, but serve also to
isolate the units from one another for acoustical and fire
control. The pattern of parallel bearing-walls is particularly
appropriate for rowhousing and townhouse schemes where
each unit is provided with two orientations.

U·SHAPED CONFIGURATION OF PLANES

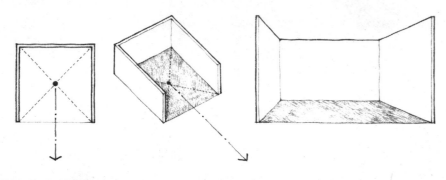

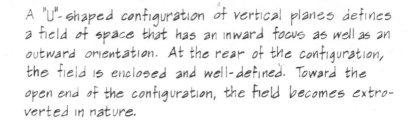

A "U"-shaped configuration of vertical planes defines a field of space that has an inward focus as well as an outward orientation. At the rear of the configuration, the field is enclosed and well-defined. Toward the open end of the configuration, the field becomes extroverted in nature.

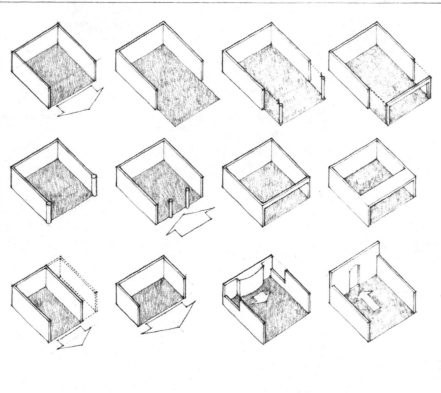

The open end is the primary aspect of the configuration by virtue of its uniqueness relative to the other three planes. It allows the field to have visual and spatial continuity with the adjoining space. The extension of the spatial field into the adjoing space can be visually reinforced by continuing the base plane beyond the open end of the configuration.

If the plane of the opening is further defined with columns or overhead elements, the definition of the original field will be reinforced, and continuity with the adjoining space will be interrupted.

If the configuration of planes is rectangular and oblong in form, the open end can be along its narrow or wide side. In either case, the open end will remain the primary "face" of the spatial field, and the plane opposite the open end will be the principal element among the three planes of the configuration.

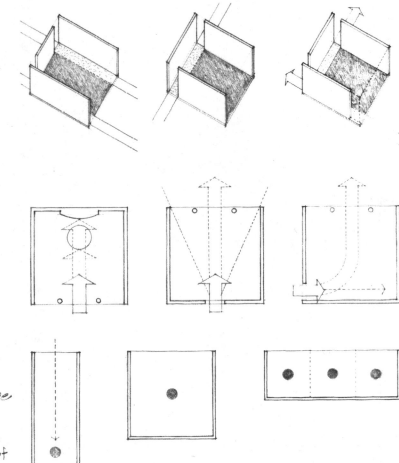

If openings are introduced at the corners of the configuration, secondary zones will be created within the field, and the field will become multidirectional and dynamic in nature.

If the field is entered through the open end of the configuration, the rear plane, or a form placed in front of it, will terminate our view of the space. If the field is entered through an opening in one of the planes, the view of what lies beyond the open end will draw our attention and terminate the sequence.

If the end of a long, narrow field is open, the space will encourage movement and be conducive to a progression or sequence of events. If the field is square, or nearly square, the space will be static and have the character of a place to be in, rather than a space to move through. If the side of a long, narrow field is open, the space will be susceptible to a subdivision into a number of zones.

Building forms and organizations can have a "U"-configuration to define and enclose an outdoor space. Their configurations can be seen to consist of linear forms. The corners of their configurations can be articulated as independent elements or be incorporated into the body of the linear forms.

U·SHAPED PLANES

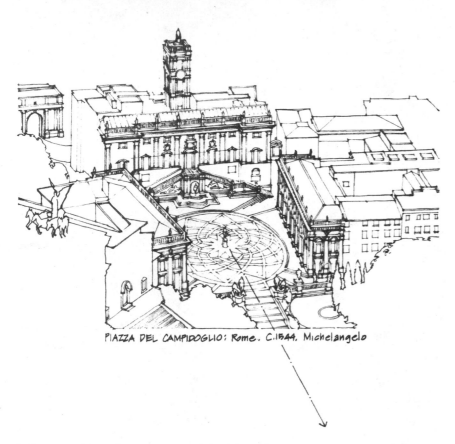

PIAZZA DEL CAMPIDOGLIO: Rome, C.1544, Michelangelo

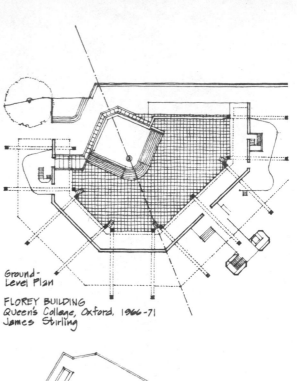

Ground-Level Plan

FLOREY BUILDING
Queen's College, Oxford, 1966-71
James Stirling

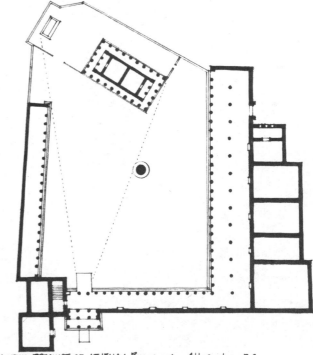

SACRED PRECINCT OF ATHENA: Pergamon. 4th Century B.C.

"U"-shaped configurations of building forms can serve to define an urban space and terminate an axial condition. They can also focus on an important or significant element within their fields. When an element is placed along the open end of its field, it gives the field a point of focus as well as a greater sense of closure.

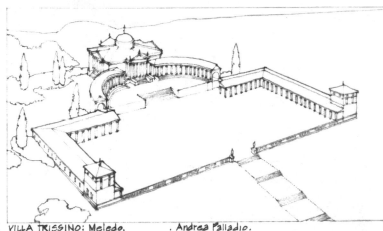

VILLA TRISSINO: Meledo. . Andrea Palladio.

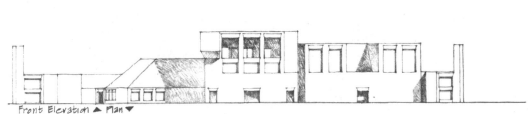

Front Elevation ▲ Plan ▼

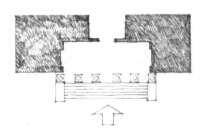

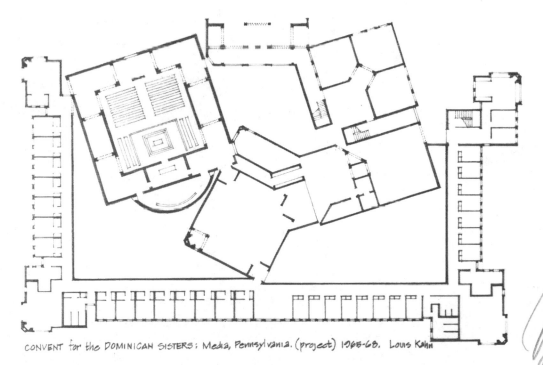

CONVENT for the DOMINICAN SISTERS; Media, Pennsylvania. (project) 1965-68. Louis Kahn

A "U"-shaped building form can also serve as a container, and organize within its field a cluster of forms and spaces.

It can define a forecourt for a building's approach as well as a recessed entrance within the volume of the building form itself.

U·SHAPED PLANES

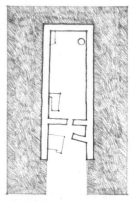

EARLY MEGARON SPACE
Principal room or hall of an early Anatolian or Aegean house.

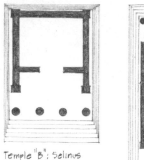

PLANS OF GREEK TEMPLES

Temple of Nemesis; Rhamnus

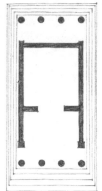

Temple "B"; Selinus

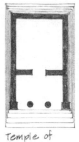

Temple on the Ilissus; Athens

"U"-shaped enclosures of interior space have a specific orientation toward their open end. They can group themselves around a central space to form an introverted organization.

The Hotel for Students at Otaniemi, by Alvar Aalto, demonstrates the use of "U"-shaped enclosures to define the basic unit of space in double-loaded schemes for dormitories, apartment, and hotels. These units are extroverted. They turn their back on the corridor and orient themselves to the exterior.

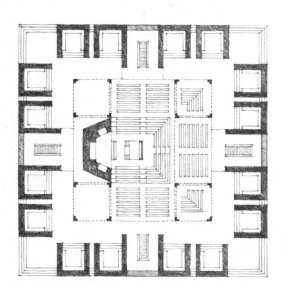

HURVA SYNAGOGUE: Jerusaleum, Israel (project) 1968. Louis Kahn

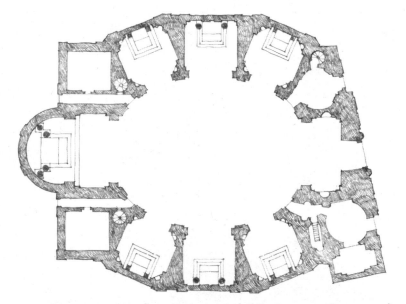

Sketch of an Oval Church by Borromini - Genisis of the organism of San Carlo Alle Quattro Fontane.

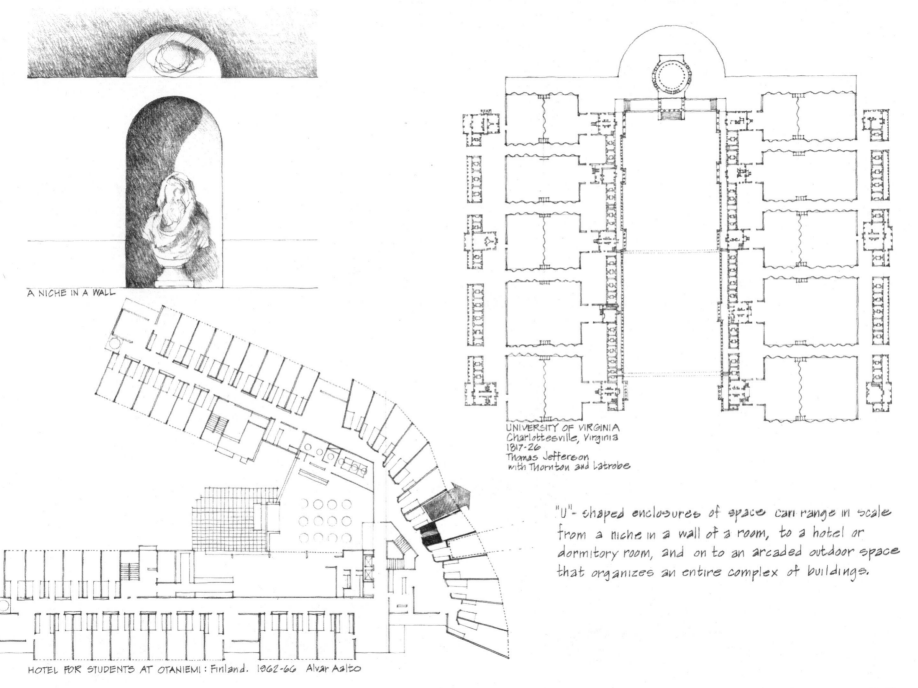

A NICHE IN A WALL

UNIVERSITY OF VIRGINIA
Charlottesville, Virginia
1817-26
Thomas Jefferson
with Thornton and Latrobe

HOTEL FOR STUDENTS AT OTANIEMI: Finland. 1962-66 Alvar Aalto

"U"- shaped enclosures of space can range in scale
from a niche in a wall of a room, to a hotel or
dormitory room, and on to an arcaded outdoor space
that organizes an entire complex of buildings.

4 PLANES: CLOSURE

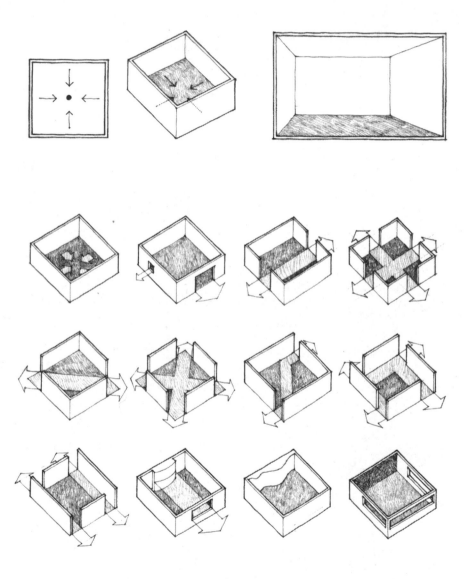

Four vertical planes completely enclosing a field of space is probably the most typical, and certainly the strongest, type of spatial definition in architecture. Since the field is completely enclosed, its space is introverted.

No spatial or visual continuity is possible with adjacent spaces without openings in the planes enclosing the field. At the same time these openings provide continuity with adjacent spaces, they can, depending on their size, number, and location, begin to weaken the enclosure of the space. These openings will also affect the orientation and flow of the space, its quality of light, its views, and the pattern of use and movement within it.

If openings are introduced between the enclosing planes at the corners of the space, the individual identity of the planes will be reinforced, and diagonal or pinwheel patterns of space, use, and movement will be encouraged.

To achieve visual dominance within the space, or become its primary face, one of the enclosing planes can be differentiated from the others by it size, form, surface articulation, or the nature of the openings within it.

Well-defined, enclosed fields of space can be found in architecture at several levels, from a large urban square, to a courtyard within a building, to a room within the building's organization. The examples on this and the following pages illustrate the uses of enclosed fields of space in urban and building-scale situations. The last section of this chapter specifically discusses enclosed spaces at the scale of a room, where the nature of the openings within the room's enclosure is a major factor in determining the quality of its space.

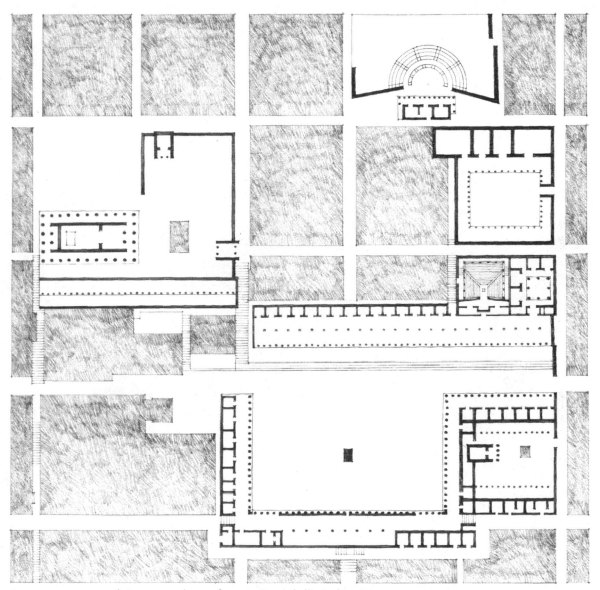

PLAN OF THE AGORA and its surroundings: Priene. Founded 4th Century B.C.

CLOSURE

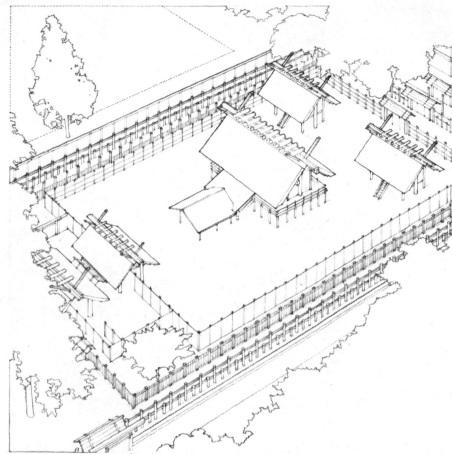

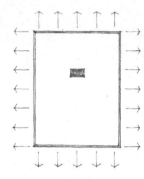
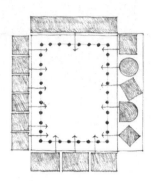

THE SACRED ENCLOSURE (NAIGU) ISE SHRINE: Mie Prefecture, Japan.
Shrine has been reconstructed every 20 years since 690 A.D.

Four planes can define a spatial and visual field for a sacred or significant building that stands as an object within the enclosure. In an urban context, the defined field of space can also organize buildings along its perimeter. In the first case, the enclosing planes are fences or walls that exclude surrounding elements from their territory. In the second case, the enclosure can consist of arcades or gallery spaces that promote the inclusion of surrounding buildings into their field. While the first enclosure isolates its field, the second activates the space it defines.

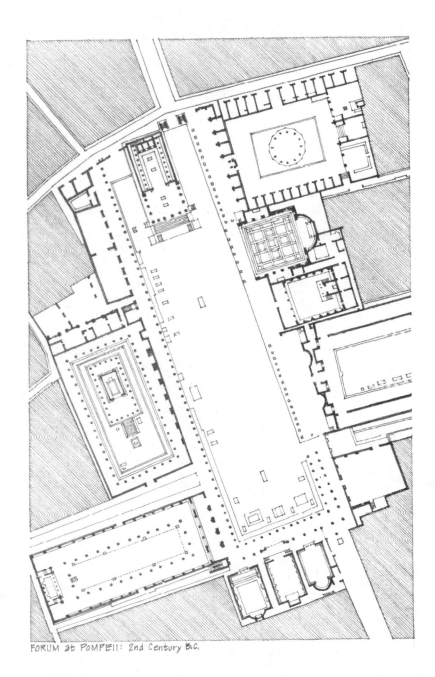

FORUM at POMPEII: 2nd Century B.C.

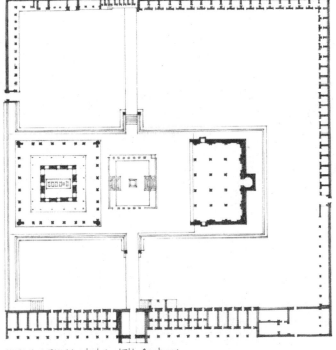

IBRAHIM RAUZA: India. 17th Century

CLOSURE

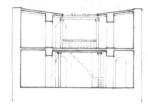

The examples on these two pages illustrate the use of enclosed fields or volumes of space as ordering elements about which a building's spaces can be clustered and organized. These organizing spaces can generally be characterized by their centrality within a building's organization, their clarity of definition, their regularity of form, and their dominating size. They are manifested here in the atrium spaces of houses, the arcaded cortile of an Italian palazzo, the cloister of a monastery, and the courtyard of a Finnish townhall.

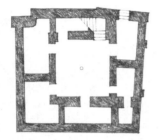

HOUSE: Ur of the Chaldees. C. 2000 B.C.

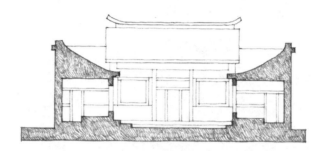

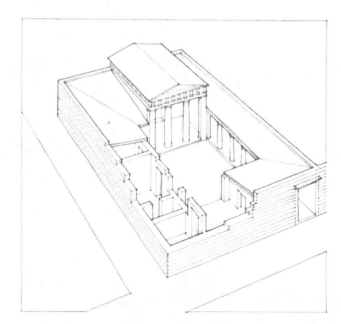

HOUSE Nº 33: Priene. C. Third Century B.C.

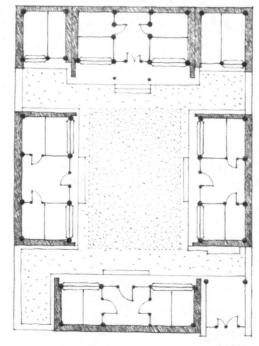

CHINESE PATIO HOUSE

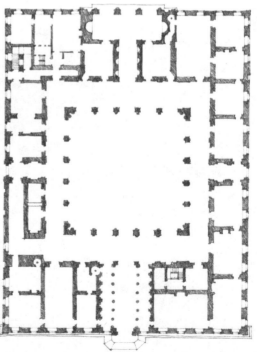

PALAZZO FARNESE: Rome. 1515 Antonio da Sangallo the Younger

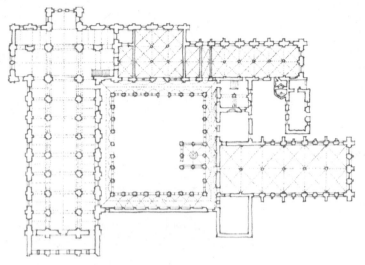

FONTENAY ABBEY: Burgundy, France. 1139 -

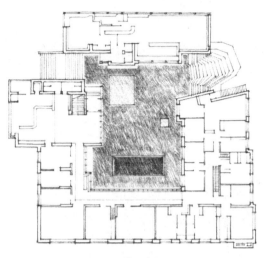

TOWN HALL: Säynätsalo, Finland. 1949-52
Alvar Aalto

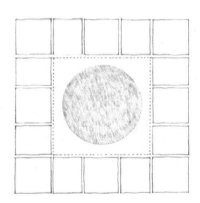

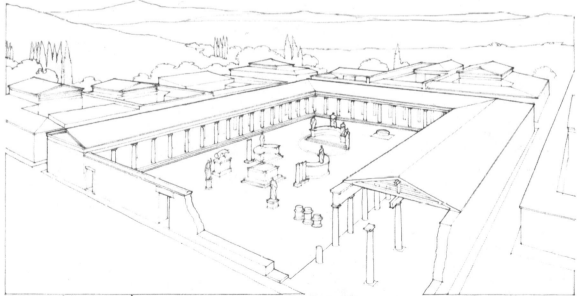

ENCLOSURE of the SHRINE of APOLLO DELPHINIOS: Miletus   c. 2nd Century B.C.

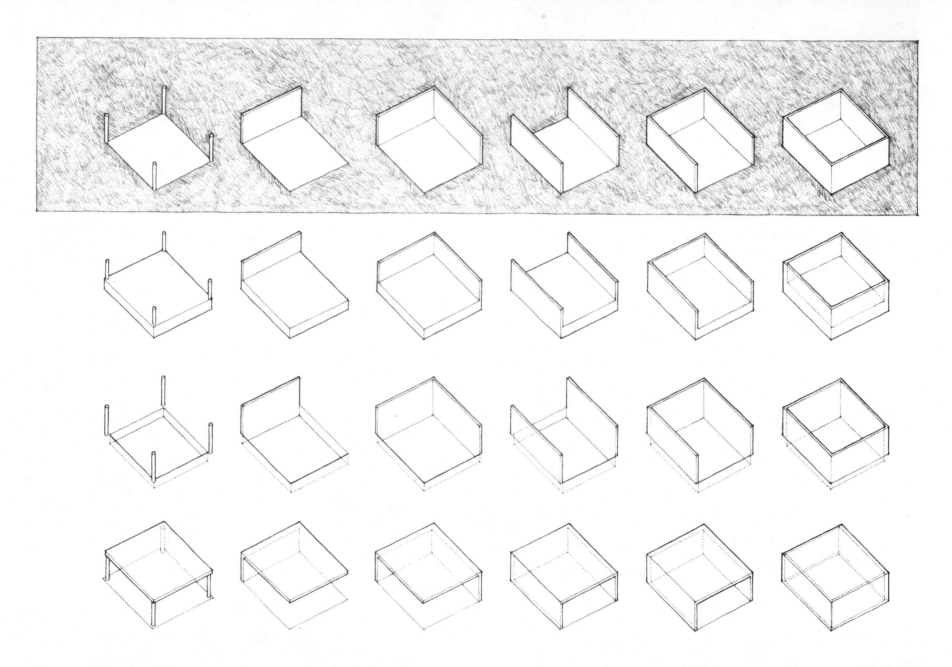

QUALITIES OF ARCHITECTURAL SPACE

The preceding categories of space-defining elements, summarized in the matrix to the left, consisted generally of simple configurations of linear and planar elements that defined basic, rectangular volumes of space. The qualities of an architectural space, however, are much richer than what the diagrams illustrate. These spatial qualities of form, proportion, scale, light, etc. will ultimately depend on the following properties of the enclosure of a space.

PROPERTIES OF ENCLOSURE

QUALITIES OF SPACE

- DIMENSIONS

- PROPORTION
- SCALE

- SHAPE
- CONFIGURATION

- FORM
- DEFINITION

- SURFACE
- EDGES

- COLOR
- TEXTURE
- PATTERN

- OPENINGS

- ENCLOSURE
- LIGHT
- VIEW

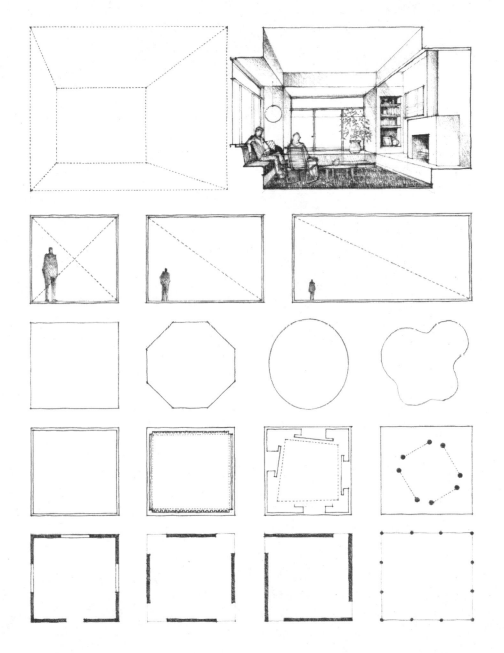

175

OPENINGS IN SPACE · DEFINING ELEMENTS

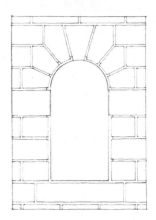 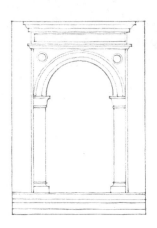 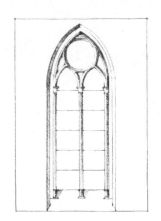  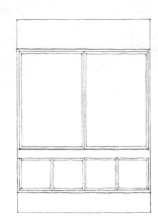

Doors offer entry into a room, and determine the patterns of movement and use within it. Windows allow light to penetrate the space and illuminate the surfaces of a room, offer views from the room to the exterior, establish visual relationships between the room and adjacent spaces, and provide ventilation for the space of the room.

The following section of this chapter discusses how the **SIZE SHAPE & LOCATION** of openings or voids within the enclosing forms of a space will affect the quality of a room's:

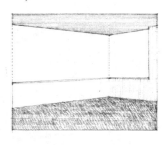

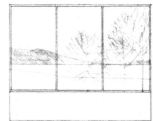

- **DEGREE OF ENCLOSURE**................the form of its space.

- **LIGHT**................the illumination of its surfaces and forms.

- **VIEW**................the focus of its space.

BAY WINDOW OF THE LIVING ROOM: HILL HOUSE. Helensburgh, Scotland. 1902-3. Charles Rennie Mackintosh.

DEGREE OF ENCLOSURE

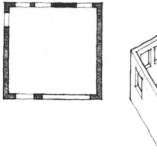

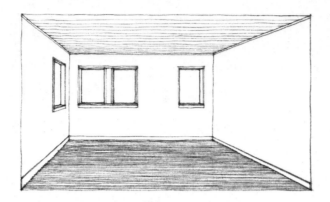

The degree of enclosure of a space, as determined by the configuration of its defining elements and the pattern of its openings, has a significant impact on our perception of the orientation and overall form of the space.

Openings lying wholly within the enclosing planes of a space do not weaken the edge definition nor the sense of enclosure of the space. The form of the space remains intact and perceptible.

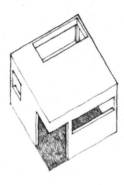
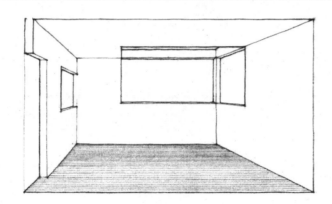

Openings located along the edges of the enclosing planes of a space will visually weaken the corner boundaries of the space. While these openings can erode the overall form of a space, they will also promote its visual continuity and interlocking with adjacent spaces.

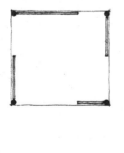

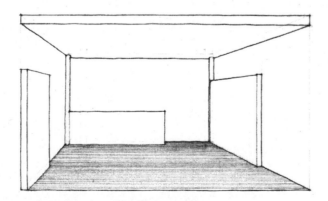

Openings between the enclosing planes of a space isolate the planes visually and articulate their individuality. As these openings increase in number and size, the space loses its sense of enclosure, becomes more diffuse, and begins to merge with adjacent spaces. The visual emphasis is on the enclosing planes rather than the volume of space defined by the planes.

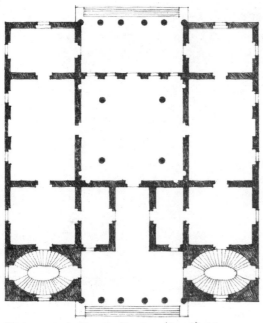

PALAZZO GARZADORE: Vicenza, (Project). 1570
Andrea Palladio

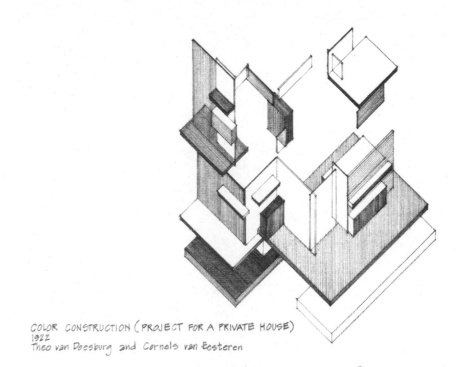

COLOR CONSTRUCTION (PROJECT FOR A PRIVATE HOUSE)
1922
Theo van Doesburg and Cornels van Eesteren

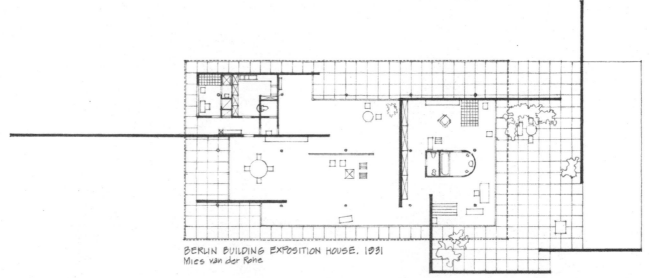

BERLIN BUILDING EXPOSITION HOUSE, 1931
Mies van der Rohe

LIGHT

NOTRE·DAME·DU·HAUT: Ronchamp, France. 1950-55. Le Corbusier

The sun is a rich source of light for the illumination of forms and spaces in architecture. The quality of its light changes with the time of day, and from season to season. And it transmits the changing colors and moods of the sky and the weather to the surfaces and forms it illuminates.

Entering a room through windows in the wall plane, or through skylights in the roof plane overhead, the sun's light falls on surfaces within the room, enlivens their colors, and articulates their textures. With the changing patterns of light and shade that it creates, the sun animates the space of the room, and articulates the forms within it. By its intensity and distribution within the room, the sun's light can clarify the form of the space or distort it; it can create a festive atmosphere within the room or instill within it a somber mood.

Since the intensity of the light the sun offers us is fairly constant, and its direction predictable, the determinants for its visual impact on the surfaces, forms, and space of a room are the size, location, and orientation of the room's windows and skylights.

Second-story west bedroom
KAUFMANN HOUSE, "FALLINGWATER"
Connelsville, Pa. 1936-37
Frank Lloyd Wright

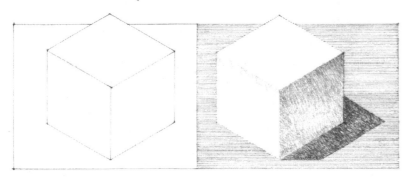

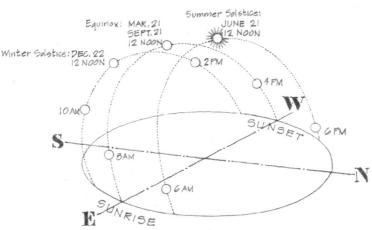

Equinox: MAR. 21 SEPT. 21 12 NOON

Summer Solstice: JUNE 21 12 NOON

Winter Solstice: DEC. 22 12 NOON

10 AM · 8 AM · 6 AM · 2 PM · 4 PM · 6 PM

S · W · N · E

SUNSET · SUNRISE

SUN PATH DIAGRAM FOR THE NORTHERN HEMISPHERE

LIGHT

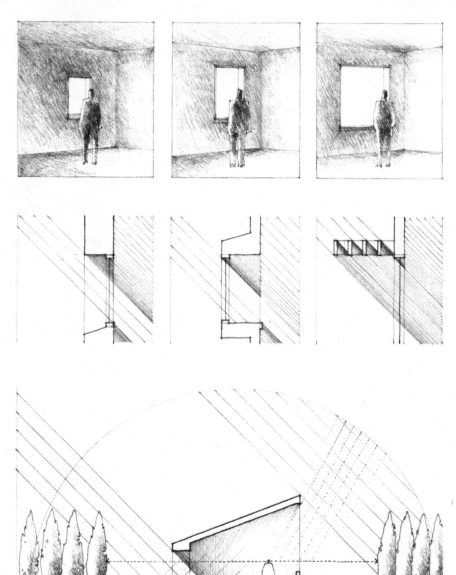

The size of a window or skylight will, of course, control the amount of daylight a room receives. The size of an opening in a wall or roof plane, however, can be determined by additional factors other than light, such as the material and construction of the wall or roof plane, requirements for visual privacy, ventilation, and enclosure of the space, or the opening's effect on the building's exterior form and appearance. The location and orientation of a window or skylight, therefore, can be more important than its size in determining the quality of daylight a room receives.

An opening can be oriented to receive direct sunlight during certain portions of the day. Direct sunlight provides a high degree of illumination that is especially intense during midday hours. It creates sharp patterns of light and dark on the surfaces of a room, and crisply articulates the forms within the space. Possible detrimental effects of direct sunlight, such as glare and excessive heat gain, can be controlled by shading devices built into the form of the opening, or provided by the foliage of nearby trees or adjacent structures.

An opening can also be oriented away from direct sunlight and receive instead the diffuse, ambient light from the "sky-vault" overhead. The "sky-vault" is a beneficial source of daylight since it remains fairly constant, even on cloudy days, and can help to soften the harshness of direct sunlight and balance the light level within a space.

The location of an opening will affect the manner in which light enters a room and illuminates its forms and surfaces. When located wholly within a wall plane, an opening will appear as a bright spot of light on a darker surface. This condition can be a source of glare if the opening's brightness contrasts greatly with the dark surface surrounding it. Conditions of glare, caused by excessive brightness ratios between adjacent surfaces or areas in a room, can be ameliorated by allowing daylight to enter the space from at least two directions.

When an opening is located along the edge of a wall, or at the corner of a room, the daylight entering through it will wash the surface of the wall adjacent and perpendicular to the plane of the opening. This illuminated surface will itself become a source of light and enhance the light level within the space.

Additional factors may also affect the quality of light within a room. The shape and articulation of an opening will be reflected in the shadow pattern it casts on the surfaces of the room. The color and texture of these surfaces will affect their reflectivity and, therefore, the ambient light level within the space.

VIEW

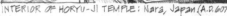

INTERIOR OF HORYU-JI TEMPLE: Nara, Japan (A.D. 607)

VISTA: Based on a sketch by Le Corbusier for the design of the Ministry of National Education and Public Health in Rio de Janeiro. 1936

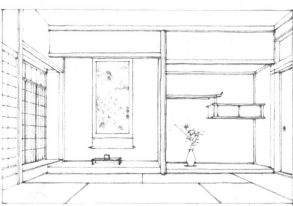

TOKONOMA in a Japanese House: AN INTERNAL FOCUS

Another quality of space that must be considered in establishing openings in the enclosure of a room is its focus and orientation. While some rooms have an internal focus, such as a fireplace, others have an outward orientation given to them by a view to the outdoors or an adjacent space. Window and skylight openings provide this view, and establish a visual relationship between a room and its surroundings. The size and location of these openings, of course, will determine the nature of the view seen through them.

A small opening tends to frame a view so that it is seen as a painting on a wall. A long, narrow opening will give only a hint of what lies beyond the room. A large opening opens a room up to a broad vista. The large scene can dominate a space or serve as a backdrop for the activities within it. A large bay window can project a person into a scene.

A window can be located in the corner of a room to give it a diagonal orientation. It can be located such that a view can be seen from only one position in the room. It can be oriented upward to offer a view of treetops and the sky. A group of windows can be sequenced to fragment a scene and encourage movement within a space.

OPENINGS: THE BASIC VARIATIONS

  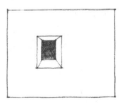 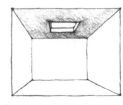

CENTERED   OFF-CENTER   GROUPED   DEEP-SET   SKYLIGHT

1. WITHIN PLANES

An opening can be located wholly within a wall or ceiling plane and be surrounded on all sides by the surface of the plane.

   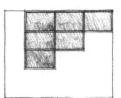 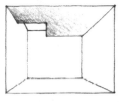

ALONG ONE EDGE   ALONG TWO EDGES   TURNING A CORNER   GROUPED   SKYLIGHT

2. AT CORNERS

An opening can be located along one edge or at a corner of a wall or ceiling plane. In either case, the opening will be at a corner of a space.

 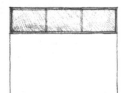 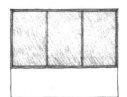 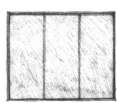 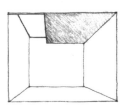

VERTICAL   HORIZONTAL   ¾ OPENING   WINDOW-WALL   SKYLIGHT

3. BETWEEN PLANES

An opening can visually span vertically between the floor and ceiling planes, or horizontally between two wall planes. It can grow in size to occupy an entire wall of a space.

OPENINGS WITHIN PLANES

An opening located wholly within a wall or ceiling plane will appear as a bright figure on a contrasting field or background. If centered within the plane, the opening will appear stable and visually organize the surface around it. Moving the opening off-center will create a degree of visual tension between the opening and the edges of the plane toward which it is moved.

The shape of the opening, if similar to the shape of the plane in which it is located, will create a redundant compositional pattern. The shape or orientation of the opening may contrast with the enclosing plane to emphasize its individuality as a figure. The individuality of an opening may also be visually reinforced with a heavy frame.

Multiple openings may be clustered to form a unified composition within a plane, or be staggered or dispersed to create visual movement along the surface of the plane.

As an opening within a plane increases in size, it will, at some point, cease to be a figure within an enclosing field, and become a positive element in itself, a transparent plane bounded by a heavy frame.

Openings within planes will appear brighter than their adjacent surfaces. If the contrast in brightness along the edges of the openings becomes excessive, the surfaces can be illuminated by a second light source from within the space, or a deep-set opening can be formed to create illuminated intermediate surfaces between the opening and the surrounding plane.

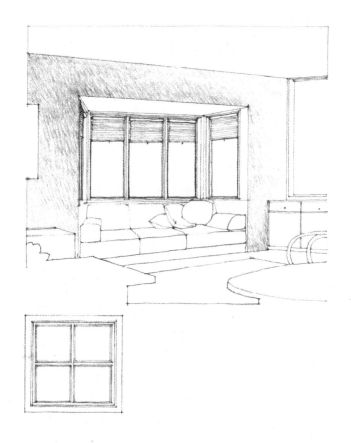

CHAPEL SPACE: NOTRE-DAME-DU-HAUT, Ronchamp, France, 1950-55. Le Corbusier.

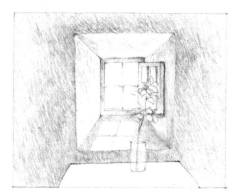

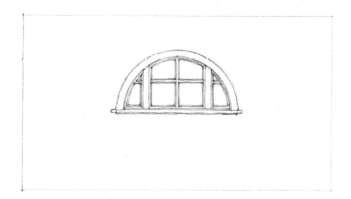

OPENINGS AT CORNERS

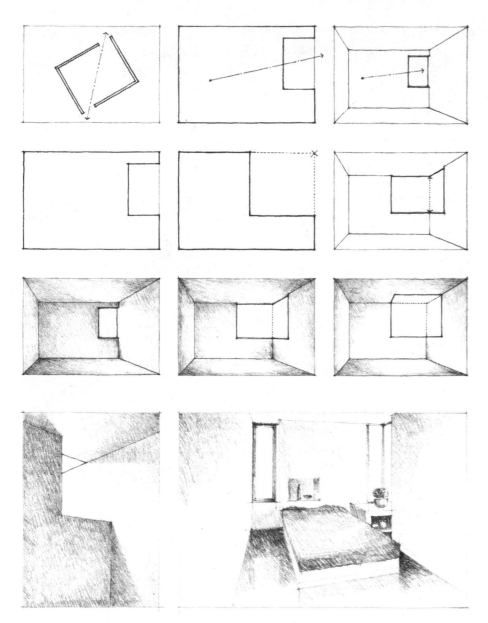

Openings that are located at corners will give a space and the planes in which they are located a diagonal orientation. This directional effect may be for compositional reasons, to capture a desirable view, or to brighten a dark corner of a space.

A corner opening will visually erode the edges of the plane in which it is located, and articulate the edge of the plane adjacent and perpendicular to it. The larger the opening, the weaker will be the definition of the corner. If the opening were to "turn the corner," the corner of the space would be implied rather than real, and the spatial field would extend beyond its enclosing planes.

The light that enters a space through a corner opening will wash the surface of the plane adjacent and perpendicular to the opening. This illuminated surface will become itself a source of light and enhance the brightness level of the space. This brightness level would be enhanced further by "turning the corner" with the opening, or adding a skylight above the opening.

STUDIO: AMÉDÉE OZENFANT HOUSE. Paris. 1922-23. Le Corbusier

OPENINGS BETWEEN PLANES

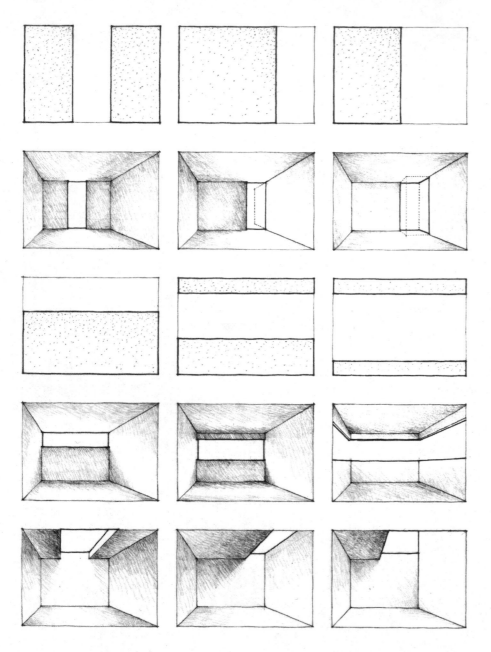

A vertical opening that extends from the floor to the ceiling plane of a space will visually separate and articulate the edges of the adjacent wall planes.

If located at a corner of a space, the vertical opening will erode the definition of the space and allow it to extend beyond the corner to the adjacent space. It will also allow incoming light to wash the surface of the wall plane perpendicular to it, and articulate the primacy of that plane in the space. If allowed to "turn the corner," the vertical opening will further erode the definition of the space, allow it to interlock with adjacent spaces, and emphasize the individuality of the enclosing planes.

A horizontal opening that extends across a wall plane will separate it into a number of horizontal layers. If the opening is not very deep, it will not erode the integrity of the wall plane. If its depth, however, increases to the point where it is greater than the bands above and below it, then the opening will become a positive element bounded at its top and bottom by heavy frames.

Turning a corner with a horizontal opening will reinforce the horizontal layering of a space, and broaden the panoramic view from within the space. If the opening continues around the space, it will visually lift the ceiling plane from the wall planes, isolate it, and give it a feeling of lightness.

Locating a linear skylight along the edge where a wall and ceiling plane meet will allow incoming light to wash the surface of the wall, illuminate it, and enhance the brightness level of the space. The form of the skylight can be manipulated to capture direct sunlight, indirect daylight, or a combination of both.

Window-wall openings provide larger views and a greater amount of light to penetrate a space than any of the previous examples of openings. If they are oriented to capture direct sunlight, sun-shading devices may be necessary to reduce glare and excessive heat gain within the space.

While a window-wall weakens the vertical boundaries of a space, it creates the potential for visually expanding the space beyond its physical boundaries.

Combining a window-wall with a large skylight overhead will create a greenhouse space in which the boundaries between inside and outside become obscure and tenuous.

LIVING ROOM: VILLA MAIREA, Noormarkku, Finland. 1938-39. Alvar Aalto

A GREENHOUSE SPACE

LIVING ROOM: SAMUEL FREEMAN HOUSE, Los Angeles, California. 1924. Frank Lloyd Wright

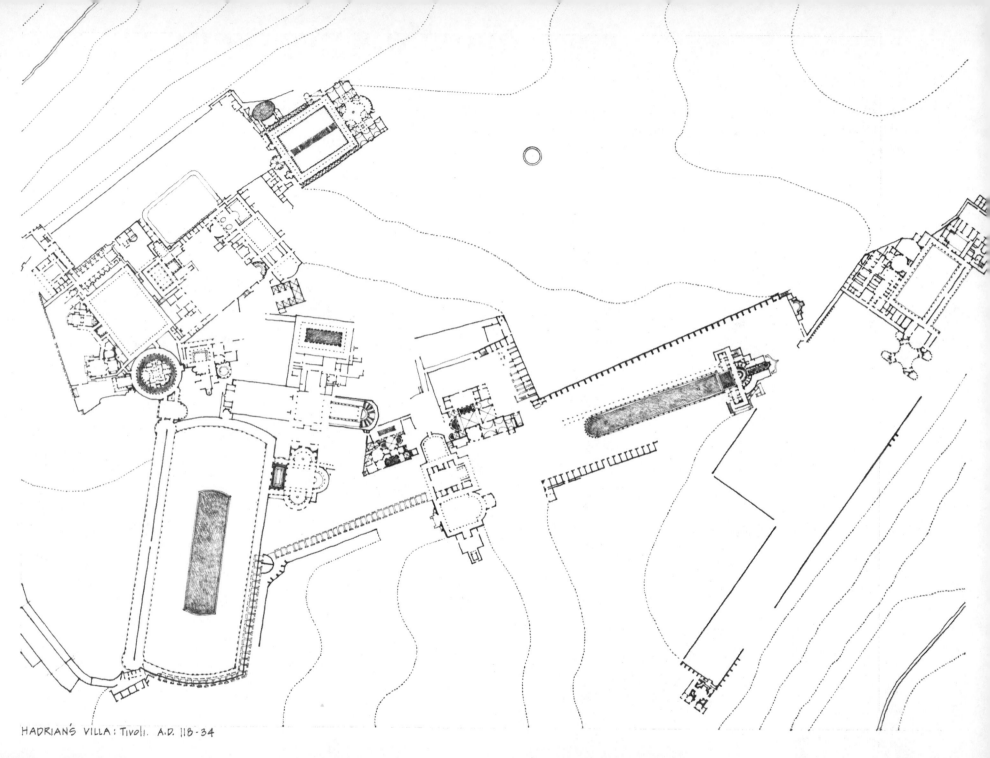

HADRIAN'S VILLA: TIVOLI. A.D. 118-34

4

ORGANIZATIONS

ORGANIZATIONS OF FORM & SPACE

The last chapter discussed how various configurations of form could be manipulated to define a solitary field or volume of space, and how their patterns of solids and voids affected the visual qualities of the defined space. Few buildings, however, consist of a solitary space. They are normally composed of a number of spaces that are related to one another by function, proximity, or a circulation path. This chapter lays out for discussion the basic ways a building's spaces can be related to one another and organized into coherent patterns of form and space.

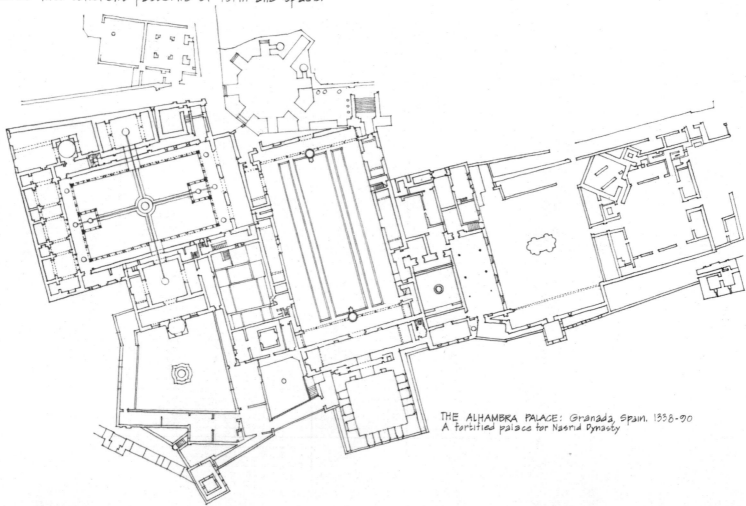

THE ALHAMBRA PALACE: Granada, Spain. 1338-90
A fortified palace for Nasrid Dynasty

SPATIAL RELATIONSHIPS

1. SPACE WITHIN A SPACE

2. INTERLOCKING SPACES

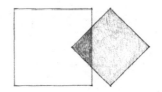

3. ADJACENT SPACES

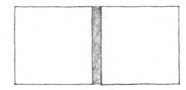

4. SPACES LINKED BY A COMMON SPACE

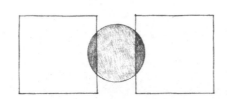

SPACE WITHIN A SPACE

 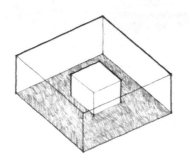

A large space can envelop, and contain within its volume, a smaller space. Visual and spatial continuity between the two spaces can be easily accommodated, but the smaller, "contained" space depends on the larger, enveloping space for its relationship to outdoor space.

In this type of spatial relationship, the larger, enveloping space serves as a three-dimensional field for the space contained within it. For this concept to be perceived, a clear differentiation in size is necessary between the two spaces. If the contained space were to increase in size, the larger space would begin to lose its impact as an enveloping form. If the contained space continued to grow, the residual space around it would become too compressed to serve as an enveloping space. It would become instead merely a thin layer or skin around the contained space. The original notion would be destroyed.

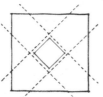 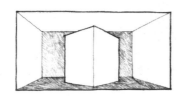

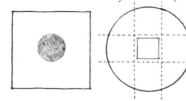 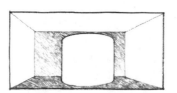

To endow itself with a higher attention-value, the contained space may share the form of the enveloping shape, but be oriented in a different manner. This would create a secondary grid and a set of dynamic, residual spaces within the larger space.

The contained space may also differ in form from the enveloping space, and strengthen its image as a freestanding object. This contrast in form may indicate a functional difference between the two spaces, or the symbolic importance of the contained space.

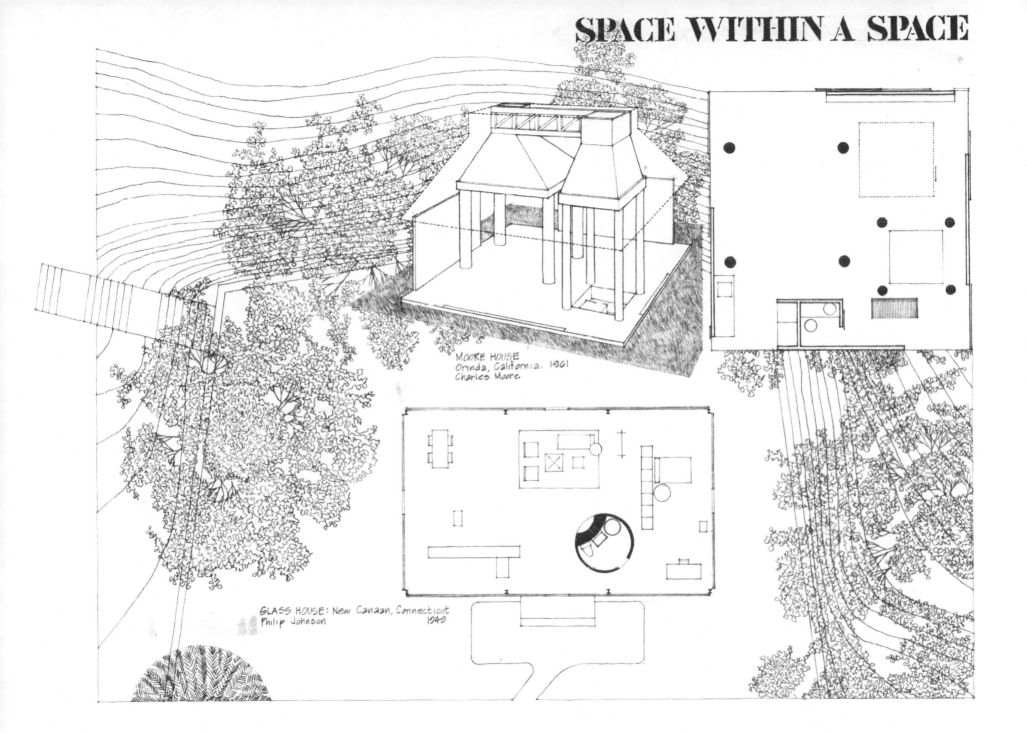

MOORE HOUSE
Orinda, California, 1961
Charles Moore

GLASS HOUSE: New Canaan, Connecticut
Philip Johnson   1949

INTERLOCKING SPACES

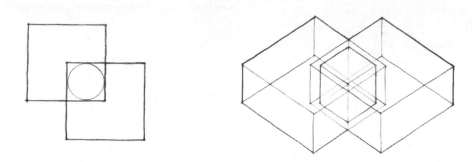

An interlocking spatial relationship consists of two spaces whose fields overlap to form a zoned of shared space. When two spaces interlock their volumes in this manner, each retains its identity and definition as a space. But the resulting configuration of the two interlocking spaces will be subject to a number of interpretations.

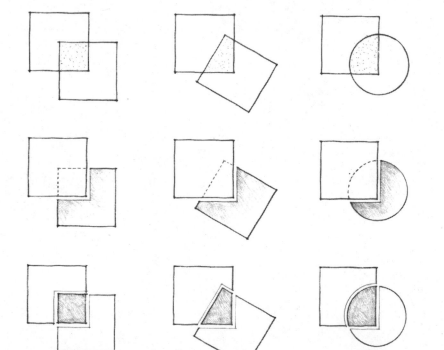

The interlocking portion of the two volumes can be shared equally by each space.

The interlocking portion can merge with one of the spaces and become an integral part of its volume.

The interlocking portion can develop its own integrity as a space that serves to link the two original spaces.

PLAN FOR ST. PETER: ROME ("Second Version") Bramante & Peruzzi

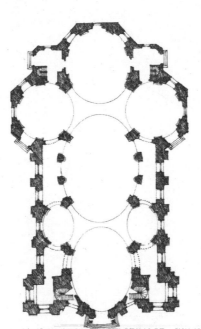

VIERZEHNHEILIGEN PILGRAMAGE CHURCH near Bamberg Germany, 1743-72 Balthasar Neumann

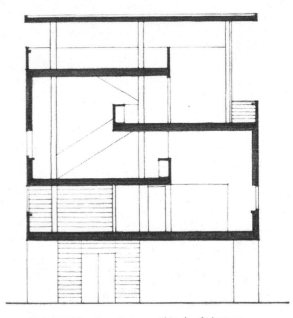

VILLA AT CARTHAGE; Tunisia, 1928 Le Corbusier

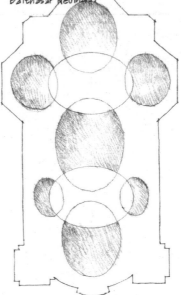

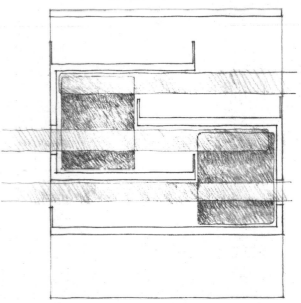

ADJACENT SPACES

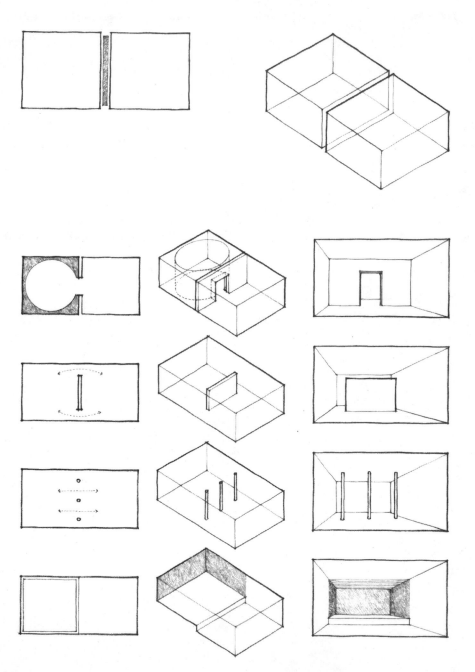

Adjacency is the most common type of spatial relationship. It allows each space to be clearly defined and to respond, each in its own way, to its functional or symbolic requirements. The degree of visual and spatial continuity that occurs between two adjacent spaces will depend on the nature of the plane that both separates and binds them together.

The separating plane may:

• limit visual and physical access between two adjacent spaces, reinforce the individuality of each space, and accommodate their differences.

• appear as a freestanding plane in a single volume of space.

• be defined with a row of columns that allows a high degree of visual and spatial continuity between the two spaces.

• be merely implied with a change in level or surface articulation between the two spaces. This and the preceding two cases can also be read as single volumes of space that are divided into two related zones.

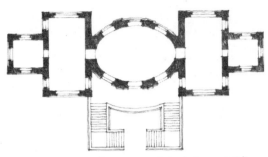

PAVILION DESIGN: Fischer von Erlach (1656-1723)

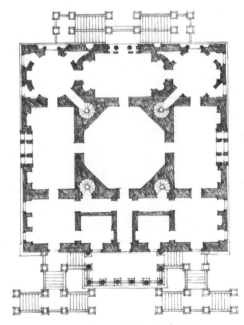

CHISWICK HOUSE: Chiswick, England. 1729
Lord Burlington

The spaces in these two buildings are individualistic in size and form.

The walls that enclose them adapt their forms to accommodate the differences between adjacent spaces.

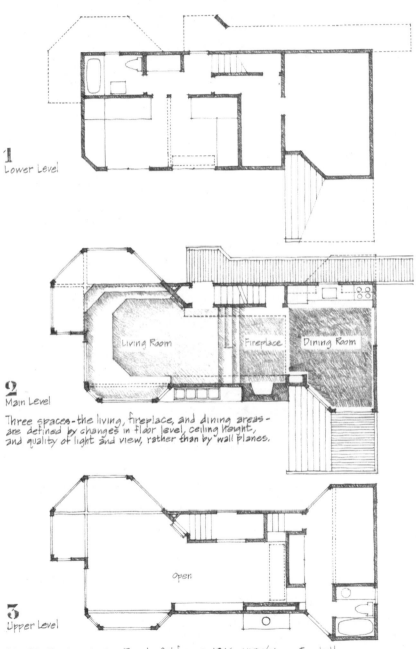

1 Lower Level

2 Main Level

Three spaces—the living, fireplace, and dining areas—are defined by changes in floor level, ceiling height, and quality of light and view, rather than by wall planes.

3 Upper Level

LAWRENCE HOUSE: Sea Ranch, California. 1966. MLTW/Moore-Turnbull

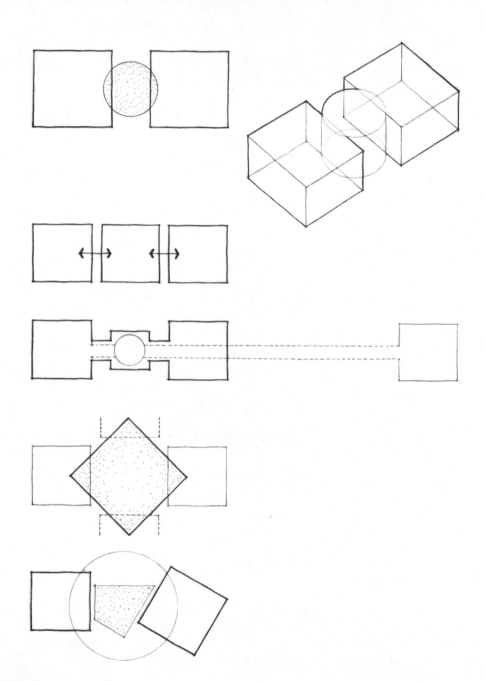

Two spaces that are separated by distance can be linked, or related to each other, by a third, intermediate space. The relationship between the two spaces will depend on the nature of the third space to which they share a common relationship.

The intermediate space can differ in form and orientation from the two spaces to express its linking function.

The two spaces, as well as the intermediate space, can be equivalent in shape and size and form a linear sequence of spaces.

The intermediate space can itself become linear in form to link two spaces that are distant from each other, or join a whole series of spaces that have no direct relationship to one another.

The intermediate space can, if large enough, become the dominant space in the relationship, and be capable of organizing a number of spaces about itself.

The form of the intermediate space may be determined solely by the forms and orientations of the two spaces being linked or related.

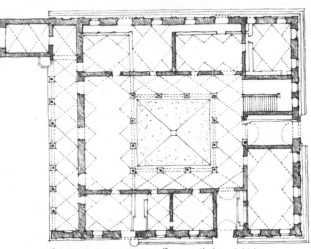

PALAZZO PICCOLOMINI: Pienza, Italy. C.1460
Bernardo Rossellino

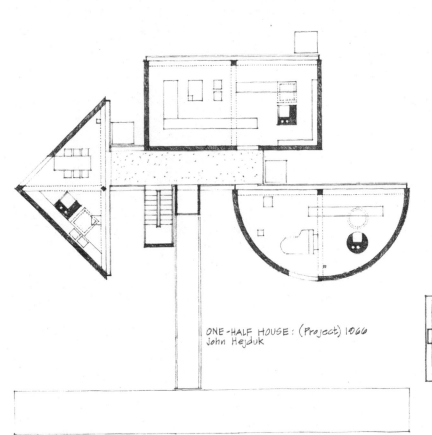

ONE-HALF HOUSE: (Project) 1966
John Hejduk

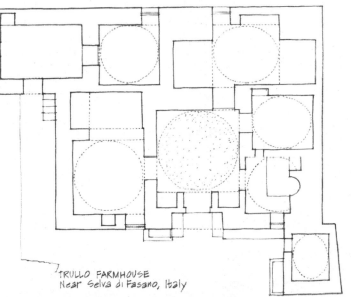

TRULLO FARMHOUSE
Near Selva di Fasano, Italy

After Edward Allen, *Stone Shelters*,
© M.I.T. Press 1969.

SPATIAL ORGANIZATIONS

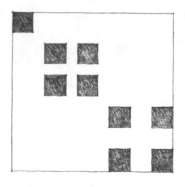

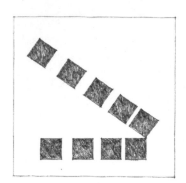
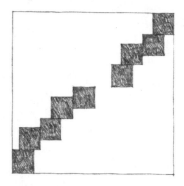

Compositions of nine squares: A Bauhaus study.

The following section lays out the basic ways we can arrange and organize a building's spaces. In a typical building program, there are usually requirements for various kinds of spaces. There may be requirements for spaces that:

- have specific functions or require specific forms,
- are flexible in use and can be freely manipulated,
- are singular and unique in their function or significance to the building organization,
- have similar functions and can be grouped into a functional cluster or repeated in a linear sequence,
- require exterior exposure for light, ventilation, view, or access to outdoor spaces,
- must be segregated for privacy,
- must be easily accessible.

The manner in which these spaces are arranged can clarify their relative importance and functional or symbolic role in a building's organization. The decision as to what type of organization to use in a specific situation will depend on:

- demands of the building program, such as functional proximities, dimensional requirements, hierarchical classification of the spaces, and requirements for access, light, or view;

- exterior conditions of the site that might limit the organization's form or growth, or that might encourage the organization to address certain features of its site and turn away from others.

Each category of spatial organization is introduced by a section that discusses the formal characteristics, spatial relationships, and contextual responses of the organization. A range of examples then illustrate the basic points made in the introduction. Each of the examples should be studied in terms of:

- What kinds of spaces are accommodated and where? How are they defined?
- What relationships are established among the spaces, one to another, and to the exterior?
- Where is the organization entered and what configuration does the circulation path have?
- What is the exterior form of the organization and how might it respond to its context?

1

CENTRALIZED

A central, dominant space about which a number of secondary spaces are grouped.

2

LINEAR

A linear sequence of repetitive spaces.

3

RADIAL

A central space from which linear organizations of space extend in a radial manner.

4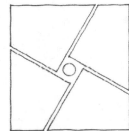

CLUSTERED

Spaces grouped by proximity or the sharing of a common visual trait or relationship.

5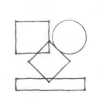

GRID

Spaces organized within the field of a structural or other three-dimensional grid.

Ideal Church by DaVinci

San Lorenzo Maggiore

A centralized organization is a stable, concentrated composition that consists of a number of secondary spaces grouped around a large, dominant, central space.

The central, unifying space of the organization is generally regular in form, and large enough in size to gather a number of secondary spaces about its form.

The secondary spaces of the organization may be equivalent to one another in function, form, and size, and create an overall configuration that is geometrically regular and symmetrical about two or more axes.

The secondary spaces may differ from one another in their form or size as a response to their individual requirements of function, relative importance, or context. This differentiation among the secondary spaces allows the form of a centralized organization to respond to varying conditions of its site.

Since the form of a centralized organization is inherently non-directional, conditions of approach and entry must be specified by its site and the articulation of one of the secondary spaces as an entrance form.

Circulation patterns within a centralized organization may be radial, loop, or spiral in form. In almost every case, however, the pattern will terminate in the central space.

Centralized organizations whose forms are relatively compact and geometrically regular can be used to:

- establish points or "places" in space;
- terminate axial compositions;
- serve as an object-form within a defined field or volume of space.

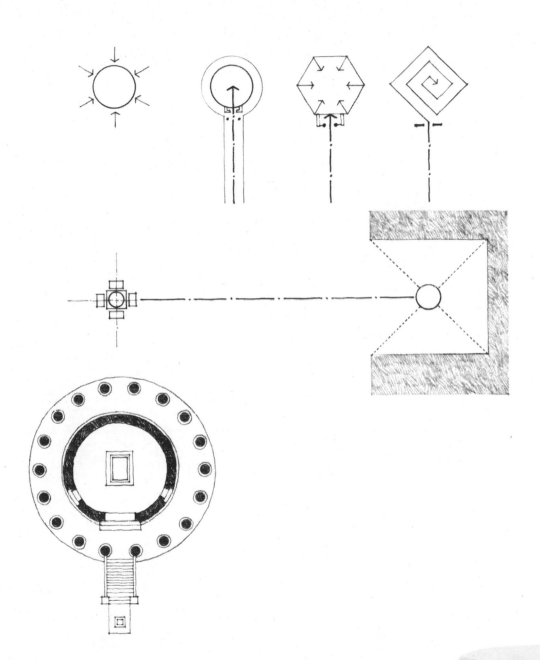

CENTRALIZED ORGANIZATIONS

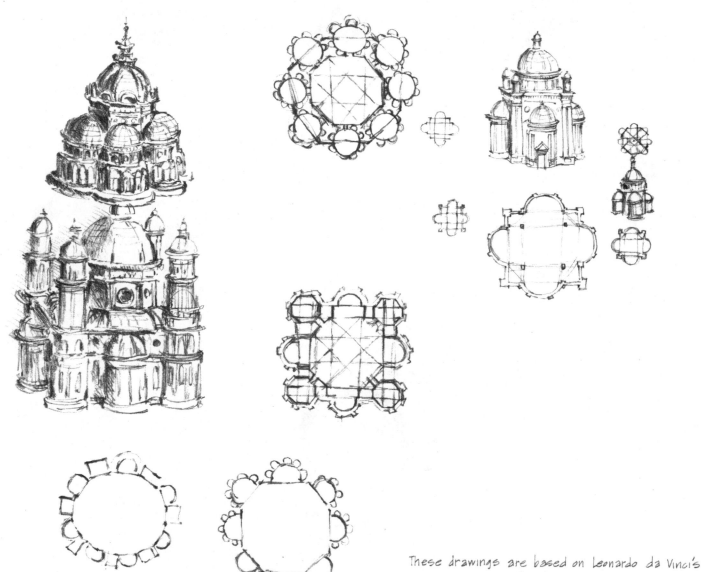

These drawings are based on Leonardo da Vinci's
sketches of "ideal" church plans. C. 1490

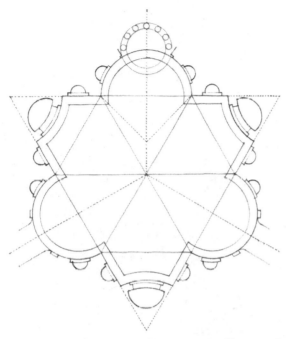

S. IVO DELLA SAPIENZA: Rome. 1642-50. Francesco Borromini

CENTRALIZED PLANS: Sebastiano Serlio. 1547

CENTRALIZED ORGANIZATIONS

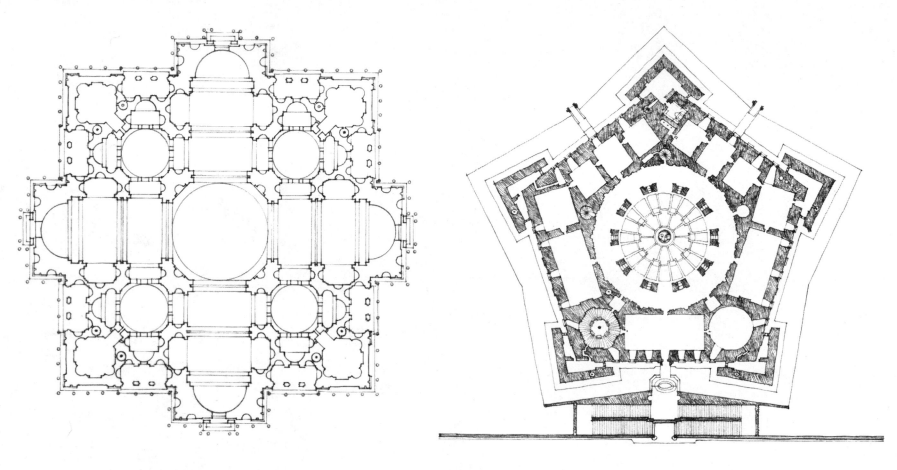

PLAN FOR ST. PETER: Rome (First version) C.1503. Bramante

PALAZZO FARNESE: Caprarola. 1547-9. Giacomo da Vignola

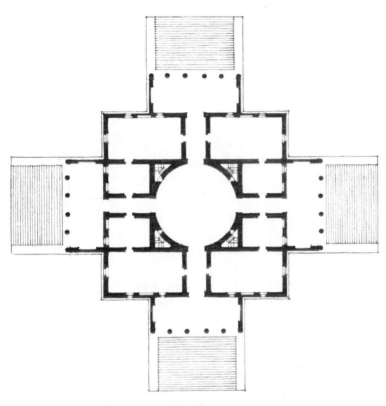

VILLA CAPRA ("ROTONDA"): Vicenza. 1552-70. Andrea Palladio

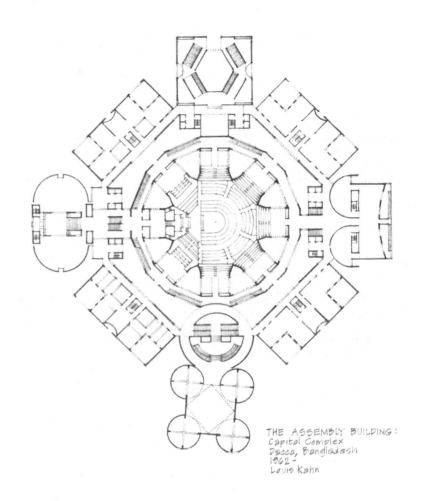

THE ASSEMBLY BUILDING:
Capitol Complex
Dacca, Bangladesh
1962-
Louis Kahn

CENTRALIZED ORGANIZATIONS

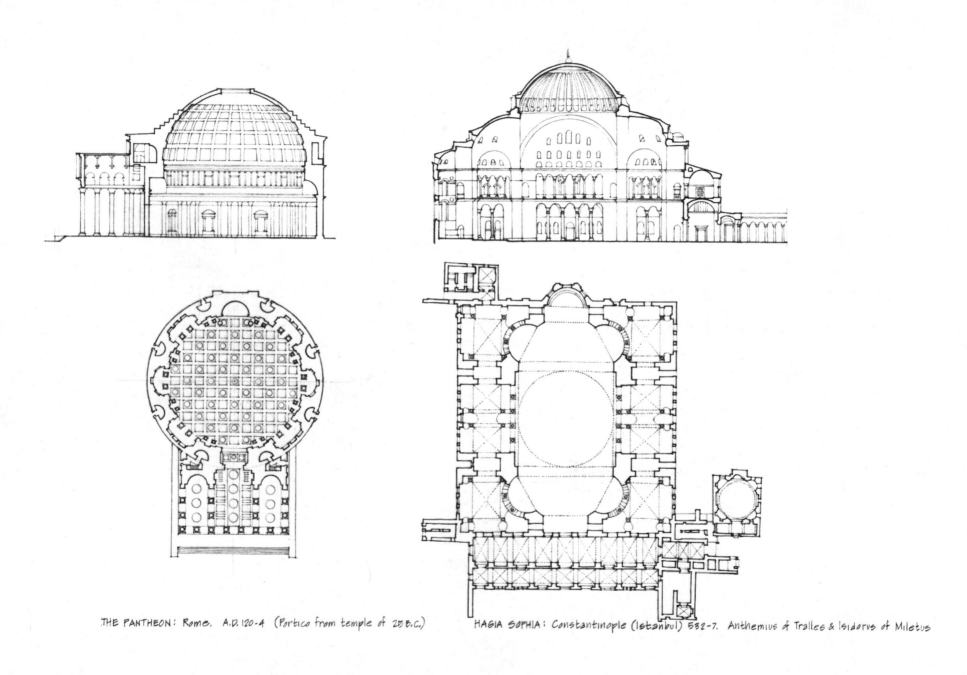

THE PANTHEON: Rome. A.D. 120-4 (Portico from temple of 25 B.C.)   HAGIA SOPHIA: Constantinople (Istanbul) 532-7. Anthemius of Tralles & Isidorus of Miletus

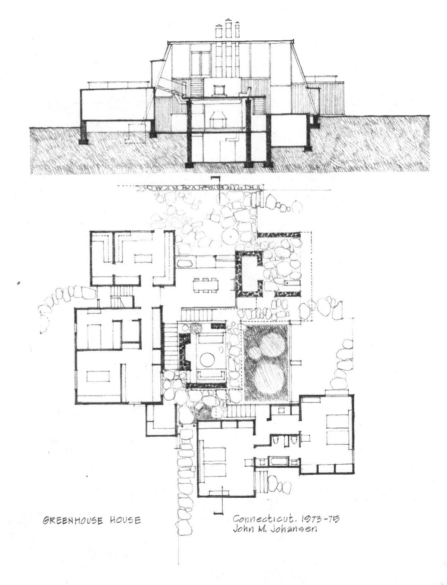

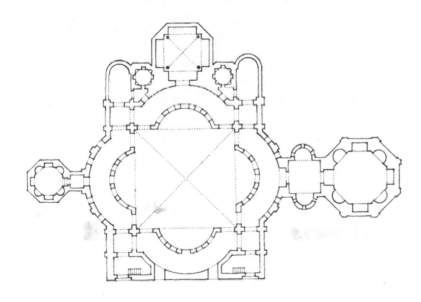

SAN LORENZO MAGGIORE: Milan, Italy. C. 480

GREENHOUSE HOUSE   Connecticut. 1973-75
John M. Johansen

LINEAR ORGANIZATIONS

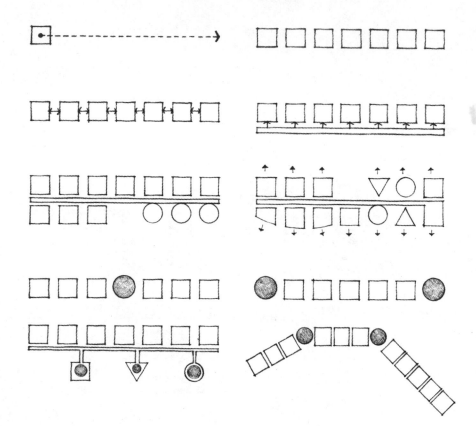

A linear organization consists essentially of a series of spaces.

These spaces can either be directly related to one another, or be linked through a separate and distinct linear space. **EXPRESSES DIRECTION**

A linear organization usually consists of repetitive spaces that are alike in size, form, and function. It can also consist of a linear space that organizes along its length a series of spaces that differ in size, form, or function. In both cases, each space along the sequence has an exterior exposure.

Spaces that are functionally or symbolically important to the organization can occur anywhere along the linear sequence and have their importance articulated by their size and form. Their significance can also be emphasized by their location: at the end of the linear sequence, offset from the linear organization, or at the pivotal points of a segmented linear form.

Because of their characteristic length, linear organizations express a direction, and signify movement, extension, and growth. To limit their growth, linear organizations can be terminated by a dominant space or form, by an elaborated or articulated entrance, or by merging with another building form or the topography of its site.

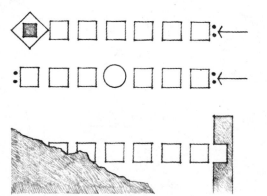

The form of a linear organization is inherently flexible and can respond readily to various conditions of its site. It can adapt to changes in topography, maneuver around a body of water or a stand of trees, or turn to orient its spaces to capture sunlight and views. It can be straight, segmented, or curvilinear. It can run horizontally across its site, or diagonally up a slope, or stand vertically as a tower.

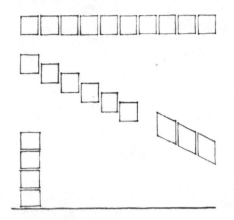

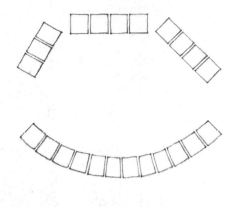

The form of a linear organization can relate to other forms in its context by:

- linking and organizing them along its length;

- serving as a wall or barrier to separate them into two different fields;

- surrounding and enclosing them within a field of space.

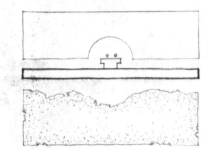

Curved and segmented forms of linear organizations enclose a field of exterior space on their concave sides and orient their spaces toward the center of the field. On their convex sides, these forms appear to front space and exclude it from their fields.

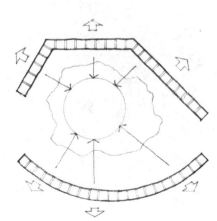

LINEAR ORGANIZATIONS

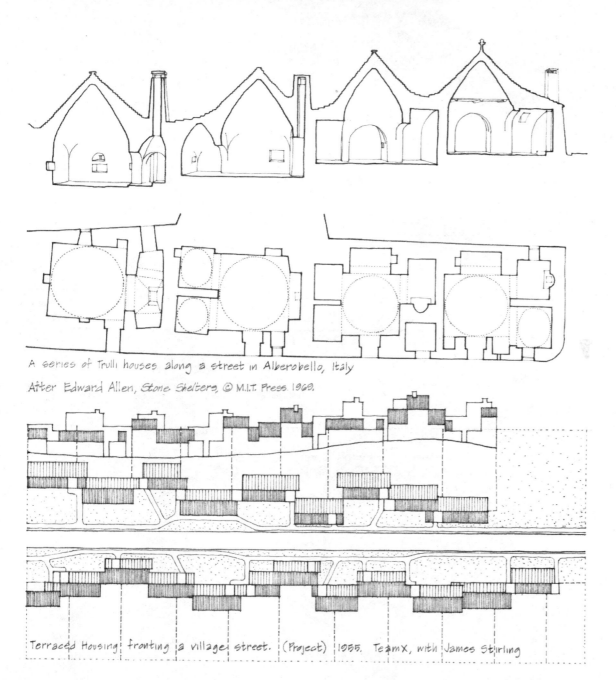

A series of Trulli houses along a street in Alberobello, Italy

After Edward Allen, *Stone Shelters,* © M.I.T. Press. 1969.

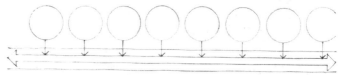

Terraced Housing fronting a village street. (Project) 1955. TeamX, with James Stirling

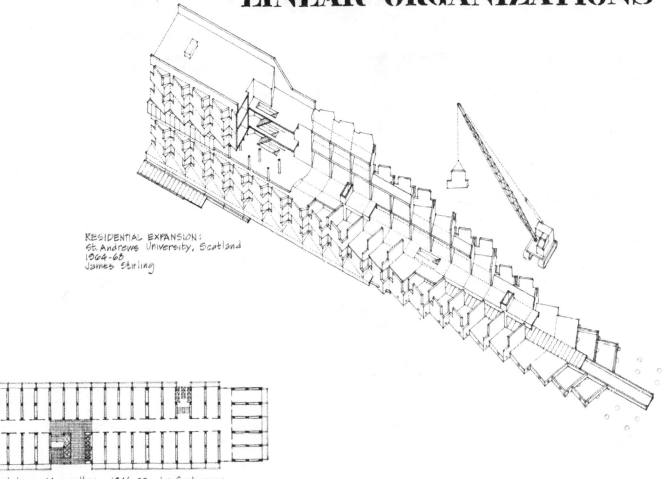

RESIDENTIAL EXPANSION:
St. Andrews University, Scotland
1964-68
James Stirling

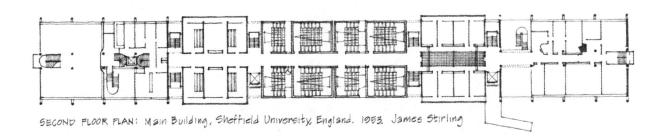

TYPICAL APARTMENT FLOOR: Unite' d'habitation, Marseilles. 1946-52. Le Corbusier

SECOND FLOOR PLAN: Main Building, Sheffield University, England. 1953. James Stirling

LINEAR ORGANIZATIONS

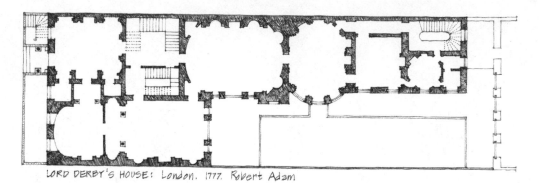

LORD DERBY'S HOUSE: London. 1777. Robert Adam

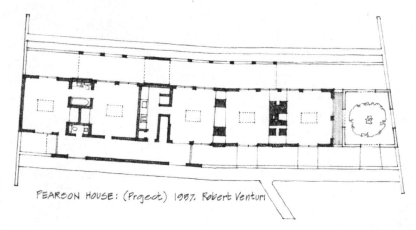

PEARSON HOUSE: (Project) 1957. Robert Venturi

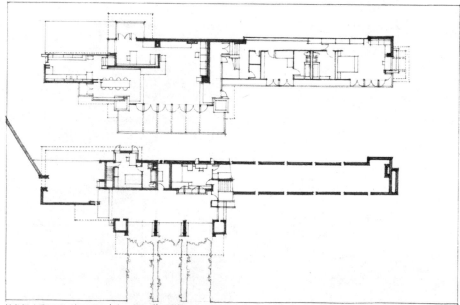

LLOYD LEWIS HOUSE: Libertyville, Illinois. 1940. Frank Lloyd Wright

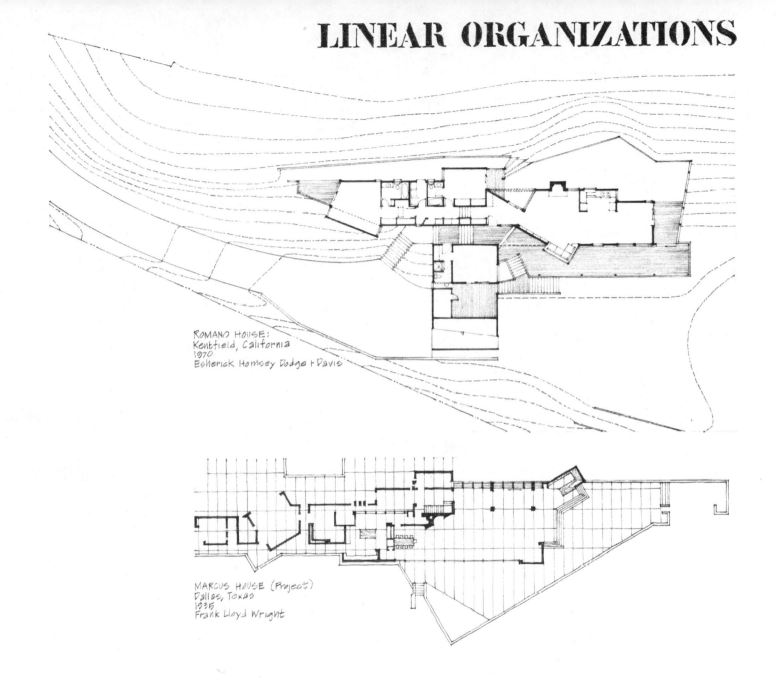

ROMANO HOUSE:
Kentfield, California
1970
Esherick Homsey Dodge + Davis

MARCUS HOUSE (Project)
Dallas, Texas
1935
Frank Lloyd Wright

LINEAR ORGANIZATIONS

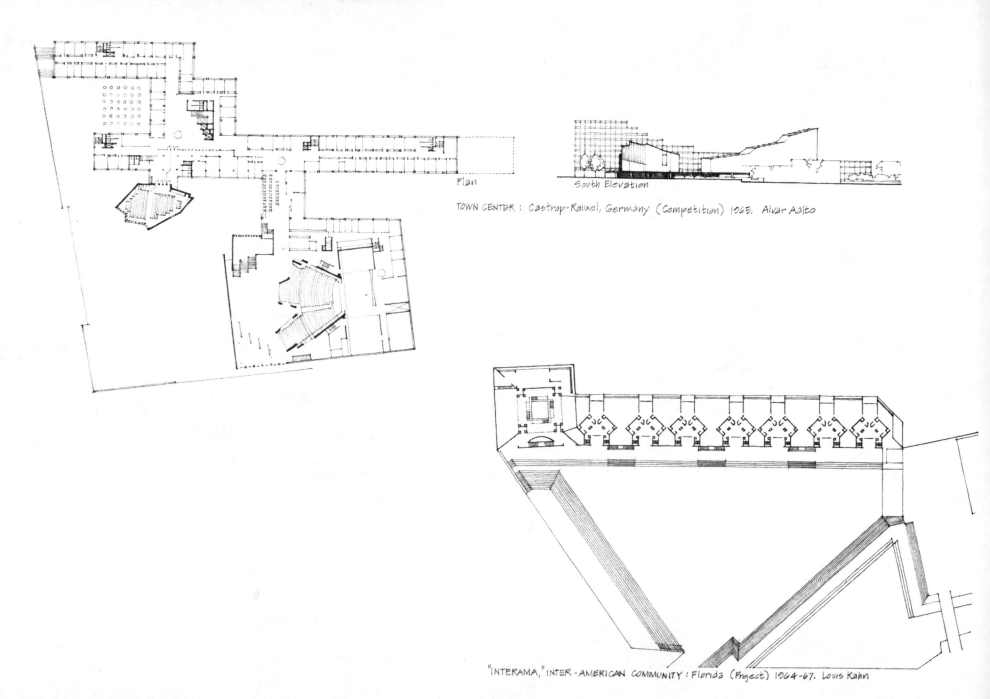

Plan

South Elevation

TOWN CENTER : Castrop-Rauxel, Germany (Competition) 1965. Alvar Aalto

"INTERAMA," INTER-AMERICAN COMMUNITY : Florida (Project) 1964-67. Louis Kahn

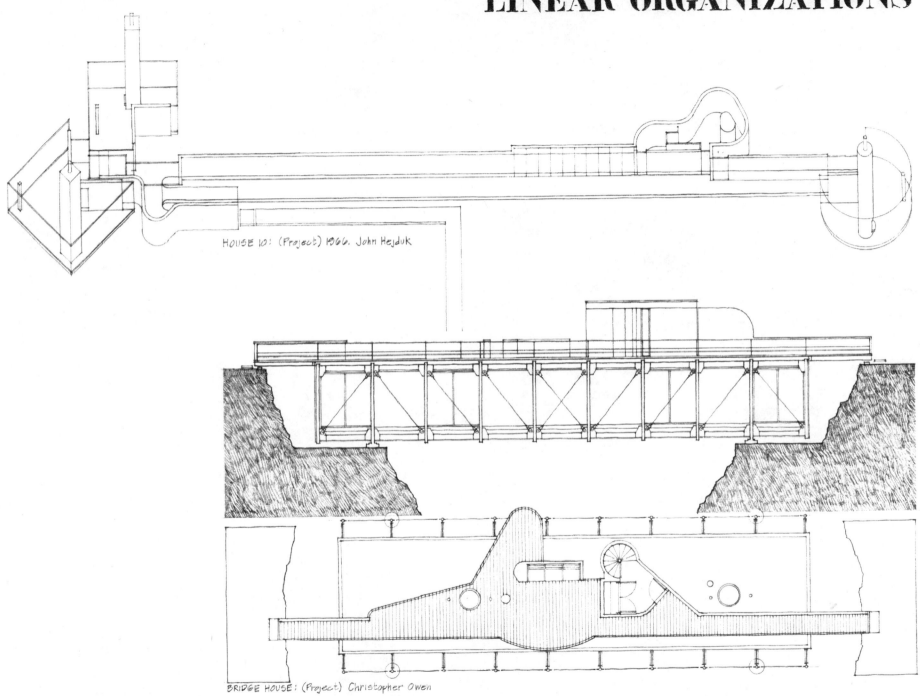

HOUSE 10: (Project) 1966. John Hejduk

BRIDGE HOUSE: (Project) Christopher Owen

LINEAR ORGANIZATIONS

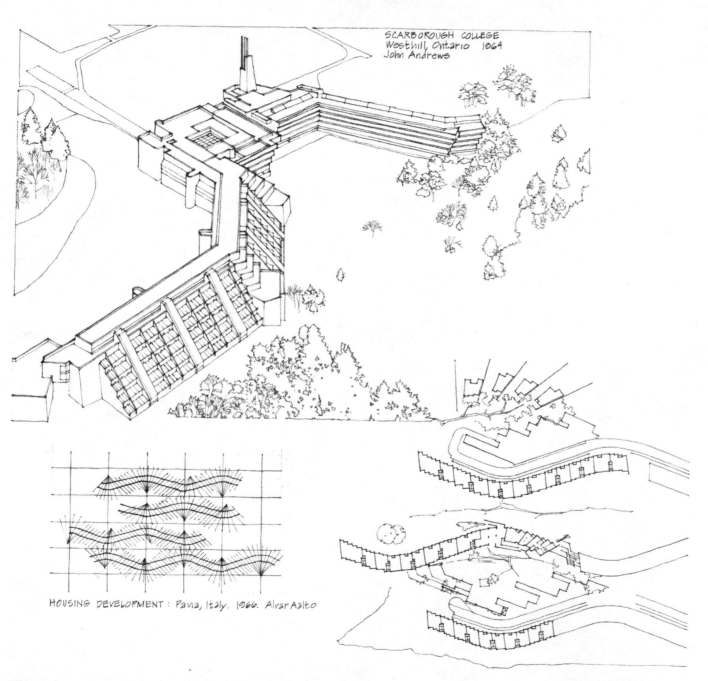

SCARBOROUGH COLLEGE
Westhill, Ontario 1964
John Andrews

HOUSING DEVELOPMENT: Pavia, Italy. 1966. Alvar Aalto

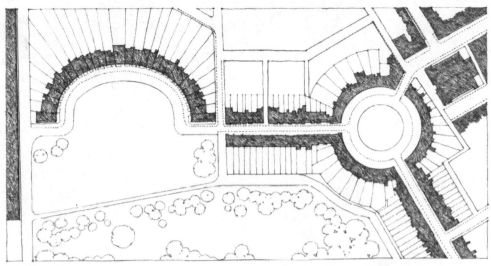

PLAN of THE ROYAL CRESCENT (1767-75, John Wood) and the CIRCUS (1754, John Wood, Sr.) at BATH

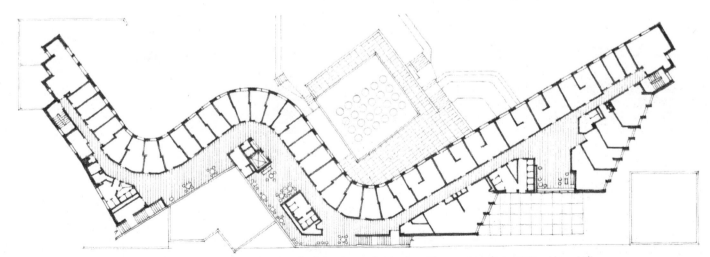

BAKER HOUSE: Massachusetts Institute of Technology, Cambridge, Massachusetts. 1948. Alvar Aalto.
Typical Upper-floor Plan

RADIAL ORGANIZATIONS

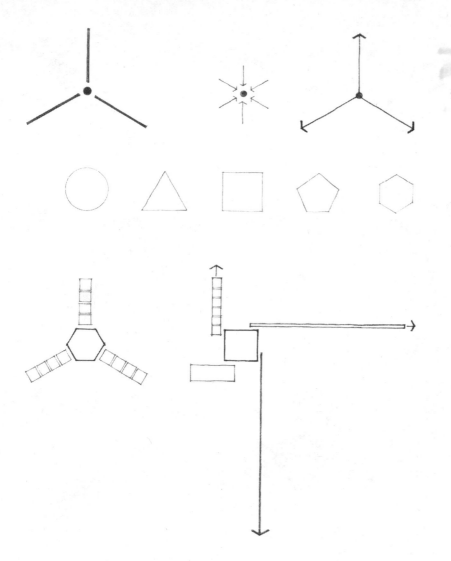

A radial organization of space combines elements of both centralized and linear organizations. It consists of a dominant central space from which a number of linear organizations extend in a radial manner. Whereas a centralized organization is an introverted scheme that focuses inward on its central space, a radial organization is an extroverted scheme that reaches out to its context. With its linear arms, it can extend and attach itself to specific elements or features of its site.

As with centralized organizations, the central space of a radial organization is generally regular in form. The linear arms, for which the central space is the hub, may be similar to one another in form and length and maintain the regularity of the organization's overall form.

The radiating arms can also differ from one another to respond to their individual requirements of function and context.

A specific variation of a radial organization is the pinwheel pattern wherein the linear arms of the organization extend from the sides of a square or rectangular central space. This arrangement results in a dynamic pattern that visually suggests a rotational movement about the central space.

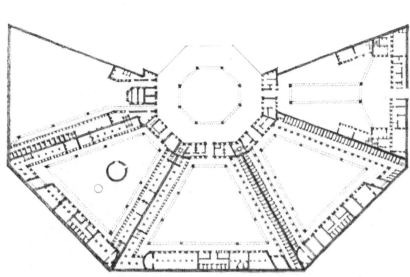

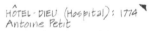

MAISON DE FORCE (Prison): Ackerghem near Ghent, 1772-75
Malfaison and Kluchman

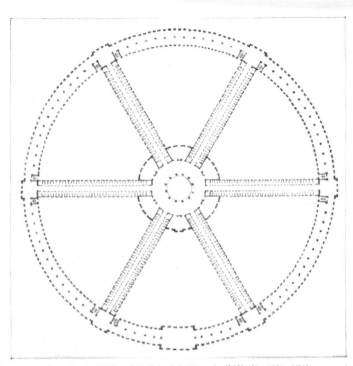

HÔTEL-DIEU (Hospital): 1774
Antoine Petit

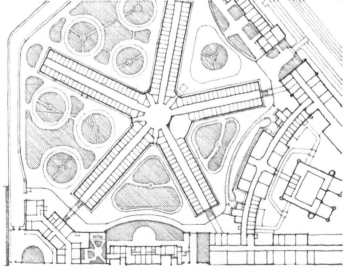

MOABIT PRISON: Berlin, 1860-70, Herrman

RADIAL ORGANIZATIONS

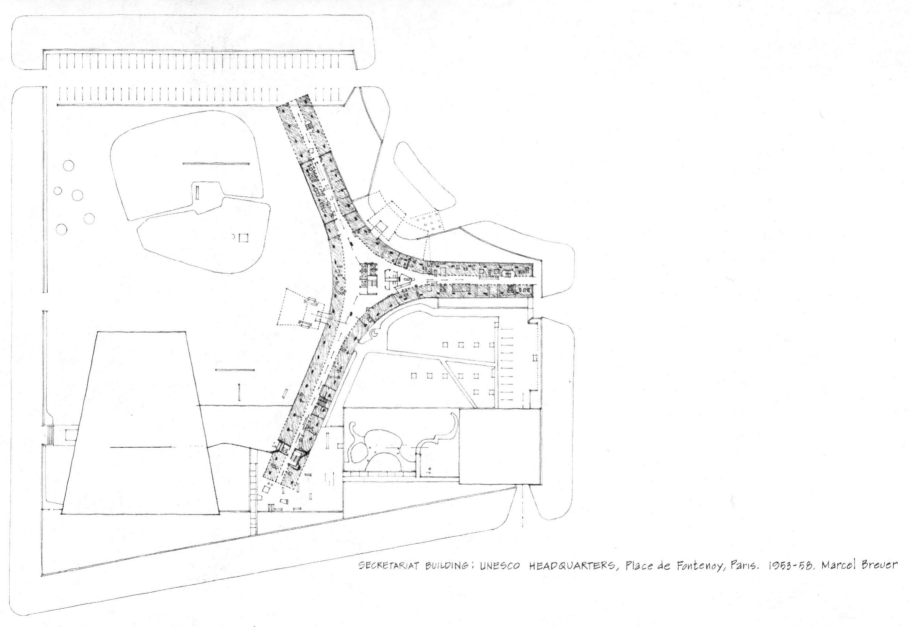

SECRETARIAT BUILDING: UNESCO HEADQUARTERS, Place de Fontenoy, Paris. 1953-58. Marcel Breuer

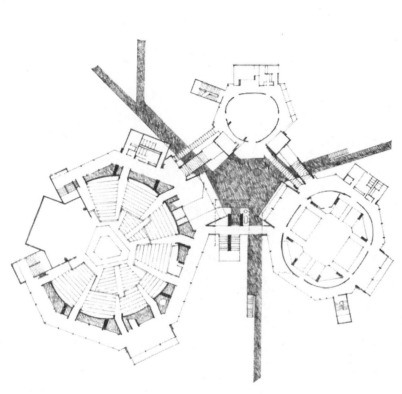

NEW MUMMERS THEATRE; Oklahoma City, Oklahoma. 1970.
John M. Johansen

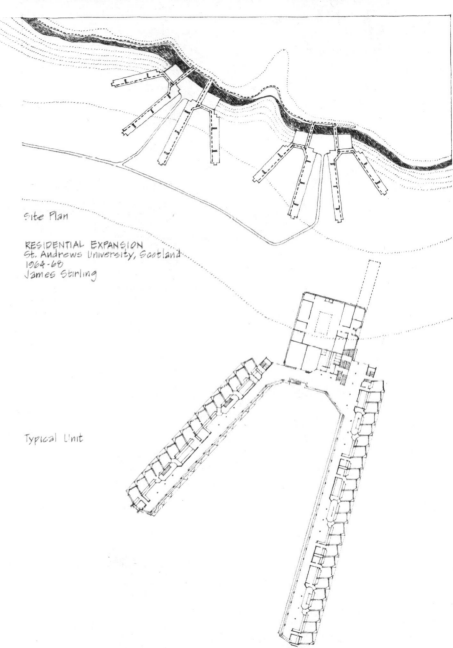

Site Plan

RESIDENTIAL EXPANSION
St. Andrews University, Scotland
1964-68
James Stirling

Typical Unit

RADIAL ORGANIZATIONS

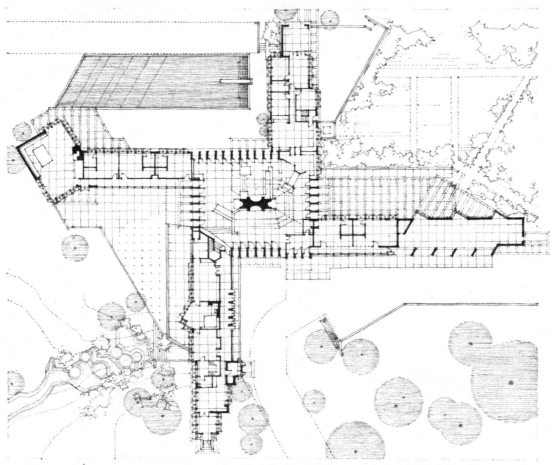

WINGSPREAD (HERBERT F. JOHNSON HOUSE): Wind Point, Wisconsin, 1937. Frank Lloyd Wright

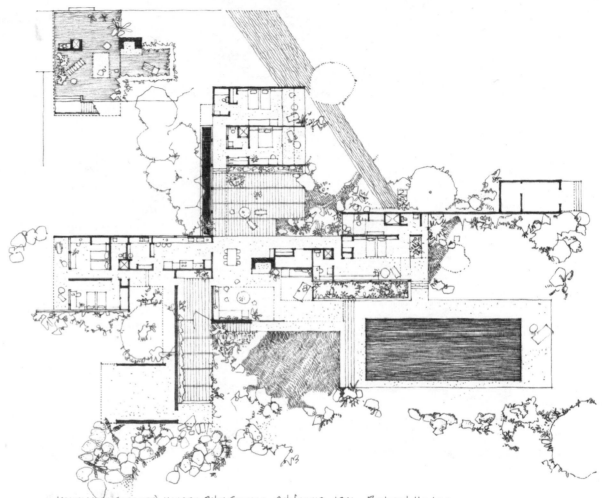

KAUFMANN (DESERT) HOUSE: Palm Springs, California, 1946. Richard Neutra.

CLUSTERED ORGANIZATIONS

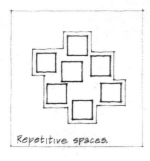
Repetitive spaces.

Sharing a common shape.

Organized by an axis.

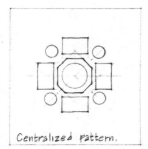
Clustered about an entry.

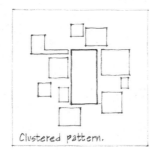
Grouped along a path.

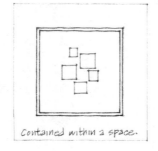
A loop path.

Centralized pattern.

Clustered pattern.

Contained within a space.

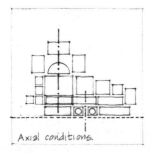
Axial conditions.

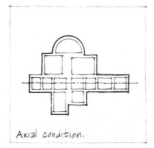
Axial condition.

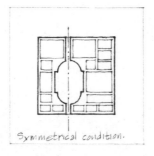
Symmetrical condition.

A clustered organization uses proximity to relate its spaces to one another. It often consists of repetitive, cellular spaces that have similar functions, and share a common visual trait such as shape or orientation. A clustered organization can also accept within its composition spaces that are dissimilar in size, form, and function, but related to one another by proximity and a visual ordering device such as symmetry or an axis. Because its pattern does not originate from a rigid, geometrical concept, the form of a clustered organization is flexible, and can accept growth and change readily without affecting its character.

Clustered spaces can be organized about a point of entry into a building, or along the path of movement through it. The spaces can also be clustered about a large, defined field or volume of space. This pattern is similar to that of a centralized organization, but it lacks the latter's compactness and geometrical regularity. The spaces of a clustered organization can also be contained within a defined field or volume of space.

Since there is no inherent place of importance within the pattern of a clustered organization, the significance of a space must be articulated by its size, form, or orientation within the pattern.

Symmetry or an axial condition can be used to strengthen and unify portions of a clustered organization and help articulate the importance of a space or group of spaces within the organization.

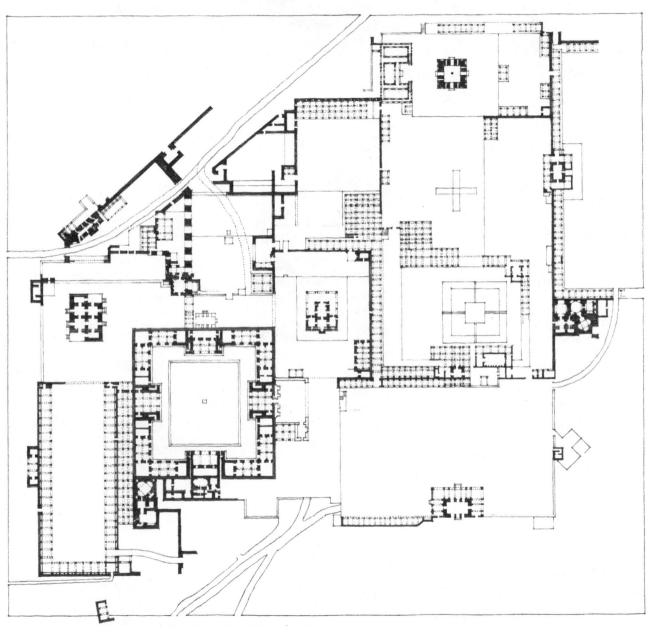

FATHEPUR SIKRI (Residence of the Great Mughul Akbar) 1569-74

CLUSTERED ORGANIZATIONS

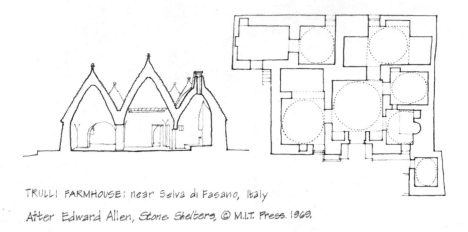

TRULLI FARMHOUSE: near Selva di Fasano, Italy

After Edward Allen, *Stone Shelters*, © M.I.T. Press. 1969.

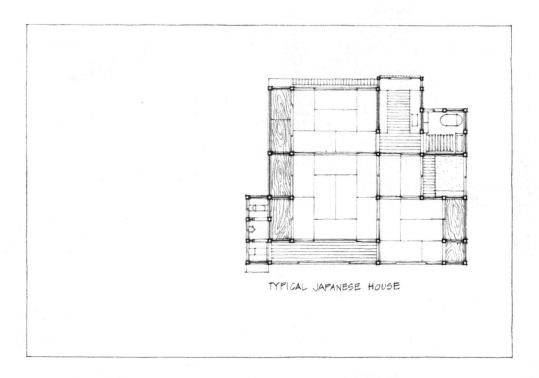

TYPICAL JAPANESE HOUSE

MORRIS HOUSE: Mount Kisco, N.Y.
(Project) 1958
Louis Kahn

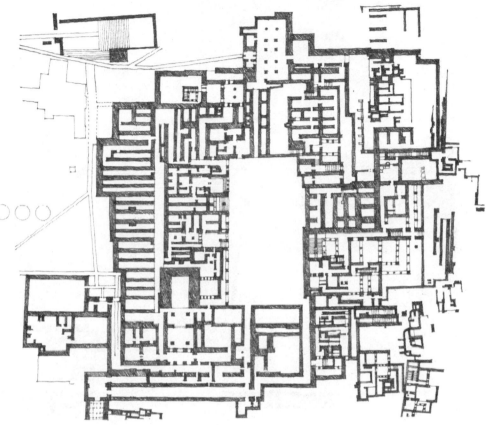

PALACE OF MINOS: Knossos, Crete. (1600-1500 B.C.)

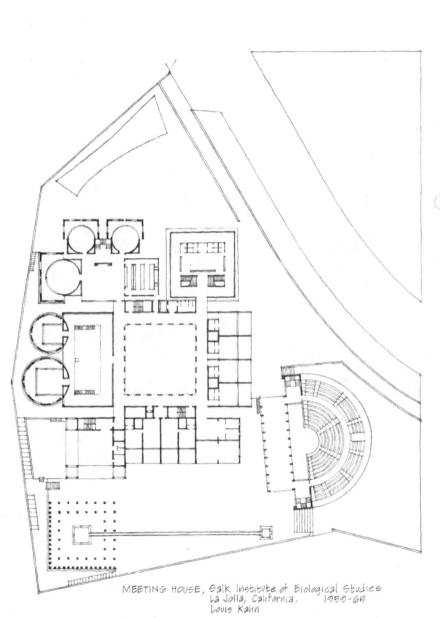

MEETING HOUSE, Salk Institute of Biological Studies
La Jolla, California.   1959-65
Louis Kahn

CLUSTERED ORGANIZATIONS

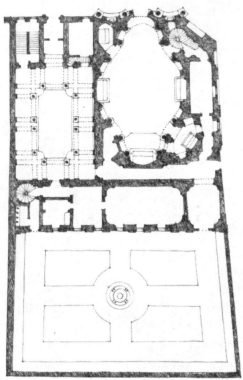

S. CARLO ALLE QUATTRO FONTANE: Rome. 1638-41
Borromini

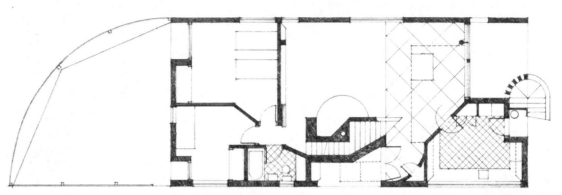

HOUSE for MRS. ROBERT VENTURI: Chestnut Hill, Pennsylvania. 1062-64. Venturi + Short

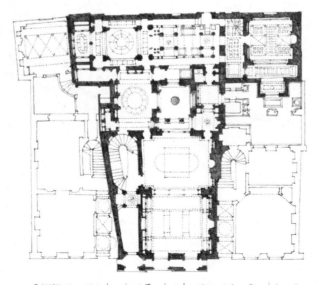

SOANE HOUSE: London, England. 1812-34. Sir John Soane

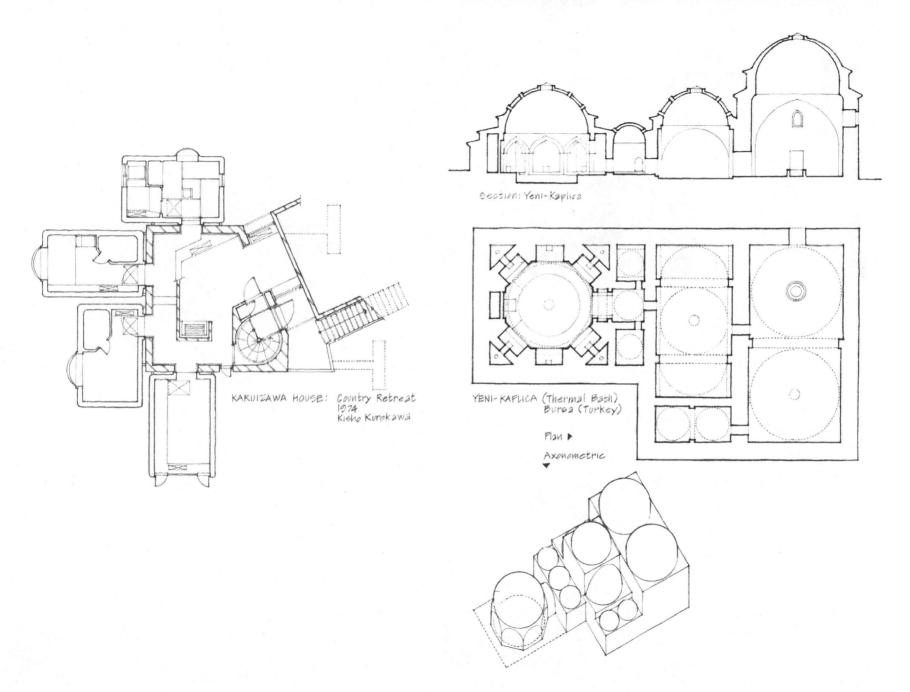

Section: Yeni-Kaplica

KARUIZAWA HOUSE: Country Retreat
1974
Kisho Kurokawa

YENI-KAPLICA (Thermal Bath)
Bursa (Turkey)

Plan ▶

Axonometric
▼

CLUSTERED ORGANIZATIONS

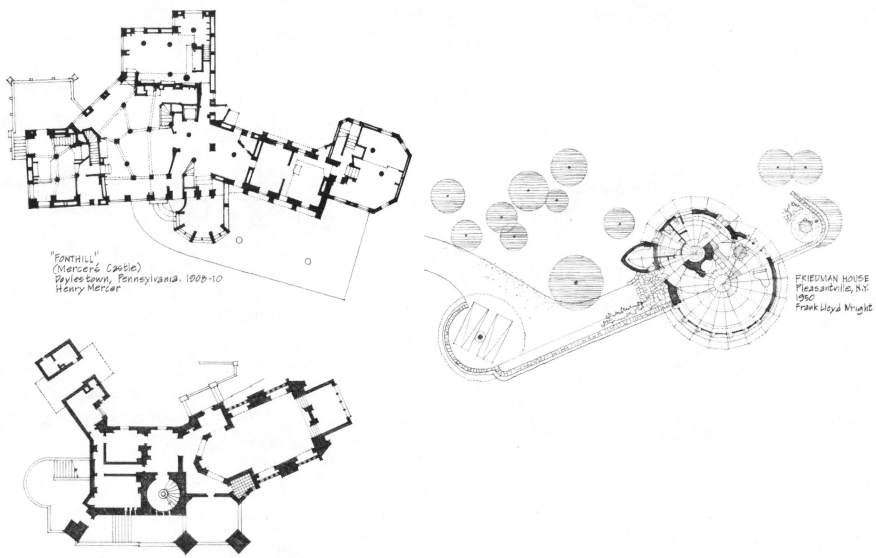

"FONTHILL"
(Mercer's Castle)
Doylestown, Pennsylvania. 1908-10
Henry Mercer

FRIEDMAN HOUSE
Pleasantville, N.Y.
1950
Frank Lloyd Wright

"WYNTOON" Country Estate for the Hearst Family in northern California
1903
Bernard Maybeck

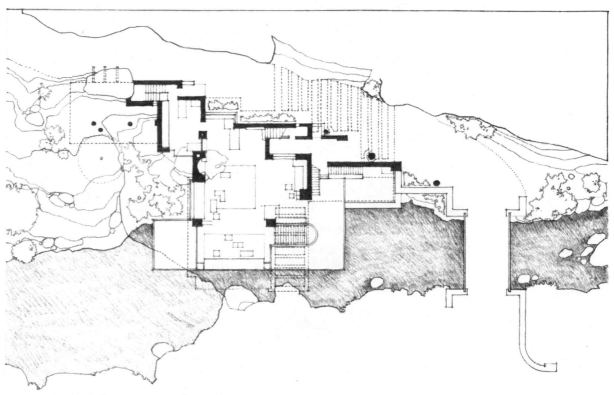

KAUFMANN HOUSE, "FALLING WATER": Connelsville, Pennsylvania. 1936-37. Frank Lloyd Wright

GRID ORGANIZATIONS

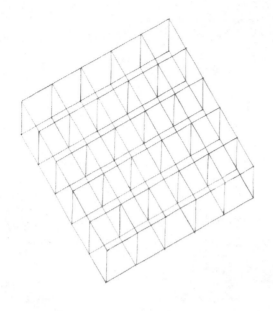

A grid organization consists of forms and spaces whose positions in space and relationships with one another are regulated by a three-dimensional grid pattern or field.

 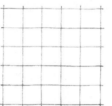 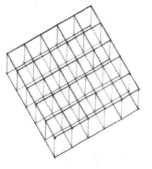

A grid is created by establishing a regular pattern of points that define the intersections of two sets of parallel lines. Projected into the third dimension, the grid pattern is transformed into a set of repetitive, modular units of space.

 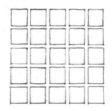 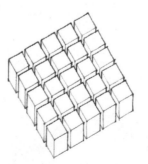

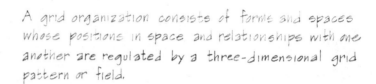

The organizing power of a grid results from the regularity and continuity of its pattern that pervades the elements it organizes. Its pattern establishes a constant set or field of reference points and lines in space with which the spaces of a grid organization, although dissimilar in size, form, or function, can share a common relationship.

A grid is established in architecture most often by a skeletal structural system of columns and beams. Within the field of this grid, spaces can occur as isolated events or as repetitions of the grid module. Regardless of their disposition within the field, these spaces, if seen as positive forms, will create a second set of negative spaces.

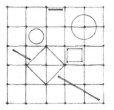 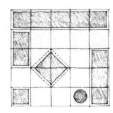 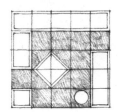

Since a three-dimensional grid consists of repetitive, modular units of space, it can be subtracted from, added to, or layered, and still maintain its identity as a grid with the ability to organize spaces. These formal manipulations can be used to adapt a grid form to its site, define an entrance or outdoor space, or allow for its growth and expansion.

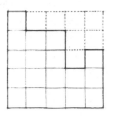 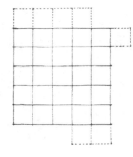 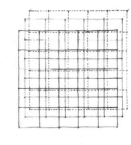

To accommodate the specific dimensional requirements of its spaces, or to articulate zones of space for circulation or service, a grid can be made irregular in one or two directions. This would create a hierarchical set of modules differentiated by size, proportion, and location.

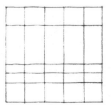 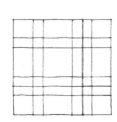 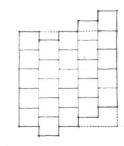

A grid can also undergo other transformations. Portions of the grid can slide to alter the visual and spatial continuity across its field. A grid pattern can be interrupted to define a major space or accommodate a natural feature of its site. A portion of the grid can be dislocated and rotated about a point in the basic pattern. The grid can transform its visual image across its field from a pattern of points — to lines, to planes, and, finally, to volumes.

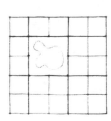 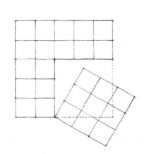 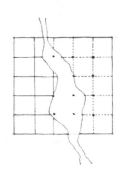

GRID ORGANIZATIONS

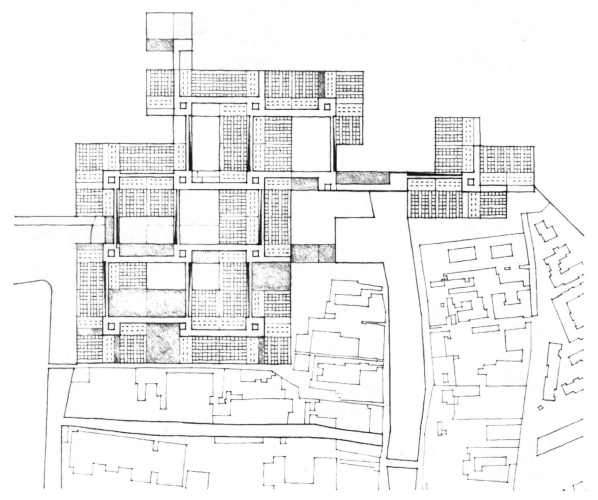

HOSPITAL PROJECT: Venice. 1964-66. Le Corbusier

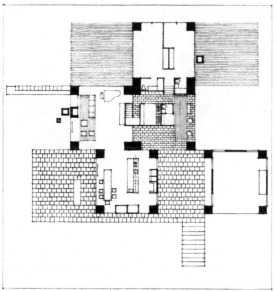

ADLER HOUSE: Philadelphia, Pennsylvania (Project)
1954
Louis Kahn

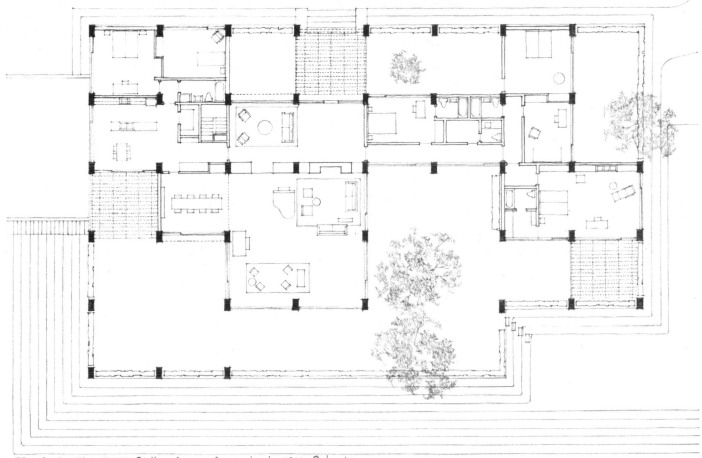

ERIC BOISSONAS HOUSE I: New Canaan, Connecticut. 1956. Philip Johnson

GRID ORGANIZATIONS

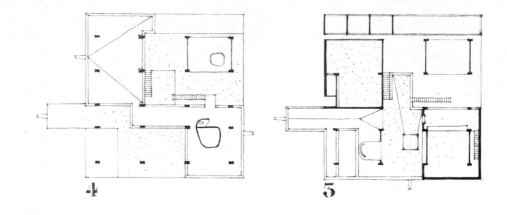

4   5

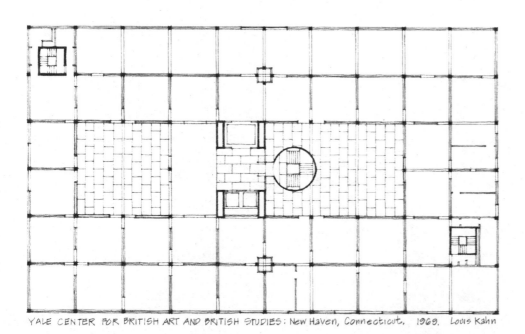

YALE CENTER FOR BRITISH ART AND BRITISH STUDIES: New Haven, Connecticut. 1969. Louis Kahn

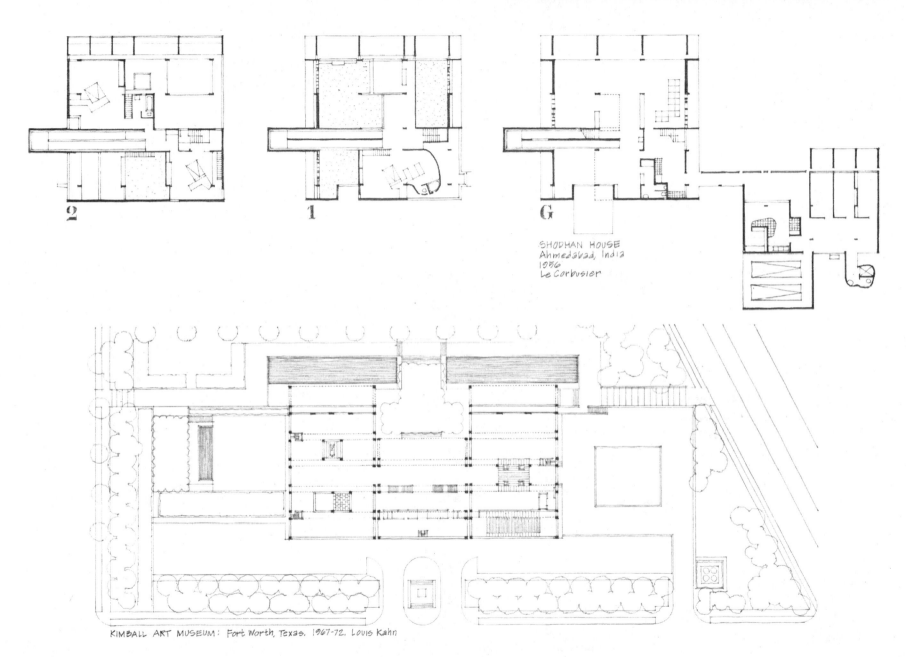

2

1

G

SHODHAN HOUSE
Ahmedabad, India
1956
Le Corbusier

KIMBALL ART MUSEUM: Fort Worth, Texas. 1967-72. Louis Kahn

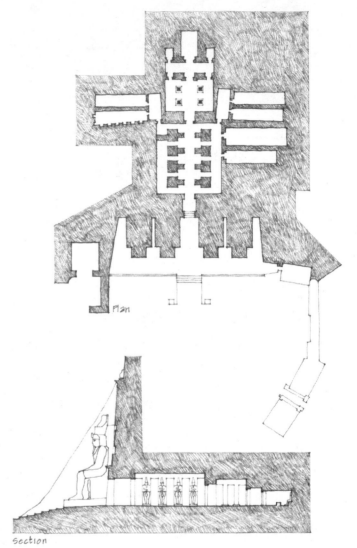

Plan

Section

GREAT TEMPLE OF RAMESES II, ABU-SIMBEL. 1301-1235 B.C.

5

CIRCULATION

CIRCULATION: MOVEMENT THROUGH SPACE

The circulation path can be conceived as the perceptual thread that links the spaces of a building, or any series of interior or exterior spaces, together.

Since we move in **TIME** through a **SEQUENCE** of **SPÃCES**,

we experience a space in relation to where we've been, and where we anticipate going. This chapter presents the principal components of a building's circulation system as positive elements that affect our perception of the building's forms and spaces.

SKYLIGHTED CONCOURSE: Olivetti Headquarters @ Milton Keynes - 1071. James Stirling + Michael Wilford

CIRCULATION ELEMENTS

1. THE BUILDING APPROACH
- THE DISTANT VIEW

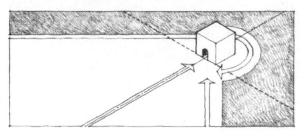

2. THE BUILDING ENTRANCE
- FROM OUTSIDE TO INSIDE

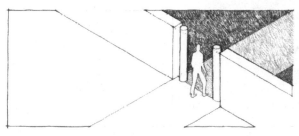

3. CONFIGURATION OF THE PATH
- THE SEQUENCE OF SPACES

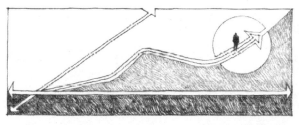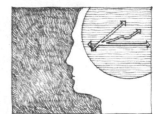

4. PATH·SPACE RELATIONSHIPS
- EDGES, NODES, & TERMINATIONS OF THE PATH

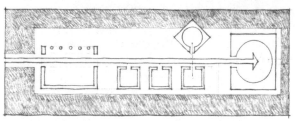

5. FORM OF THE CIRCULATION SPACE
- CORRIDORS, BALCONIES, GALLERIES, STAIRS, & ROOMS

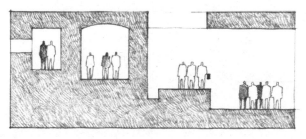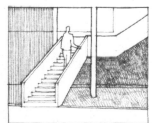

THE BUILDING APPROACH

APPROACH TO NOTRE·DU·HAUT, Ronchamp, France. 1950·55. Le Corbusier

Prior to actually entering a building's interior, we approach its entrance along a path. This is the first phase of the circulation system, during which we are prepared to see, experience, and use the building's spaces.

The approach to a building and its entrance may vary in duration, from a few paces through a compressed space to a lengthy and circuitous route. It can be frontal to a building's face, or oblique to it. The nature of the approach may contrast with what is confronted at its termination, or it may be continued on into the building's interior sequence of spaces, obscuring the distinction between inside and outside.

1. FRONTAL

- A frontal approach leads directly to a building's entrance along a straight, axial path.
- The visual goal that terminates the approach is clear; it can be the entire front facade of a building or an elaborated entrance within it.

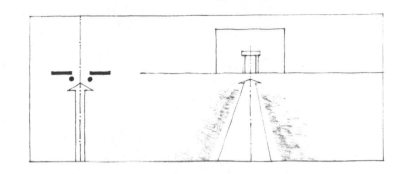

2. OBLIQUE

- An oblique approach enhances the effect of perspective on a building's front facade and form.
- The path can be re-directed one or more times to delay and prolong the sequence of the approach.
- If a building is approached at an extreme angle, its entrance can project beyond its facade to be more clearly visible.

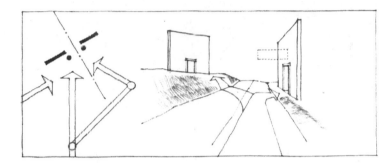

3. SPIRAL

- A spiral path prolongs the sequence of the approach, and emphasizes the three-dimensional form of a building as it moves around the building's perimeter.
- The building's entrance might be viewed intermittently during the approach to clarify its position, or it can be hidden until the point of arrival.

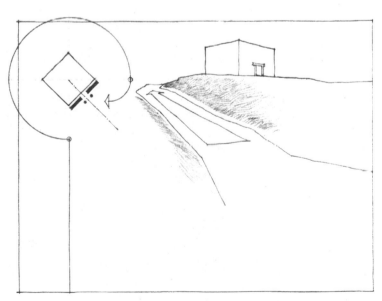

VILLA BARBARO; Maser, Italy. 1560-8. Andrea Palladio.

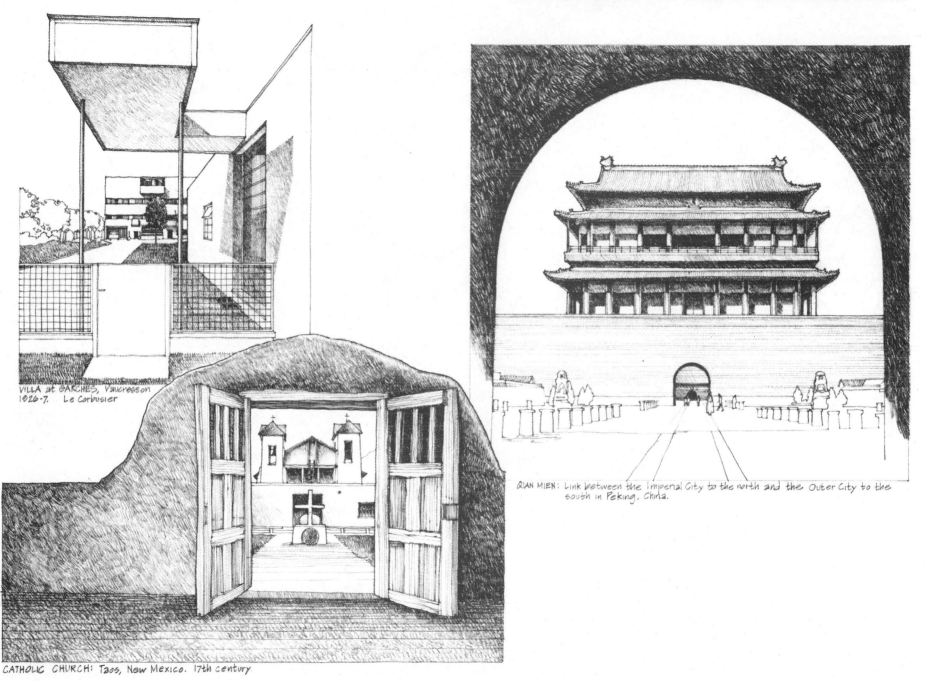

VILLA at GARCHES, Vaucresson
1926-7.   Le Corbusier

CATHOLIC CHURCH: Taos, New Mexico. 17th century.

QIAN MIEN: Link between the Imperial City to the north and the Outer City to the south in Peking, China.

BUILDING APPROACHES

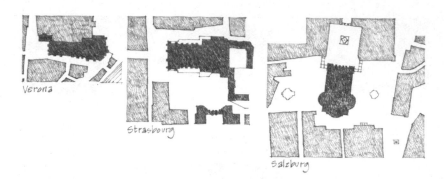

Verona

Strasbourg

Salzburg

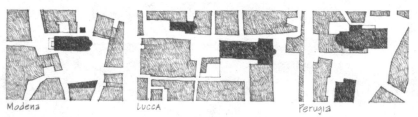

Modena

Lucca

Perugia

Drawings of church-dominated, urban spaces by Camillo Sitte that illustrate the assymetrical, picturesque approach to the siting of buildings. Only fragments of the churches can be seen from various points in the squares.

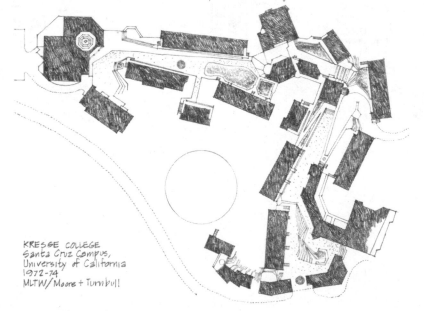

KRESGE COLLEGE
Santa Cruz Campus,
University of California
1972-74
MLTW/Moore + Turnbull

Street in Siena, Italy

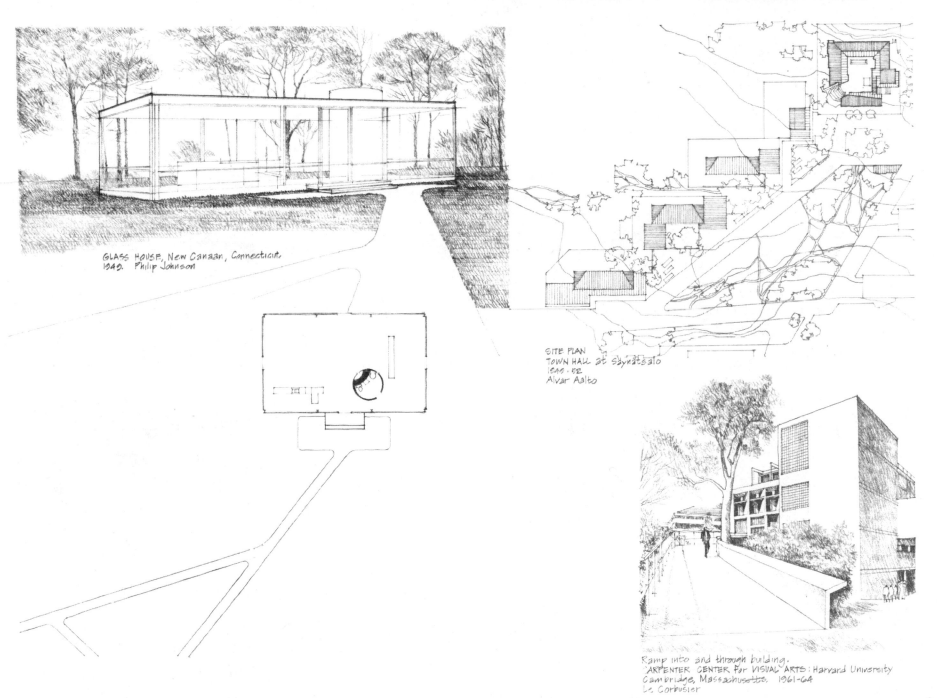

GLASS HOUSE, New Canaan, Connecticut.
1949. Philip Johnson

SITE PLAN
TOWN HALL at Säynätsalo
1949-52
Alvar Aalto

Ramp into and through building.
CARPENTER CENTER for VISUAL ARTS; Harvard University
Cambridge, Massachusetts. 1961-64
Le Corbusier

BUILDING APPROACHES

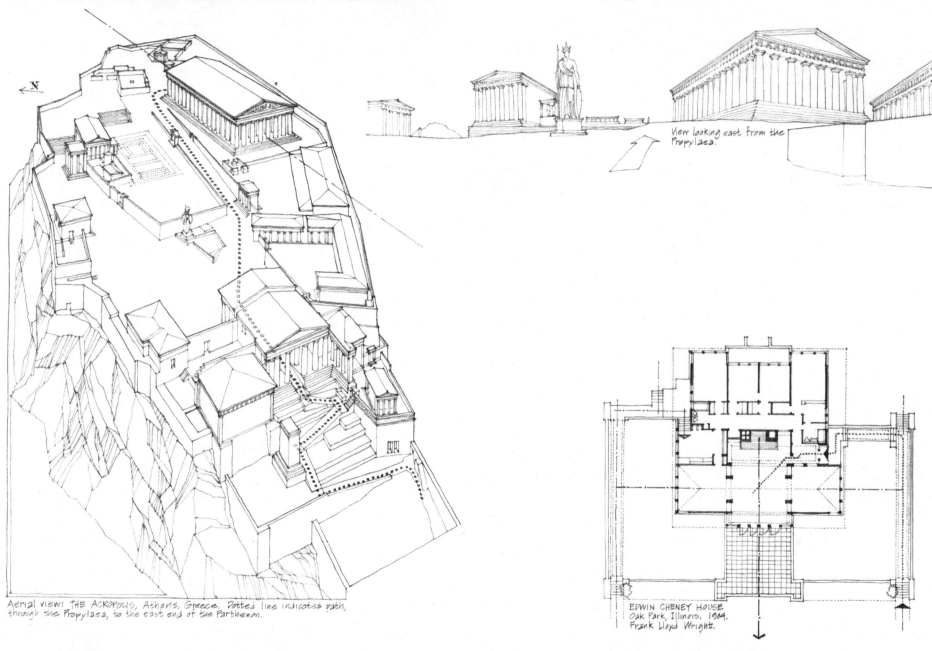

View looking east from the Propylaea.

Aerial view: THE ACROPOLIS, Athens, Greece. Dotted line indicates path, through the Propylaea, to the east end of the Parthenon.

EDWIN CHENEY HOUSE
Oak Park, Illinois, 1904.
Frank Lloyd Wright.

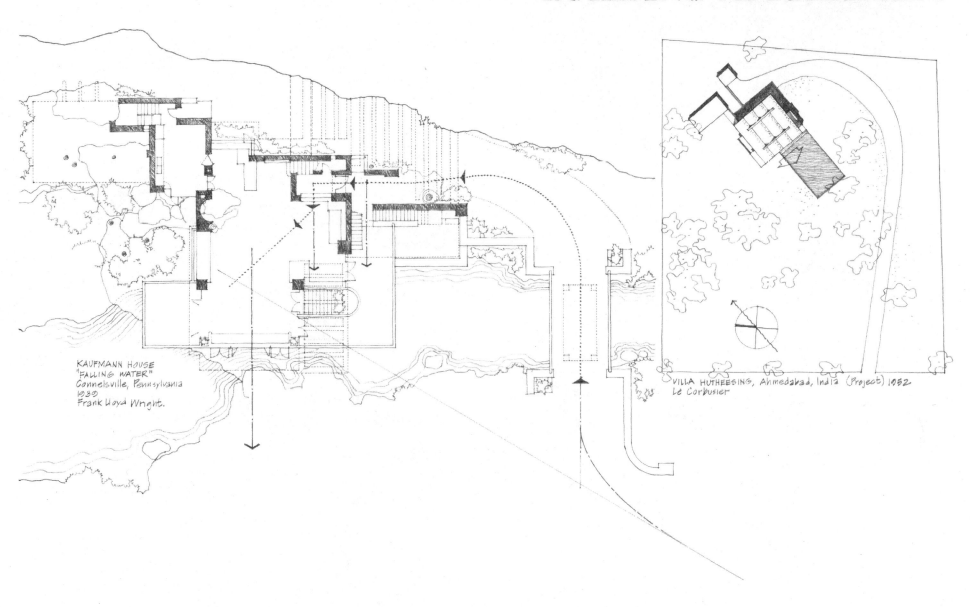

KAUFMANN HOUSE
"FALLING WATER"
Connelsville, Pennsylvania
1930
Frank Lloyd Wright.

VILLA HUTHEESING, Ahmedabad, India (Project) 1952
Le Corbusier

BUILDING ENTRANCES

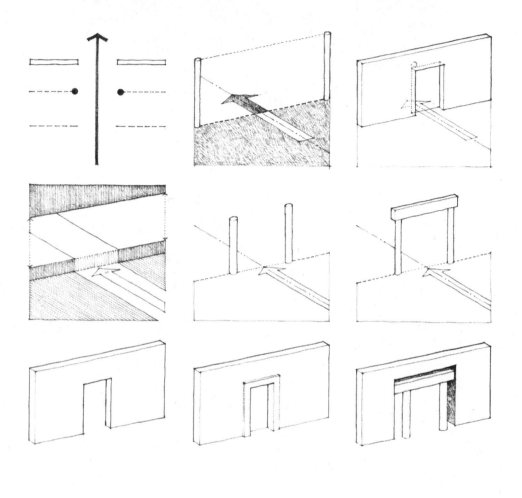

Entering a building, a room within a building, or a defined field of exterior space, involves the act of penetrating a vertical plane that distinguishes one space from another, and separates "here" from "there."

Since the act of entry is essentially one of piercing a vertical plane, it can be signified in more subtle ways than punching a hole in a wall. It can be the passage through an implied, rather than real, plane, established by two pillars or an overhead beam. In more subtle situations, where visual and spatial continuity between two spaces is desired, a change in level can mark the passage from one place to another.

In the normal situation where a wall is used to define and enclose a space or series of spaces, an entrance is accommodated by an opening in the plane of the wall. The form of the opening, however, can range from a simple hole in the wall to an elaborate, articulated gateway.

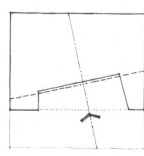
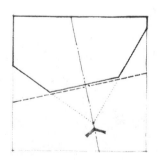

Regardless of the form of the space being entered, or the form of its enclosure, the entrance into the space is best signified by establishing a real or implied plane perpendicular to the path of the approach.

Entrances may be grouped formally into the following categories: flush, projected, and recessed. Flush entrances maintain the continuity of a wall's surface, and can be, if desired, deliberately obscured. Projected entrances announce their function to the approach and provide shelter overhead. Recessed entrances also provide shelter and receive a portion of exterior space into the realm of the building.

In each of the categories above, the form of the entrance can be similar to, and serve as a preview of, the form of the space being entered. Or it can contrast with the form of the space to reinforce its boundaries and emphasize its character as a place.

In terms of location, an entrance can be centered within the frontal plane of a building, or it can be placed off-center and create its own symmetrical condition about its opening. The location of an entrance, relative to the form of the space entered, will determine the configuration of the path and the pattern of the activities within the space.

The notion of an entrance can be visually reinforced by:
• making the opening lower, wider, or narrower than anticipated;
• making the entrance extra-deep or circuitous;
• articulating the opening with ornamentation or decorative embellishment.

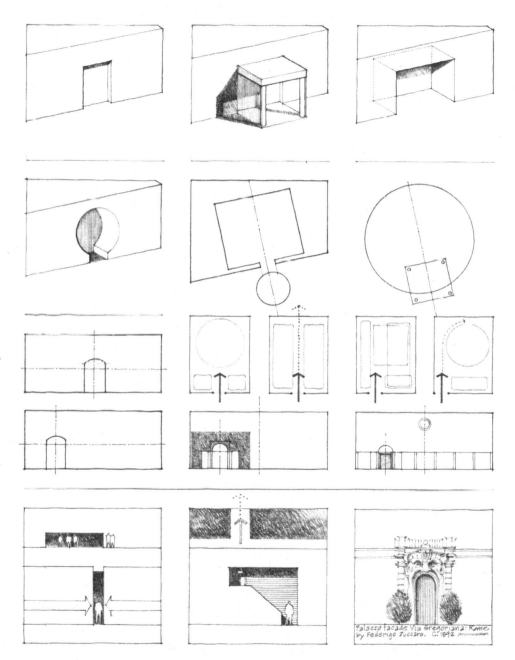

Palazzo facade Via Gregoriana: Rome, by Federigo Zuccaro. C. 1592

257

ENTRANCES

PIAZZA SAN MARCO, Venice: View of sea framed by the Doges Palace on the left and Scamozzi's Library on the right. The entrance to the Piazza is marked by two granite columns, the Lion's Column (1180) and the Column of St. Theodore (1329).

"Ō-torii", the first gate to the Tōshōgū Shrine, Tochigi Prefecture, Japan. 1636.

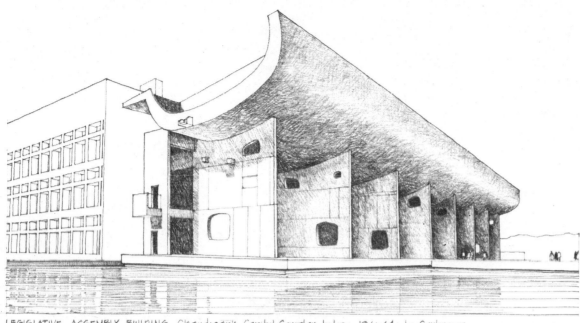

LEGISLATIVE ASSEMBLY BUILDING, Chandigarh Capitol Complex, India. 1961-64. Le Corbusier.

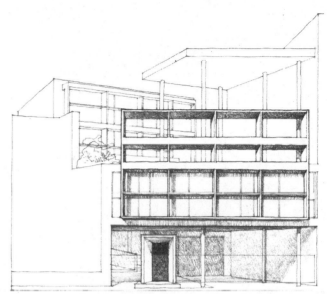

DR. CURRUTCHET'S HOUSE, La Plata, Argentina. 1949. Le Corbusier.

VON STERNBERG HOUSE, Los Angeles, California. 1936. Richard Neutra.

S. GIORGIO MAGGIORE, Venice. 1566-1610. Andrea Palladio

ENTRANCES

While the fence separates, the gateway and the stepping stones provide continuity between the Imperial Carriage Stop and the Gepparo (Moon-Wave Pavilion) beyond. KATSURA IMPERIAL VILLA, Kyoto, Japan.

MORRIS GIFT SHOP, San Francisco, California. 1948-49
Frank Lloyd Wright.

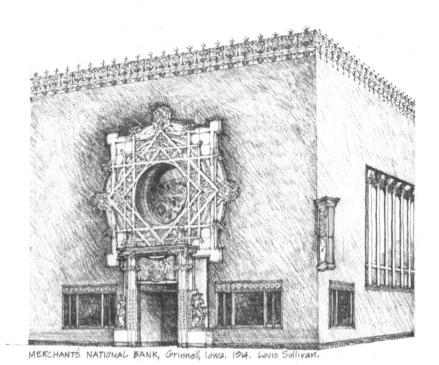

MERCHANTS' NATIONAL BANK, Grinnell, Iowa. 1914. Louis Sullivan.

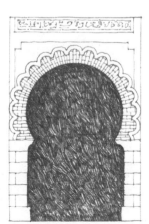

ENTRANCES

Entrance Pylons:
TEMPLE OF HORUS at EDFU. 237-57 B.C.

JOHN F. KENNEDY MEMORIAL, Dallas, Texas. 1970. Philip Johnson.

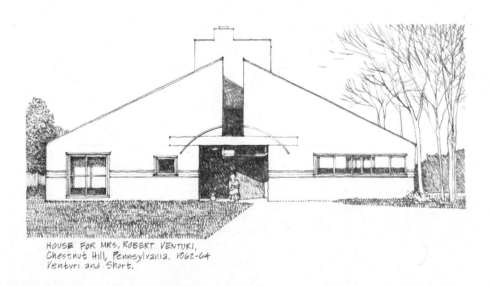

HOUSE FOR MRS. ROBERT VENTURI,
Chestnut Hill, Pennsylvania. 1962-64
Venturi and Short.

Entrance to the S.C. Johnson and Son, Inc. Administration Building, Racine, Wisconsin. 1936-39. Frank Lloyd Wright.

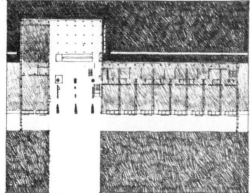

Plan Diagram

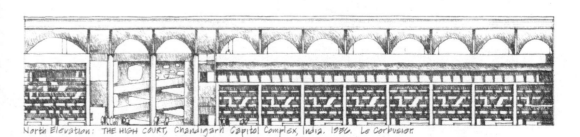

North Elevation: THE HIGH COURT, Chandigarh Capitol Complex, India. 1956. Le Corbusier.

ENTRANCES

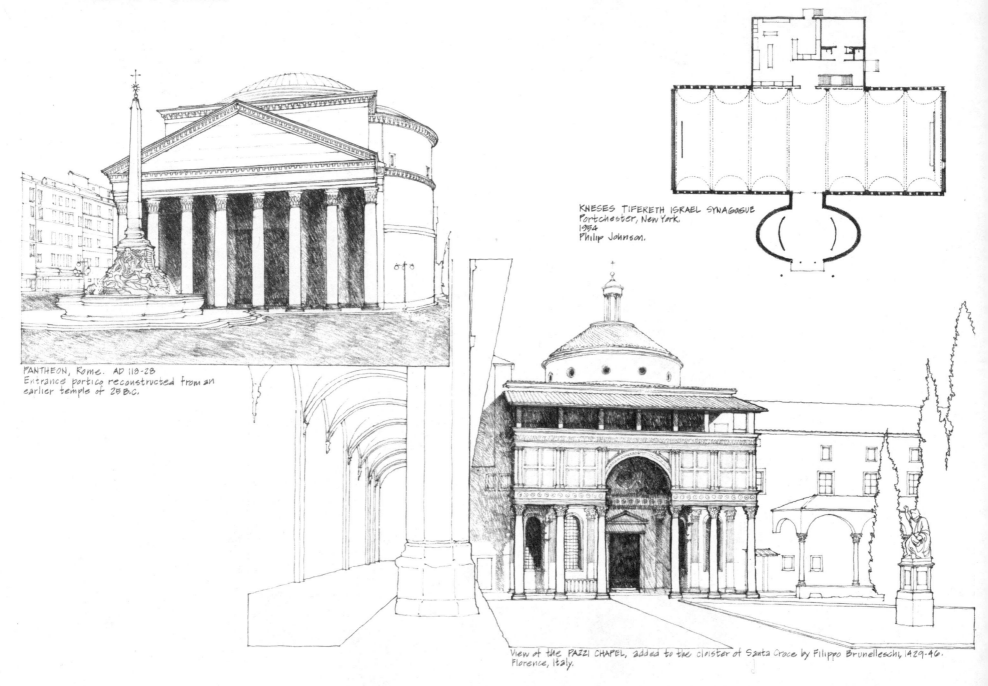

PANTHEON, Rome. AD 118-28
Entrance portico reconstructed from an
earlier temple of 25 B.C.

KNESES TIFERETH ISRAEL SYNAGOGUE
Portchester, New York.
1954
Philip Johnson.

View of the PAZZI CHAPEL, added to the cloister of Santa Croce by Filippo Brunelleschi, 1429-46.
Florence, Italy.

S. VITALE, Ravenna, Italy, 526-47

THE ORIENTAL THEATRE: Milwaukee, Wisconsin. 1927. Dick + Bauer

ENTRANCES

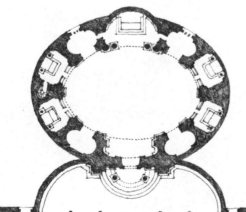

CHIESA DI S. ANDREA DEL QUIRINALE
Rome. 1670
Giovanni Bernini

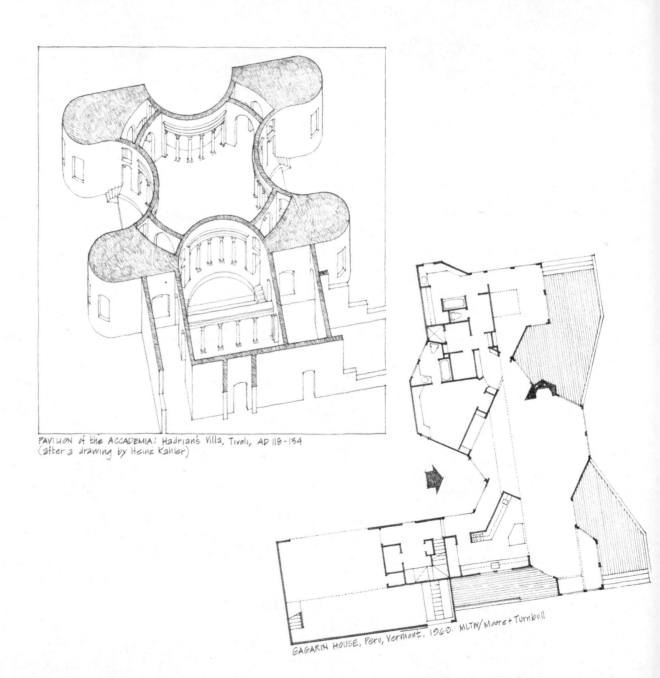

PAVILION of the ACCADEMIA: Hadrian's Villa, Tivoli, AD 118-134
(after a drawing by Heinz Kähler)

GAGARIN HOUSE, Peru, Vermont. 1960. MLTW/Moore + Turnbull

EAST BUILDING, NATIONAL GALLERY OF ART, Washington, D.C. 1978. I.M. PEI & Partners

S. ANDREA, Mantua, Italy. 1472-94. Leon Battista Alberti

ENTRANCES

Rowhouses in Galena, Illinois

TALIESIN WEST, near Phoenix, Arizona. 1938 —
Frank Lloyd Wright

MILLOWNER'S ASSOCIATION BUILDING, Ahmedabad, India. 1954. Le Corbusier

Interior doorway by Francesco Borromini

MAIN ENTRANCE to the SANTA BARBARA COURTHOUSE, California, by William Mooser, 1929, with view to the garden and hills beyond.

A stele and tortoise guarding the tomb of Emperor Wan Li (1563-1620), northwest of Peking, China.

CONFIGURATION OF THE PATH

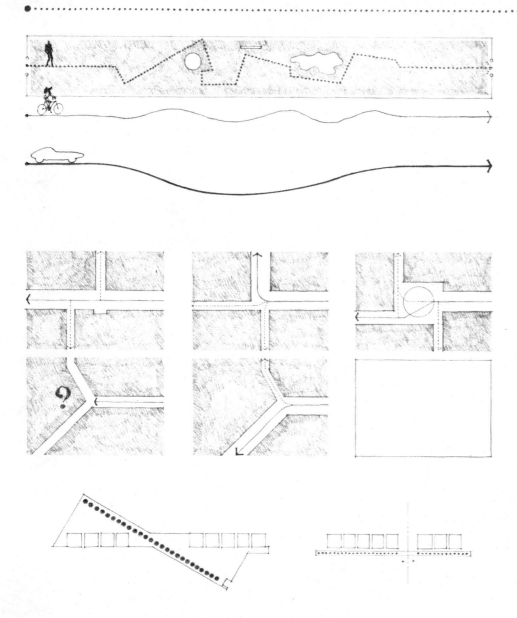

All paths of movement, whether of people, cars, goods or services, are linear in nature. And all paths have a starting point, from which we are taken through a sequence of spaces to our destination. The contour of a path depends on our mode of transportion. While we, as pedestrians, can turn, pause, stop, and rest at will, a bicycle has less freedom, and a car even less, in changing its pace and direction abruptly. Interestingly, though, while a wheeled vehicle may require a path with smooth contours that reflect its turning radius, the width of the path can be tailored tightly to its dimensions. Pedestrians, on the other hand, although able to tolerate abrupt changes in direction, require a greater volume of space than their bodily dimensions, and greater freedom of choice along a path.

The intersection or crossing of paths is always a point of decision-making for the person approaching it. The continuity and scale of each path at an intersection can help us distinguish between major routes leading to major spaces and secondary paths leading to lesser spaces. When the paths at a crossing are equivalent to one another, sufficient space should be provided to allow people to pause and orient themselves.

The nature of a path's configuration influences, or is influenced by, the organizational pattern of the spaces it links. The config- uration of a path may reinforce a spatial organization by paral- leling its pattern. Or the configuration can contrast with the form of the spatial organization, and serve as a visual counter- point to it. Once we can map out in our minds the overall config- uration of the paths in a building, our orientation within the building and our understanding of its spatial layout will be clear.

1. LINEAR

All paths are linear. A straight path, however, can be the primary organizing element for a series of spaces. In addition, it can be curvi-linear or segmented, intersect other paths, have branches, form a loop.

2. RADIAL

A radial configuration has paths extending from, or terminating at, a central, common point.

3. SPIRAL

A spiral configuration is a single, continuous path that originates from a central point, revolves around it, and becomes increasingly distance from it.

4. GRID

A grid configuration consists of two sets of parallel paths that intersect at regular intervals and create square or rectangular fields of space.

5. NETWORK

A network configuration consists of random paths that connect established points in space.

6. COMPOSITE

In reality, a building normally employs a combination of the preceding patterns. To avoid the creation of a disorienting maze, a hierarchical order among the paths can be achieved by differentiating their scale, form, and length.

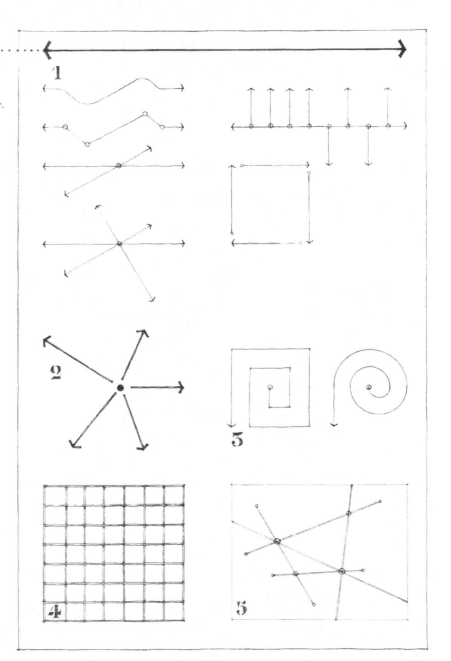

PATH CONFIGURATIONS

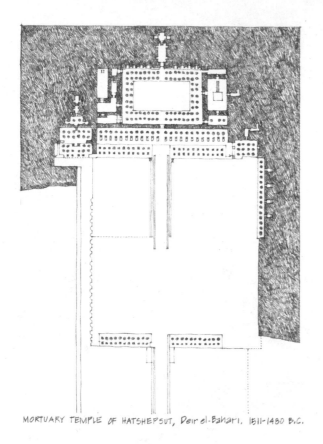

MORTUARY TEMPLE OF HATSHEPSUT, Deir el-Bahari, 1511-1480 B.C.

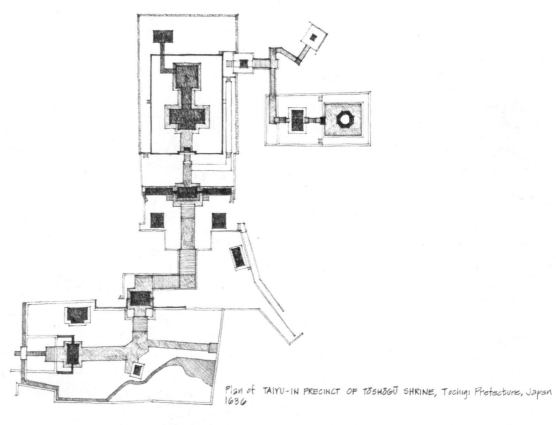

Plan of TAIYU-IN PRECINCT OF TŌSHŌGŪ SHRINE, Tochigi Prefecture, Japan 1636

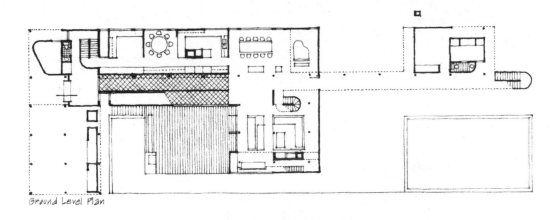

Ground Level Plan

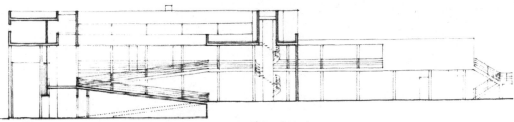

Section: HOUSE IN OLD WESTBURY, New York, 1969-71 Richard Meier.

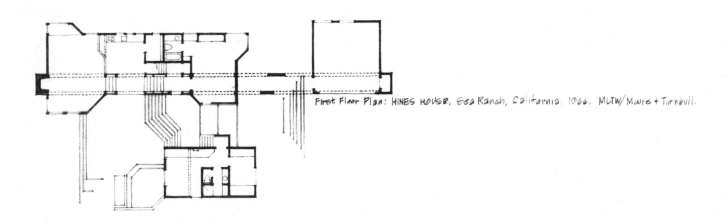

First Floor Plan: HINES HOUSE, Sea Ranch, California. 1966. MLTW/Moore + Turnbull.

PATH CONFIGURATIONS

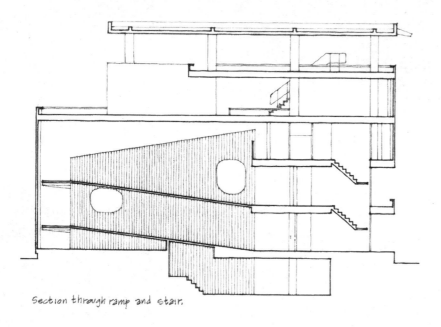

Section through ramp and stair.

SHODHAN HOUSE, Ahmedabad, India. 1956. Le Corbusier.

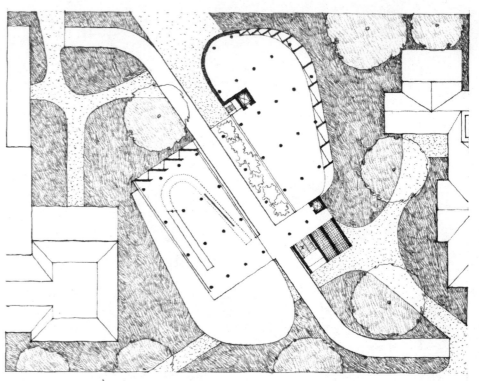

CARPENTER CENTER for VISUAL ARTS, Harvard University, Cambridge, Massachusetts. 1961-64. Le Corbusier

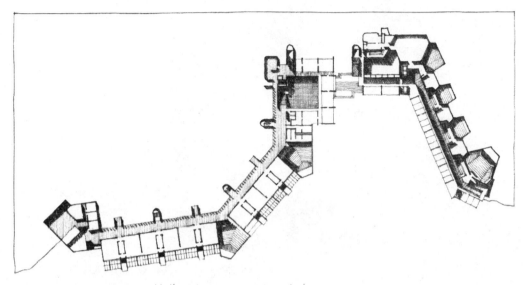

SCARBOROUGH COLLEGE, Westhill, Ontario. 1964. John Andrews

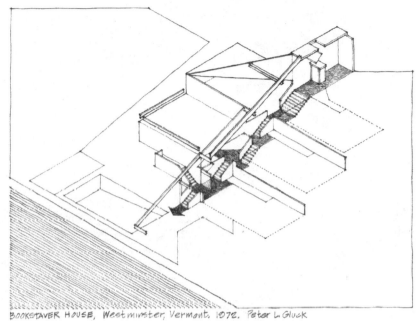

BOOKSTAVER HOUSE, Westminster, Vermont. 1972. Peter L. Gluck

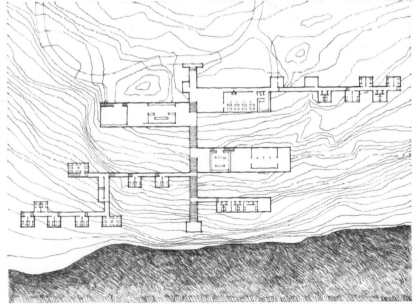

HAYSTACK MOUNTAIN SCHOOL OF ARTS AND CRAFTS, Deer Isle, Maine. 1960. Edward Larrabee Barnes.

PATH CONFIGURATIONS

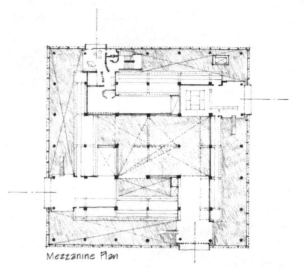

Mezzanine Plan

MUSEUM OF WESTERN ART: TOKYO. 1957-59. Le Corbusier

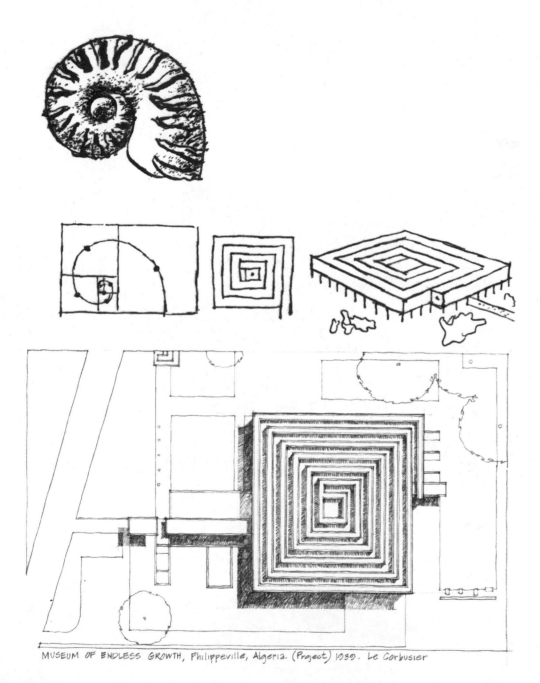

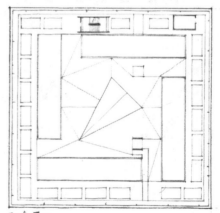

Roof Plan

MUSEUM OF ENDLESS GROWTH, Philippeville, Algeria. (Project) 1939. Le Corbusier

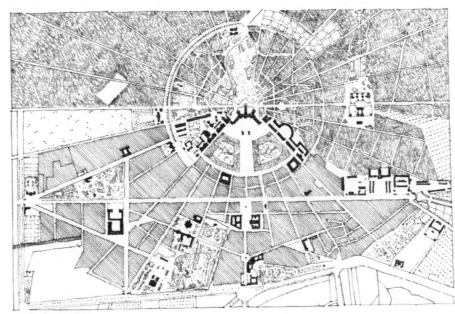

KARLSRUHE, 1834

City on a Plain

City on a Hill

PLANS OF IDEAL CITIES, by Franceso di Giorgi Martini, 1451-1464.

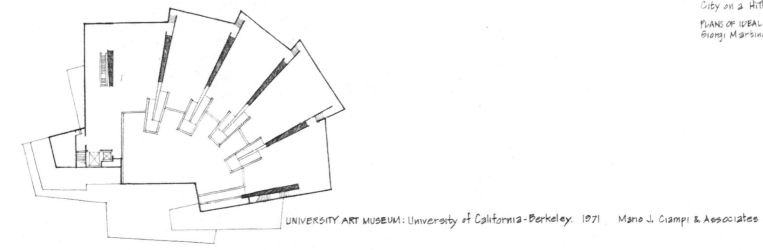

UNIVERSITY ART MUSEUM: University of California-Berkeley. 1971   Mario J. Ciampi & Associates

PATH CONFIGURATIONS

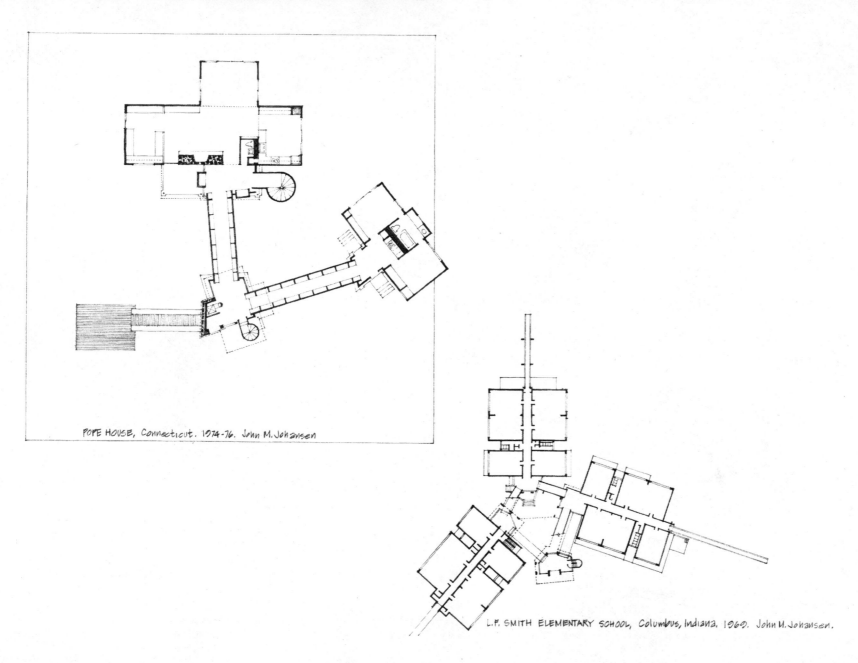

POPE HOUSE, Connecticut. 1974-76. John M. Johansen

L.F. SMITH ELEMENTARY SCHOOL, Columbus, Indiana. 1960. John M. Johansen.

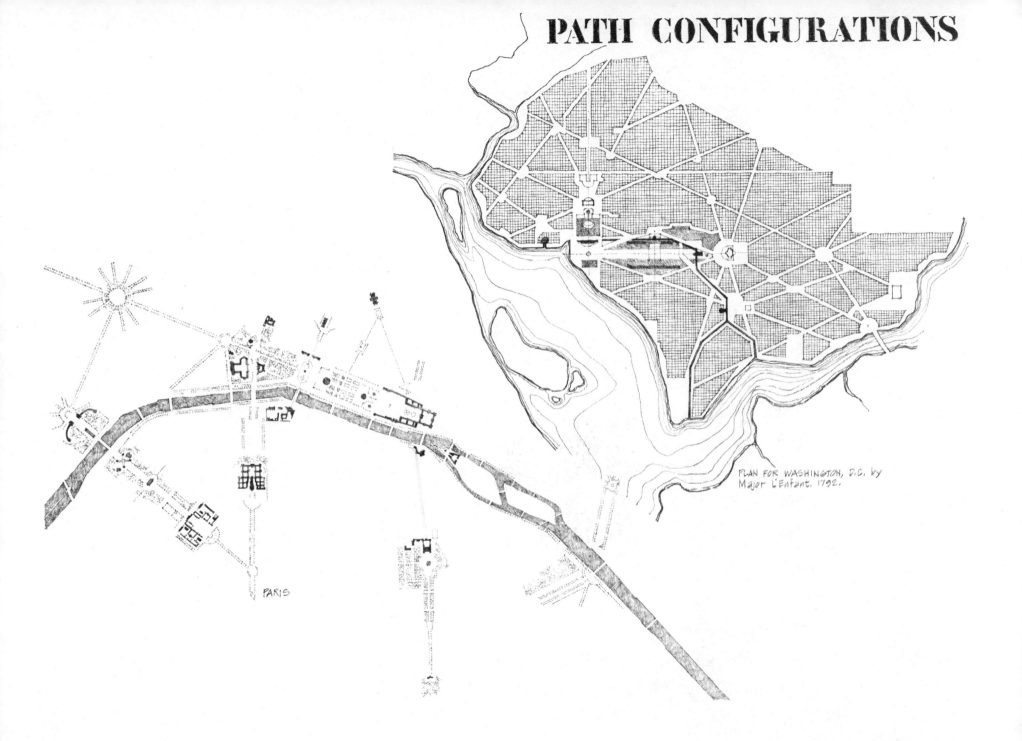

PLAN FOR WASHINGTON, D.C. by
Major L'Enfant. 1792.

PARIS

PATH CONFIGURATIONS

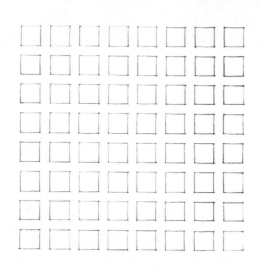

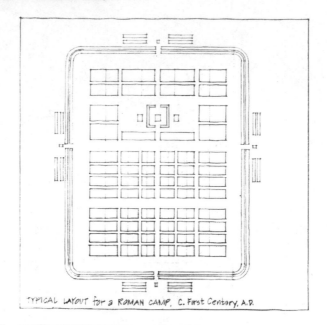

TYPICAL LAYOUT for a ROMAN CAMP, C. First Century, A.D.

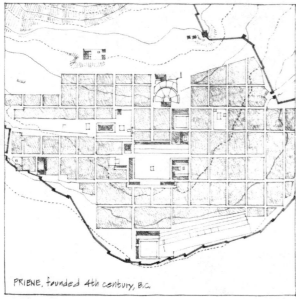

PRIENE, founded 4th century, B.C.

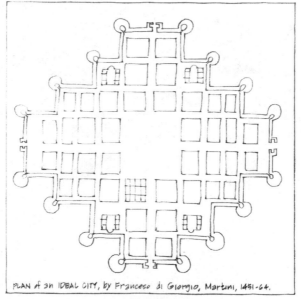

PLAN of an IDEAL CITY, by Franceso di Giorgio, Martini, 1451-64.

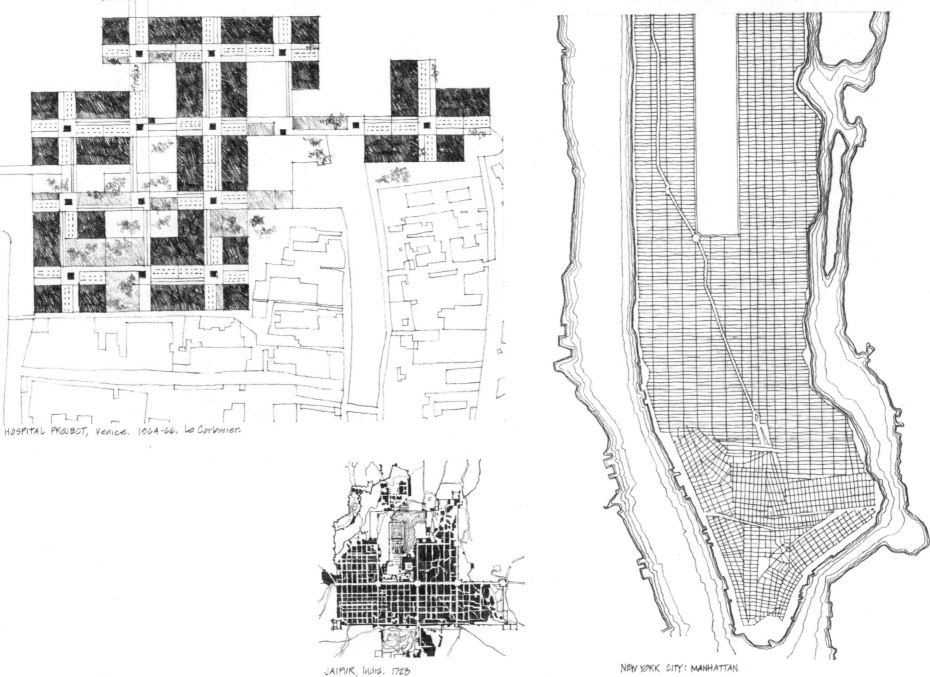

HOSPITAL PROJECT, Venice. 1064-66. Le Corbusier.

JAIPUR, India, 1728

NEW YORK CITY: MANHATTAN

PATH · SPACE RELATIONSHIPS

Paths may be related to the spaces they link in the following ways.   Paths may:

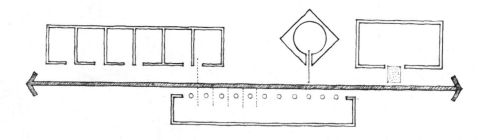

1. PASS BY SPACES

- The integrity of each space is maintained.
- The configuration of the path is flexible.
- Mediating spaces can be used to link the path with the spaces

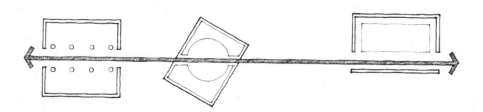

2. PASS THROUGH SPACES

- The path may pass through a space axially, obliquely, or along its edge.
- In cutting through a space, the path creates patterns of rest and movement within it.

3. TERMINATE IN A SPACE

- The location of the space establishes the path.
- This path-space relationship is used to approach and enter functionally or symbolically important spaces.

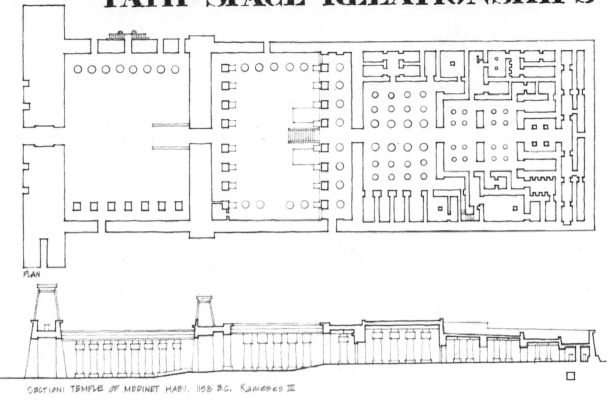

PLAN

SECTION: TEMPLE OF MEDINET HABU, 1198 B.C. Rameses III

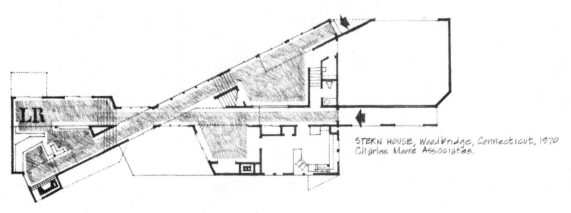

LR

STERN HOUSE, Woodbridge, Connecticut, 1970
Charles Moore Associates.

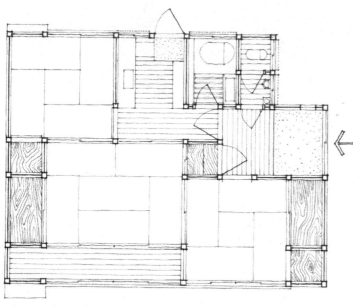

TYPICAL JAPANESE HOUSE

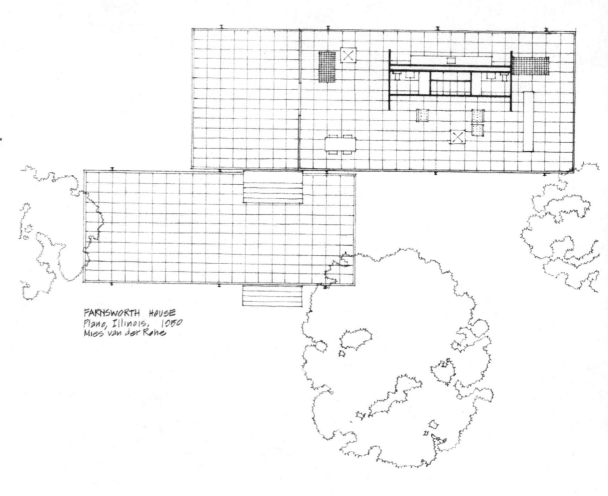

FARNSWORTH HOUSE
Plano, Illinois, 1950
Mies van der Rohe

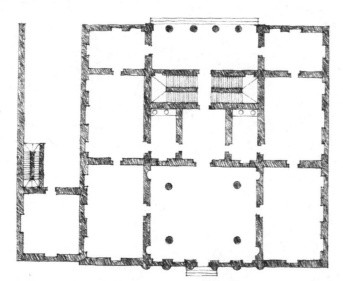

PALAZZO ANTONINI, Udine, Italy, 1570 (Project) Andrea Palladio

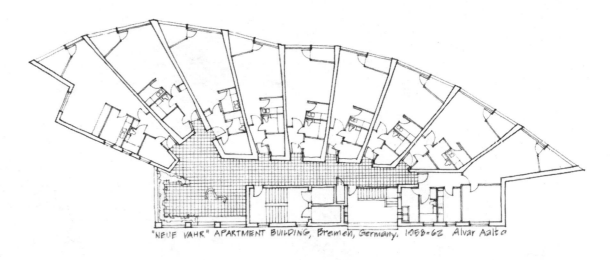

"NEUE VAHR" APARTMENT BUILDING, Bremen, Germany. 1958-62. Alvar Aalto

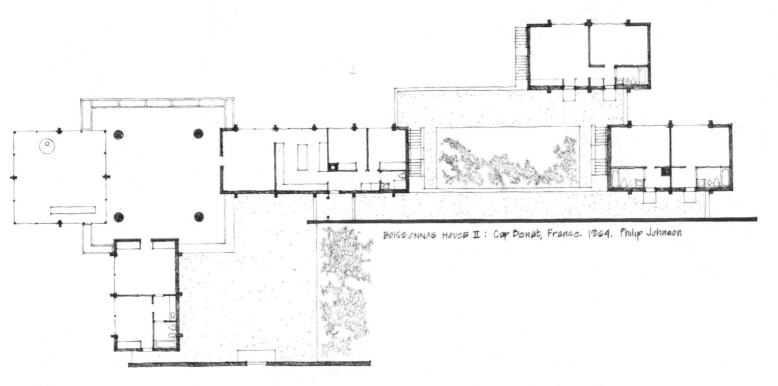

BOISSONNAS HOUSE II : Cap Benat, France. 1964. Philip Johnson

FORM OF THE CIRCULATION SPACE

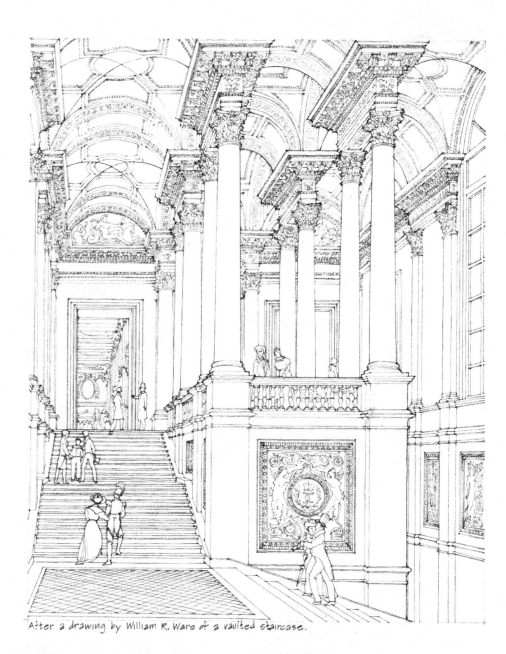

After a drawing by William R. Ware of a vaulted staircase.

Circulation spaces form an integral part of any building organization, and occupy a significant amount of space within the building's volume. If considered merely as functional linking-devices, then circulation paths would be endless, corridor-like spaces. The form and scale of a circulation space, however, must accommodate the movement of people as they promenade, pause, rest, or take in a view, along its path.

The form of a circulation space can vary according to how:

- its boundaries are defined;
- its form relates to the form of the spaces it links;
- its qualities of scale, proportion, light, and view are articulated;
- entrances open onto it;
- it handles changes in level with stairs and ramps.

A circulation space may be:
- ENCLOSED, forming a corridor that relates to the spaces it links through entrances in the wall plane;
- OPEN ON ONE SIDE, to provide visual and spatial continuity with the spaces it links;
- OPEN ON BOTH SIDES, to become a physical extension of the space it passes through.

The width and height of a circulation space should be proportionate with the type and amount of traffic it must handle. A narrow, enclosed path will encourage movement. A path can be widened not only to accommodate more traffic but also to create spaces for pausing, resting, or viewing. It can be enlarged by merging with the spaces it passes through. Within a large space, a path can be random, without form or definition, and determined by the activities within the space.

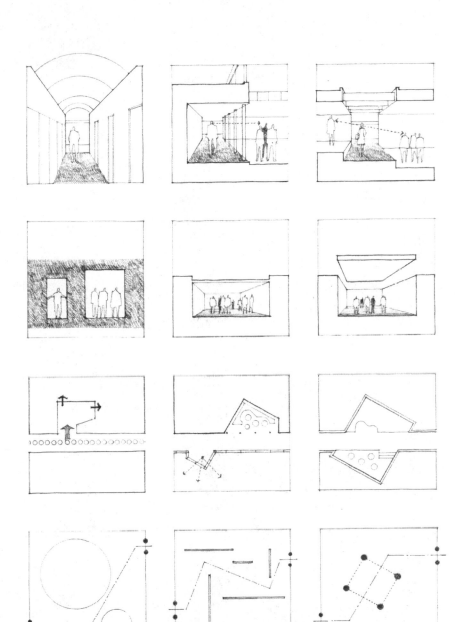

CIRCULATION SPACES

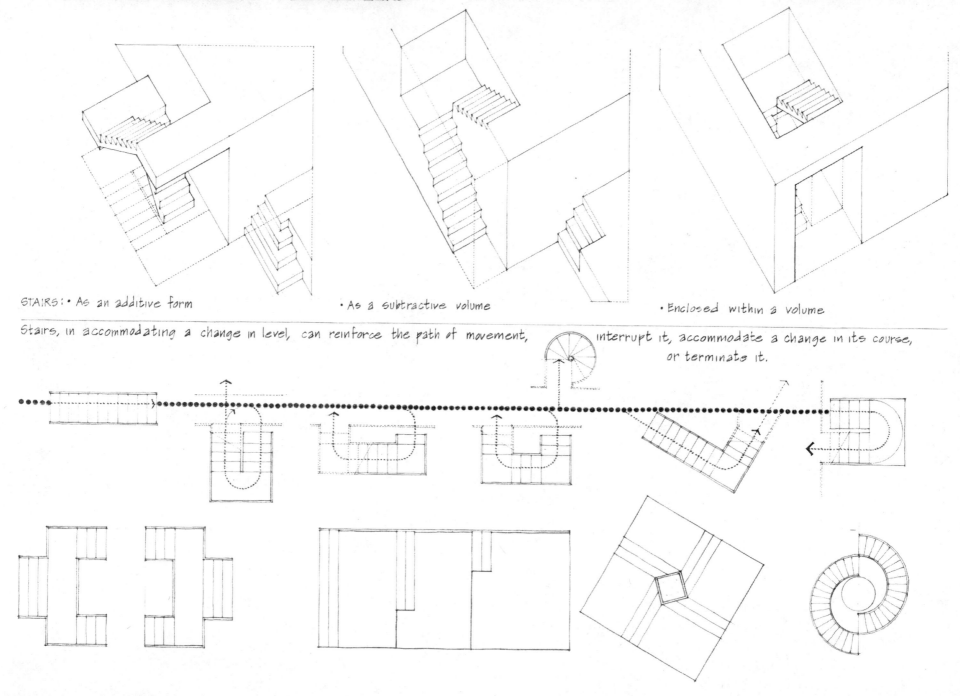

STAIRS: • As an additive form   • As a subtractive volume   • Enclosed within a volume

Stairs, in accommodating a change in level, can reinforce the path of movement, interrupt it, accommodate a change in its course, or terminate it.

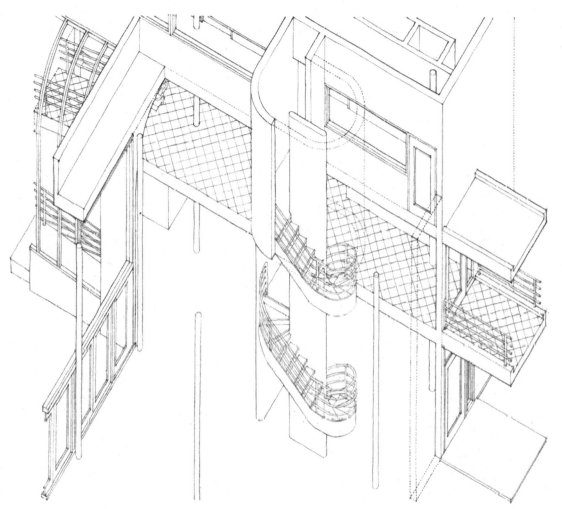

Grand Staircase
PARIS OPERA HOUSE, 1861-74
Charles Garnier

Axonometric of Living Room Stair
HOUSE IN OLD WESTBURY, New York, 1969-71
Richard Meier.

6

PROPORTION & SCALE

PROPORTION

MATERIAL PROPORTIONS

All building materials in architecture have distinct properties of stiffness, hardness, and durability. And they all have an ultimate strength beyond which they cannot extend themselves without fracturing, breaking, or collapsing. Since the stresses in a material, due to the force of gravity, increase with its size, all materials also have a rational size beyond which they cannot go. For example, a stone slab that is four-inches thick and eight-feet long can be reasonably expected to support itself as a bridge between two supports. But if its size were to increase fourfold, to sixteen-inches thick and thirty-two feet long, it would probably collapse under its own weight. Even a strong material like steel has lengths beyond which it cannot span without exceeding its ultimate strength.

All materials also have rational proportions that are dictated by their inherent strengths and weaknesses. Masonry units like brick, for example, are strong in compression and depend on their mass for strength, and are, therefore, volumetric in form. Materials like steel are strong in both compression and tension, and can, therefore, be formed into linear columns and beams as well as planar sheet material. Wood, being a flexible and fairly elastic material, can be used as linear posts and beams, planar boards, and as a volumetric element in log cabin construction.

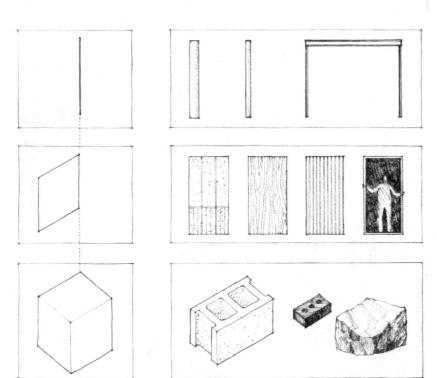

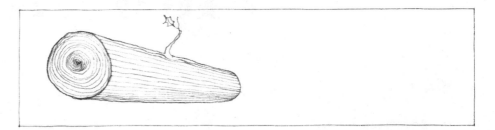

STRUCTURAL PROPORTIONS

In the construction of architecture, structural elements are called upon to span over spaces, and transmit their loads through vertical supports to a building's foundation system. The size and proportion of these elements are directly related to the structural tasks they perform and can be, therefore, visual indicators of the size and scale of the spaces they help enclose.

Beams, for example, transmit their loads horizontally across space to their vertical supports. If a beam's span or load is doubled, its bending stresses would likewise double, possibly causing it to collapse. But if its depth were doubled, its strength would increase four-fold. Depth, therefore, is a beam's critical dimension, and its depth-to-span ratio, a good indicator of its structural role.

Similarly, columns become thicker as their loads and unsupported height increase. Together, beams and columns form a skeletal structural framework that defines modules of space. By their size and proportion, columns and beams articulate space, and give it scale and a hierarchical structure. This can be seen in the way joists are supported by beams, and the beams, in turn, are supported by girders. Each element increases in depth as its load and span increases in size.

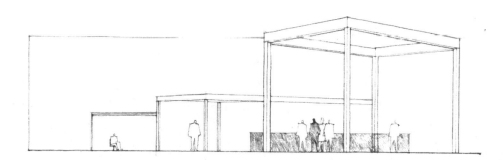

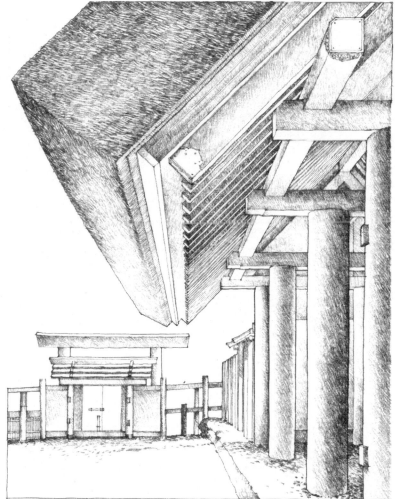

ISE SHRINE: South gateway of third fence of Naiku, the inner shrine. Near Ise-City, Japan. 3rd century, A.D.

PROPORTION

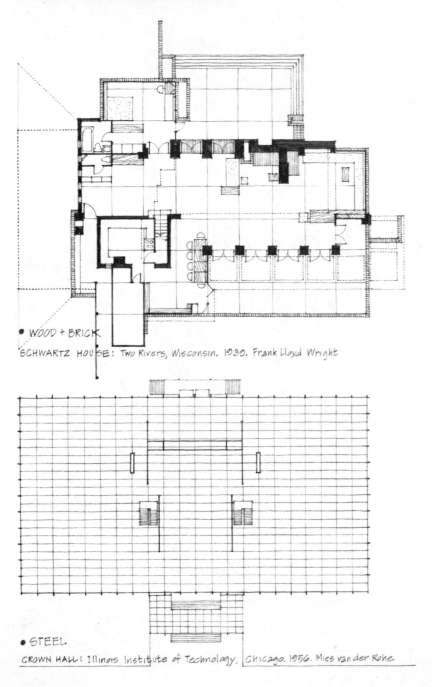

● WOOD + BRICK

SCHWARTZ HOUSE: Two Rivers, Wisconsin. 1939. Frank Lloyd Wright

● STEEL

CROWN HALL: Illinois Institute of Technology, Chicago. 1956. Mies van der Rohe

Other structural forms, such as bearing walls, floor and roof slabs, vaults, and domes, also give us visual clues with their proportion as to their role in a structural system as well as the nature of their material. A masonry wall, being strong in compression but relatively weak in bending, will be thicker than a reinforced concrete wall doing the same work. A steel column will be thinner than a wood post supporting the same load. A four-inch reinforced-concrete slab will span farther than four-inch wood decking.

As a structure depends less on the weight and stiffness of a material and more on its geometry for stability, as in the case of membrane structures and space frames, its elements will get thinner and thinner until they lose their ability to give a space scale and dimension.

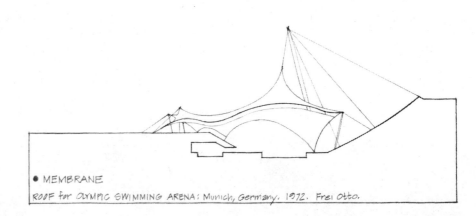

● MEMBRANE

ROOF for OLYMPIC SWIMMING ARENA: Munich, Germany. 1972. Frei Otto.

MANUFACTURED PROPORTIONS

Many architectural elements are sized and proportioned
not only according to their structural properties and function,
but also by the process through which they are manufactured.
Because these elements are mass-produced in factories,
they have standard sizes and proportions imposed on
them by the individual manufacturers or industry standards.

Concrete block and common brick, for example, are produced
as modular building blocks. Although they differ from each
other in size, both are proportioned on a similar basis. Plywood
and other sheathing materials are also manufactured as modular units with fixed proportions. Steel sections have fixed
proportions generally agreed upon by the steel manufacturers
and the American Institute of Steel Construction. Window and
door units have proportions that are set by the individual
manufacturers.

Since these and other materials must ultimately come
together and achieve a high degree of fit in the construction
of a building, the standard sizes and proportions of factory-
produced elements will affect the size, proportion, and spacing
of other materials as well. Standard door and window units
must be sized and proportioned to fit into modular masonry
openings. Wood or metal studs and joists must be spaced to
accept modular sheathing materials.

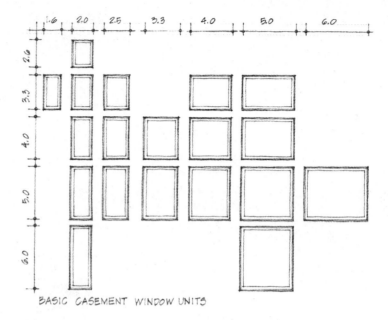

BASIC CASEMENT WINDOW UNITS

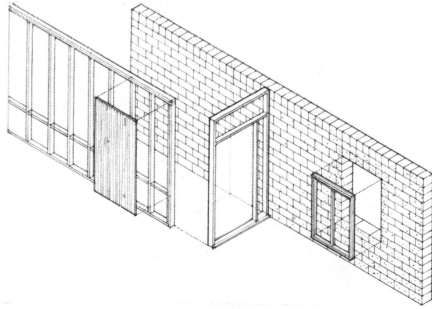

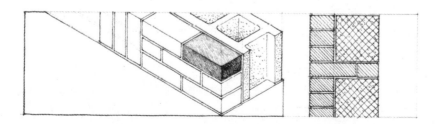

PROPORTIONING SYSTEMS

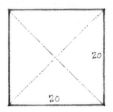 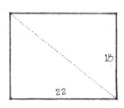 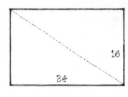

400 S.F.

A square space, having four equal faces, is static in nature. If its length expands and dominates its width, it becomes more dynamic. While square and oblong spaces define "places" for activity, linear spaces encourage movement, and are susceptible to subdivision into a number of zones.

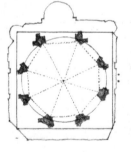 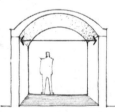 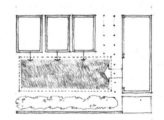

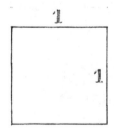 

Even considering the proportional restraints imposed on a form by the nature of its material, its structural function, or by the manufacturing process, the designer still has the ability to control the proportion of a building's forms and spaces. The decision to make a room square or oblong, low or high, or to endow a building with an imposing, higher-than-normal facade, legitimately falls to the designer. But on what basis are these decisions made?

If a space 400 square feet in area were required, what dimensions, width to length, length to height, should it have? Of course, the functioning of the space, the nature of the activities to be accommodated, will influence its form and proportion. A technical factor, such as its structure, might limit one or more of its dimensions. Its context, the exterior environment or an adjacent interior space, might pressure its form. The decision might be to recall another space from another time and place, and simulate its proportions. Or the decision might be based finally on aesthetic judgment, a visual judgement of the "desirable" dimensional relationships between the parts, and a part and the whole, of a building. To this end a number of theories of "desirable" proportions have been developed in the course of history.

In truth, our perception of the physical dimensions of architecture, of proportion and scale, is imprecise. It is distorted by the foreshortening of perspective and distance, and by cultural biases, and is thus difficult to control and predict in an objective and precise manner.

Small or slight differences in a form's dimensions are especially difficult to discern. While a square, by definition, has four equal sides and four right angles, a rectangle can appear to be exactly square, almost a square, or very much unlike a square. It can appear to be long, short, stubby, or squat, depending on our point of view. We use these terms to give a form or figure a visual quality that is largely a result of how we perceive its proportions. It is not, however, an exact science.

If the precise dimensions and relationships of a design that is regulated by a proportioning system cannot be objectively perceived in a similar manner by everyone, why are proportioning systems useful and of particular significance in architectural design?

The intent of all theories of proportion is to create a sense of order among the elements in a visual construction. According to Euclid, a ratio refers to the quantitative comparison of two similar things, while proportion refers to the equality of ratios. Underlying any proportioning system, therefore, is a characteristic ratio, a permanent quality that is transmitted from one ratio to another. Thus, a proportioning system establishes a consistent set of visual relationships between the parts of a building, as well as between the parts and their whole. Although these relationships may not be immediately perceived by the casual observer, the visual order they create can be sensed, accepted, or even recognized through a series of repetitive experiences. Over a period of time, we might begin to see the whole in the part, and the part in the whole.

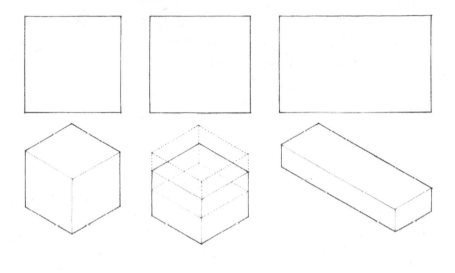

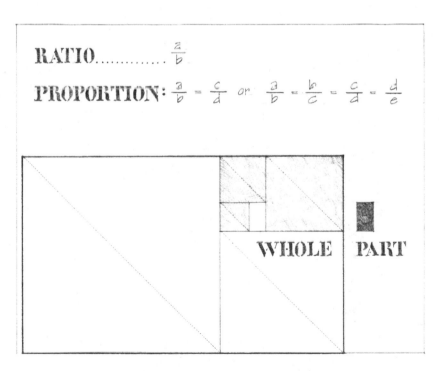

RATIO.............$\frac{a}{b}$

PROPORTION: $\frac{a}{b} = \frac{c}{d}$ or $\frac{a}{b} = \frac{b}{c} = \frac{c}{d} = \frac{d}{e}$

WHOLE | PART

PROPORTIONING SYSTEMS

Proportioning systems go beyond the functional and technical determinants of architectural form and space to provide an aesthetic rationale for their dimensions. They can visually unify the multiplicity of elements in an architectural design by having all of its parts belong to the same family of proportions. They can provide a sense of order in, and heighten the continuity of, a sequence of spaces. They can establish relationships between the exterior and interior elements of a building.

The notion of devising a system for design and communicating its means is common to all periods in history. Although the actual system varies from time to time, the principles involved and their value to the designer remain the same.

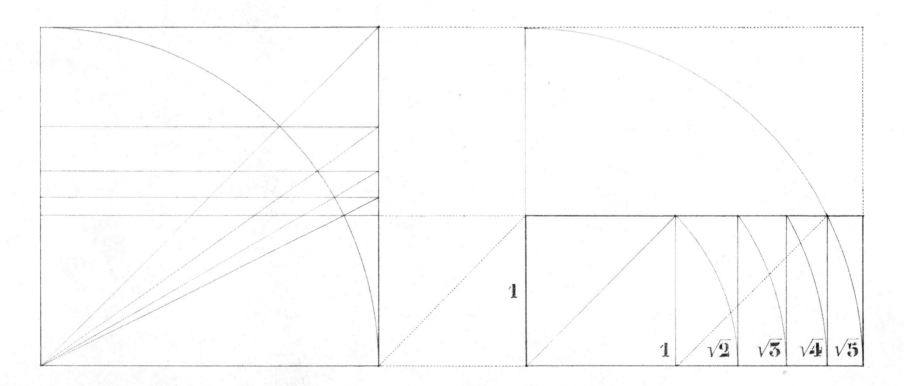

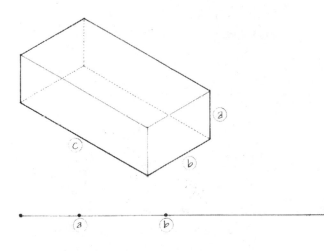

TYPES OF PROPORTION:

1. GEOMETRIC : $\dfrac{c-b}{b-a} = \dfrac{c}{b}$ (eg. 1, 2, 4)

2. ARITHMETIC : $\dfrac{c-b}{b-a} = \dfrac{c}{c}$ (eg. 1, 2, 3)

3. HARMONIC : $\dfrac{c-b}{a-b} = \dfrac{c}{a}$ (eg. 2, 3, 6)

THEORIES OF PROPORTION:

- **THE GOLDEN SECTION**

- **THE ORDERS**

- **RENAISSANCE THEORIES**

- **THE MODULOR**

- **THE 'KEN'**

- **ANTHROPOMORPHIC PROPORTIONS**

- **SCALE:** A fixed proportion used in determining measurements and dimensions.

THE GOLDEN SECTION

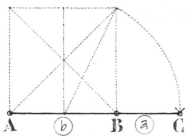 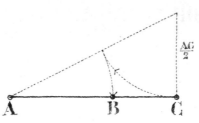

Geometrically constructing the Golden Section, first by extension, and then by division.

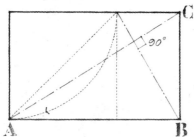

AB = b
BC = a

Φ = GOLDEN SECTION

$\Phi = \dfrac{a}{b} = \dfrac{b}{a+b} = 1.618\ldots\ldots$

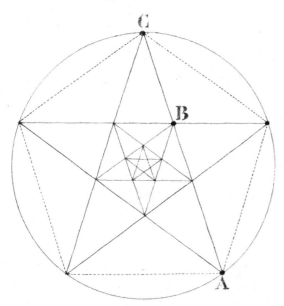

Mathematical systems of proportion originate from the Pythagorean concept of "all is number" and the belief that certain numerical relationships manifest the harmonic structure of the universe. One of these relationships that has been in use ever since the days of antiquity is the proportion known as the Golden Section. The Greeks recognized the dominating role the Golden Section played in the proportioning of the human body. Believing that both man and his temples should belong to a higher universal order, these same proportions were reflected in their temple structures. The Golden Section was also explored in the work of Renaissance architects. In more recent times, Le Corbusier based his Modulor system on the Golden Section. And its use in architecture endures even today.

The Golden Section can be defined geometrically as a line that is divided such that the lesser portion is to the greater as the greater is to the whole. It can be expressed algebraically by the equation of two ratios: $\frac{a}{b} = \frac{b}{a+b}$.

The Golden Section has some remarkable algebraic and geometric properties that account for its existence in architecture as well as in the structure of living organisms. Any progression based on the Golden Section is at once additive and geometrical. In the numerical progression: $1, \phi^1, \phi^2, \phi^3 \ldots \phi^n$, each term is the sum of the two preceding ones. Another progression that closely approximates the Golden Section in whole numbers is the Fibonacci Series: 1, 1, 2, 3, 5, 8, 13, ... etc. Each term again is the sum of the two preceding ones, and the ratio between two consecutive terms tends to approximate the Golden Section as the series progresses.

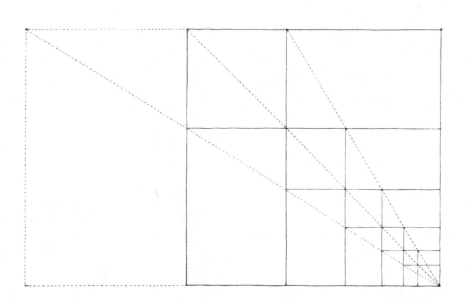

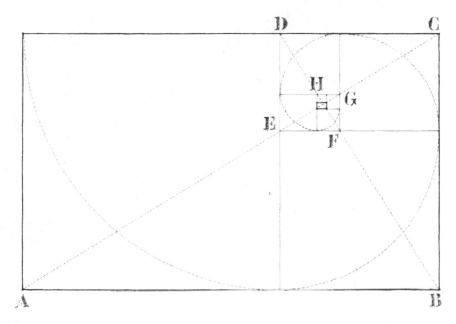

A rectangle whose sides are proportioned according to the Golden Section is known as a Golden Rectangle. If a square is constructed on its smaller side, the remaining portion of the original rectangle would be a smaller but similar Golden Rectangle. This operation can be repeated indefinitely to create a gradation of squares and Golden Rectangles. During this transformation, each part remains similar to all of the other parts, as well as to the whole. The diagrams on this page illustrate this additive and geometrical growth pattern of progressions based on the Golden Section.

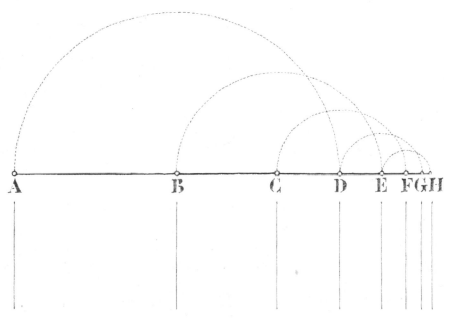

$$\frac{AB}{BC} = \frac{BC}{CD} = \frac{CD}{DE} \cdots = \phi$$

$$AB = BC + CD$$
$$BC = CD + DE$$

etc.

THE GOLDEN SECTION

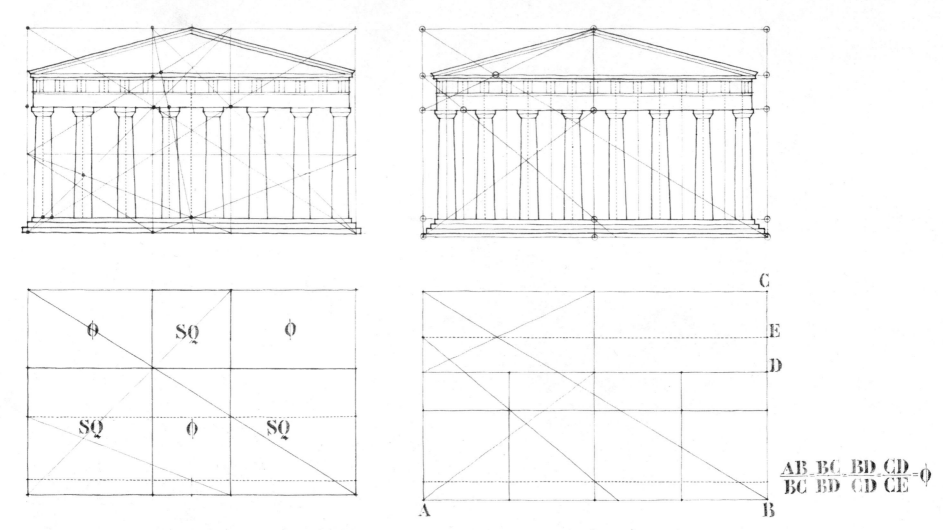

$$\frac{AB}{BC} = \frac{BC}{BD} = \frac{BD}{CD} = \frac{CD}{CE} = \phi$$

These two graphic analyses illustrate the use of the Golden Section in the proportioning of the facade of the Parthenon (Athens, 447-432 B.C., Ictinus and Callicrates). It is interesting to note that while both analyses begin by fitting the facade into a Golden Rectangle, each analysis then varies from the other in its approach to proving the existence of the Golden Section and its effect on the facade's dimensions and distribution of elements.

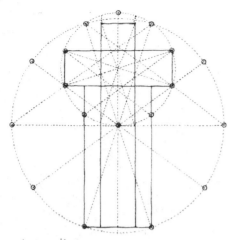

▲ (Moessel)

▼ (F.M. Lund)

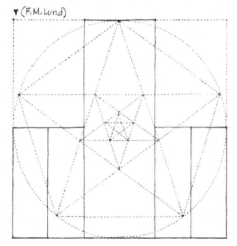

STANDARD GOTHIC PLAN and SECTION

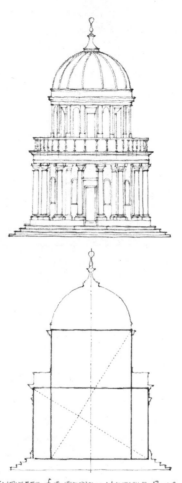

TEMPIETTO of S. PIETRO in MONTORIO, Rome.
1502-10. Donato Bramante

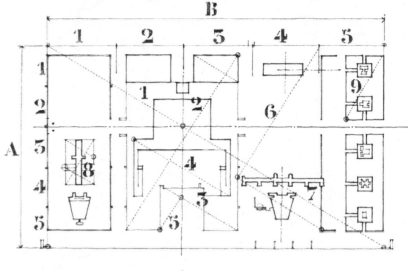

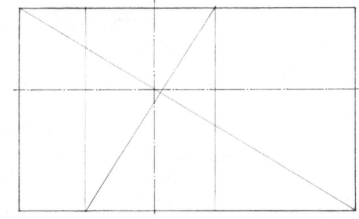

WORLD MUSEUM: Geneva (Project) 1929. Le Corbusier

REGULATING LINES

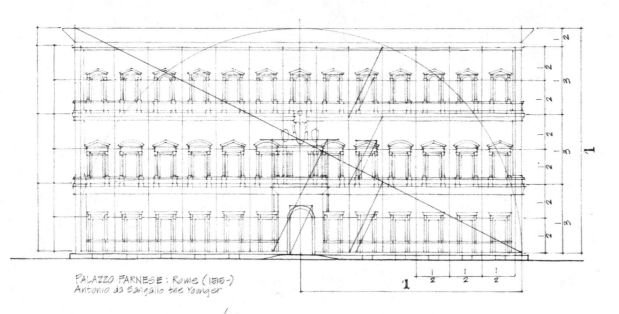

PALAZZO FARNESE : Rome (1515-)
Antonio da Sangallo the Younger

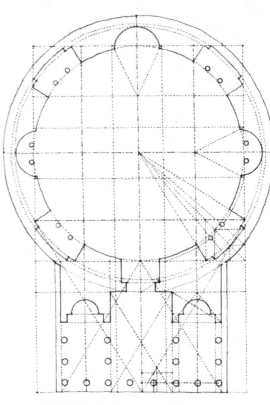

THE PANTHEON : Rome. A.D. 120-4

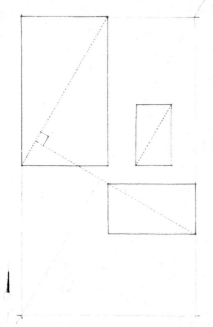

If the diagonals of two rectangles are either parallel or perpendicular to each other, they indicate that the two rectangles have similar proportions. These diagonals, as well as lines that indicate the alignment of elements with one another, are called regulating lines. They were seen previously in the discussion of the Golden Section, but they can also be used to control the proportion and placement of elements in other proportioning systems as well. Le Corbusier, in Towards a New Architecture, stated the following:

"A regulating line is an assurance against capriciousness; it is a means of verification which can ratify all work created in a fervour... It confers on the work the quality of rhythm. The regulating line brings in this tangible form of mathematics which gives the reassuring perception of order. The choice of a regulating line fixes the fundamental geometry of the work... It is a means to an end; it is not a recipe."

A·B = B:(A·B)

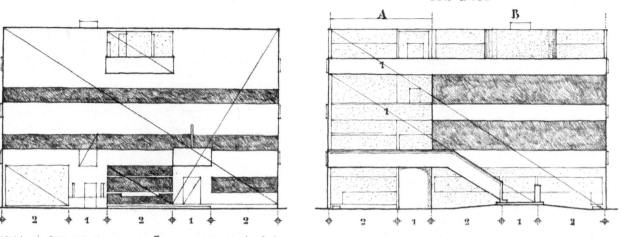

VILLA at GARCHES, Vaucresson, France. 1926-26. Le Corbusier

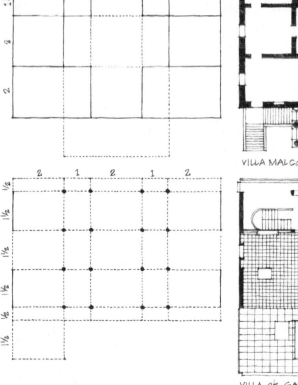

In his essay," The Mathematics of the Ideal Villa," 1947, Colin Rowe pointed out the similarity between the spatial subdivision of a Palladian villa and the structural grid of a villa by Le Corbusier. While both villas shared a similar proportioning system and a relationship to a higher (mathematical) order, Palladio's villa consisted of spaces with fixed shapes and harmonic inter-relationships. Le Corbusier's villa was composed of horizontal layers of free space defined by the floor and roof slabs. The rooms varied in shape and were asymmetrically arranged at each level.

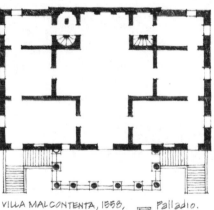

VILLA MALCONTENTA, 1558,   Palladio.

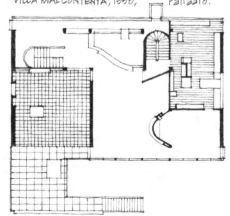

VILLA at GARCHES

THE ORDERS

IONIC ORDER: From the Temple on the Ilissus, Athens. 440 B.C.
Callicrates.   After a drawing by William R. Ware

To the Greeks and Romans of classical antiquity, the Orders represented in their proportioning of elements the perfect expression of beauty and harmony. The basic unit of dimension was the diameter of the column. From this module were derived the dimensions of the shaft, the capital, as well as the pedestel below, and the entablature above, down to the smallest detail. Intercolumniation, the spacing between the columns, was also based on the diameter of the column.

Since the size of columns varied according to the size of a building, the Orders were not based on a fixed unit of measurement. Rather, the intention was to ensure that all of the parts of any one building were proportioned and in harmony with one another.

Vitruvius, in the time of Augustus, studied actual examples of the Orders and presented his "ideal" proportions for each in his treatise, The Ten Books on Architecture. Vignola re-codified these rules for the Italian Renaissance, and his forms for the Orders are probably the best known today.

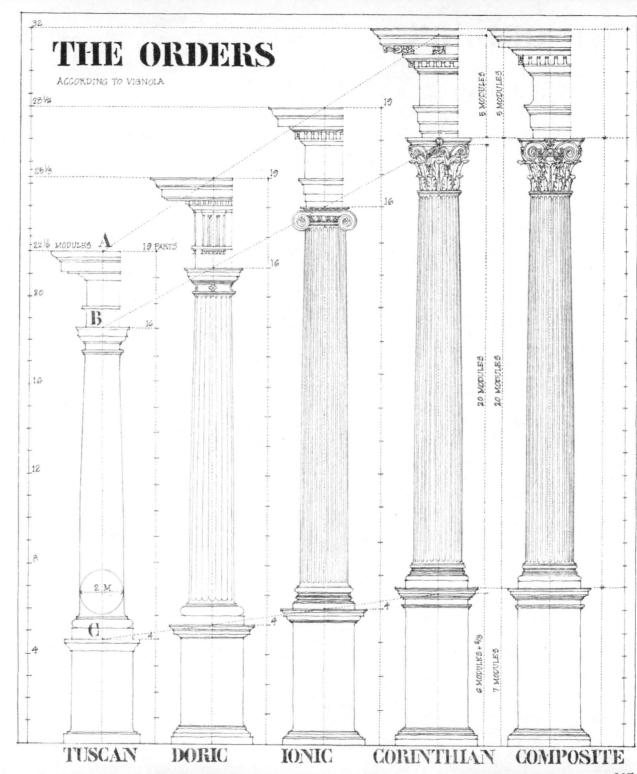

THE ORDERS

ACCORDING TO VIGNOLA

TUSCAN   DORIC   IONIC   CORINTHIAN   COMPOSITE

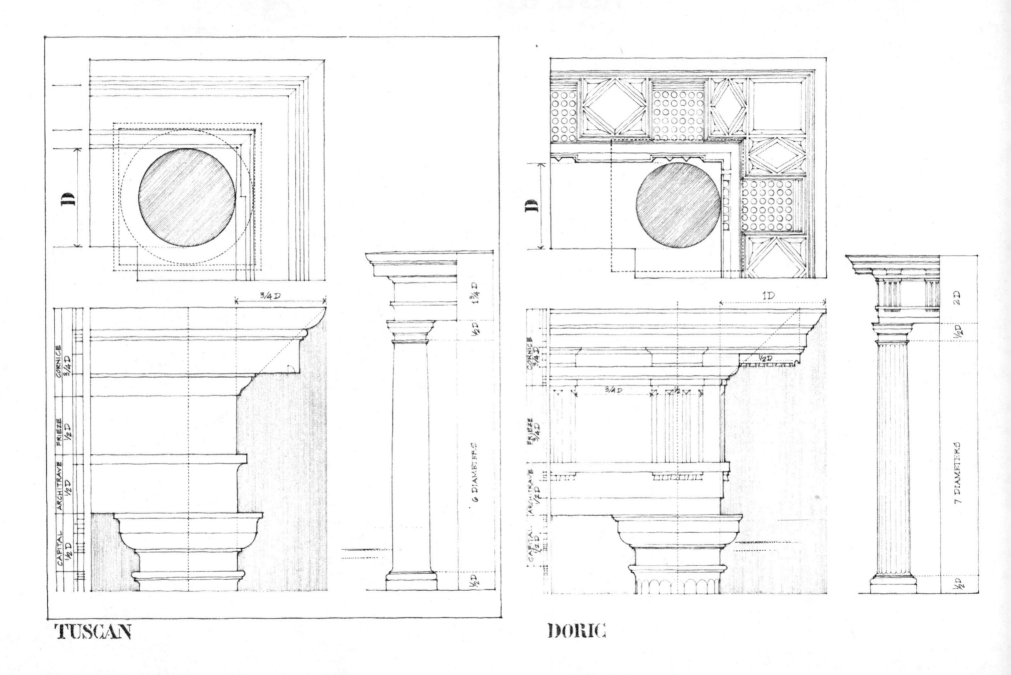

TUSCAN

DORIC

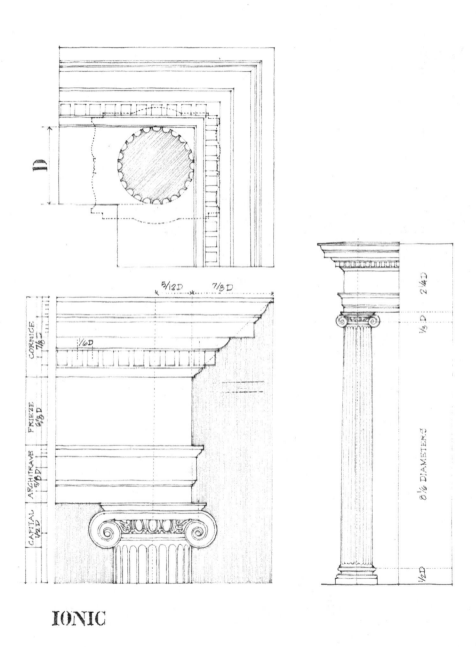

IONIC

5/12D   7/8D

CORNICE 7/8D

1/6D

FRIEZE 9/8D

ARCHITRAVE 5/6D

CAPITAL 1/2D

2 1/4 D

1/3 D

8 1/2 DIAMETERS

1/2D

CORINTHIAN

6/5D 5/12D 1D

CORNICE 1D

1/4 1/8 5/12

FRIEZE 3/4D

ARCHITRAVE 3/4D

CAPITAL 7/6D

2 1/2 D

7/6 D

8 1/3 DIAMETERS

1/2D

309

THE ORDERS

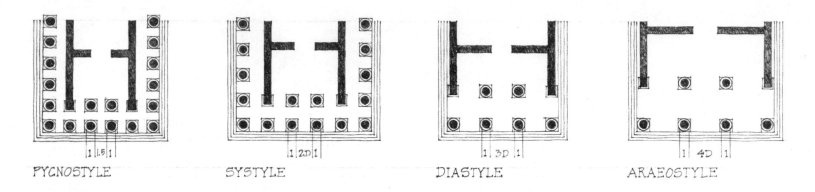

PYCNOSTYLE   SYSTYLE   DIASTYLE   ARAEOSTYLE

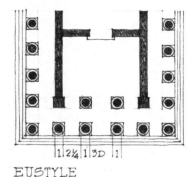

CLASSIFICATION of TEMPLES ACCORDING TO THEIR INTERCOLUMNIATION

EUSTYLE

VITRUVIUS' RULES FOR THE DIAMETER, HEIGHT, & SPACING OF COLUMNS

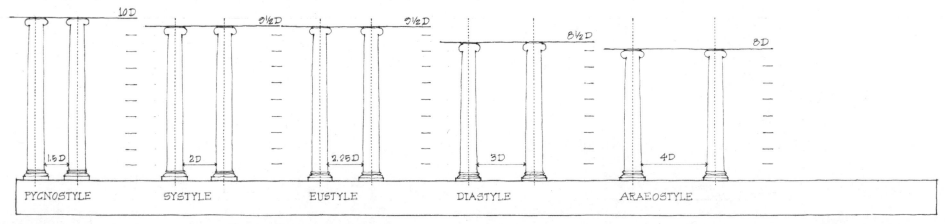

PYCNOSTYLE   SYSTYLE   EUSTYLE   DIASTYLE   ARAEOSTYLE

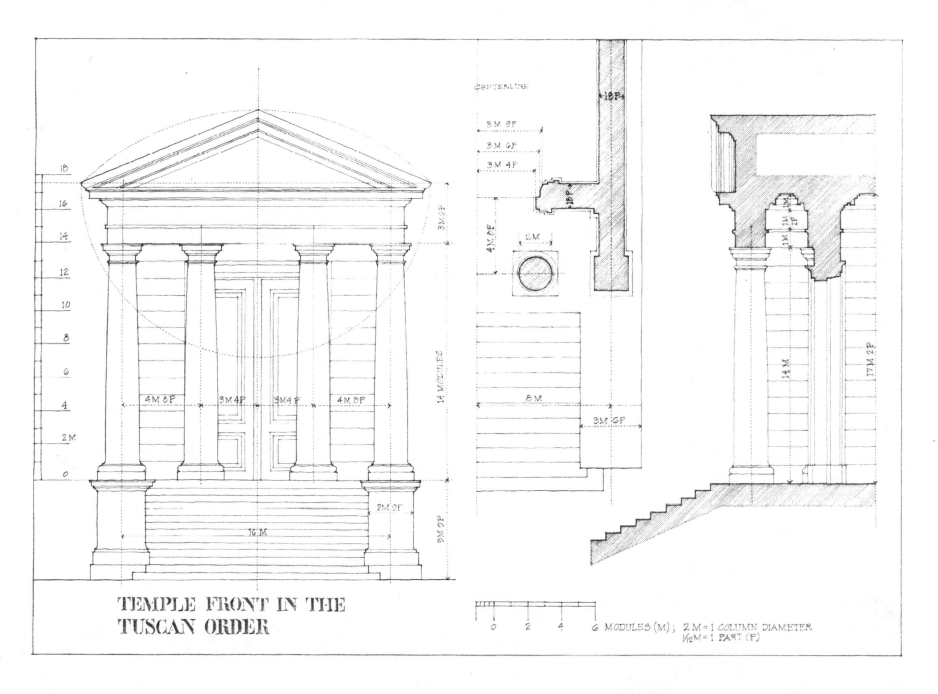

TEMPLE FRONT IN THE
TUSCAN ORDER

CENTERLINE

3 M 9 P

3 M 6 P

3 M 4 P

18 P

12 P

4 M 8 P

2 M

18

16

14

12

10

8

6

4

2 M

0

4 M 8 P   3 M 4 P   3 M 4 F   4 M 8 P

14 MODULES

3 M 2 P

2 M 0 P

16 M

3 M 0 P

8 M

3 M 6 P

14 M

17 M 2 P

0   2   4   6 MODULES (M);   2 M = 1 COLUMN DIAMETER
1/12 M = 1 PART (P)

311

RENAISSANCE THEORIES

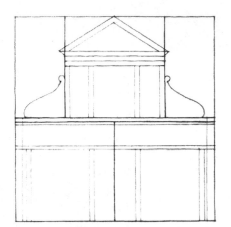

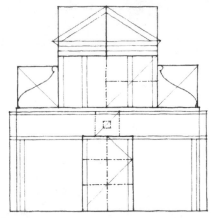

S. MARIA NOVELLA: Florence. Renaissance facade (1456-70) was designed by Alberti to complete a Gothic church (1278-1350)

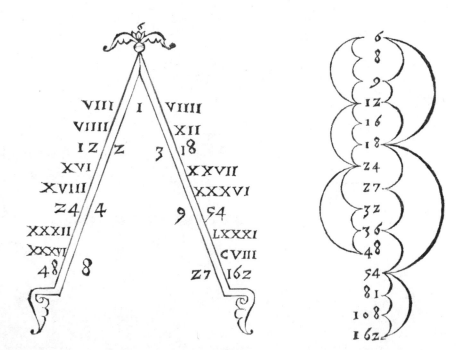

DIAGRAM BY FRANCESCO GIORGI, 1525, illustrating the series of interlocking ratios that results from apply Pythagoras' theory of means to the intervals of the Greek musical scale.

Pythagoras discovered that the consonances of the Greek musical system could be expressed by the simple numerical progression, 1:2:3:4, and their ratios, 1:2, 1:3, 2:3, 3:4. This relationship led the Greeks to believe they had found the key to the mysterious harmony that pervaded the universe. The Pythagorean creed was: "Everything is arranged according to numbers." Plato later developed Pythagoras' aesthetics of numbers into an aesthetics of proportion. He squared and cubed the simple numerical progression to produce the double and triple progressions, 1, 2, 4, 8, and 1, 3, 9, 27. For Plato, these numbers and their ratios not only contained the consonances of the Greek musical scale but also expressed the harmonic structure of his universe.

The architects of the Renaissance, believing that their buildings had to belong to a higher order, returned to the Greek mathematical system of proportions. Just as the Greeks conceived music to be geometry translated into sound, Renaissance architects believed that architecture was mathematics translated into spatial units. Applying Pythagoras' theory of means to the ratios of the intervals of the Greek musical scale, they developed an unbroken progression of ratios that formed the basis for the proportions of their architecture. These series of ratios manifested themselves not only in the dimensions of a room or a facade, but also in the interlocking proportions of a sequence of spaces or an entire plan.

CIRCLE

SQUARE

1:√2

3:4

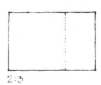
2:3

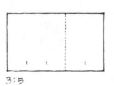
3:5

1:2

7 IDEAL PLAN · SHAPES FOR ROOMS

Andrea Palladio (1508-80) was probably the most influential architect of the Italian Renaissance. In <u>The Four Books on Architecture</u>, first published in Venice in 1570, he followed in the footsteps of his predecessors, Albert and Serlio, and proposed seven "most beautiful and proportionable manners of rooms."

DETERMINING THE HEIGHTS OF ROOMS

Palladio also proposed several methods for determining the proper height of a room so that it would be in proper proportion to the room's width and length. For rooms with flat ceilings, their height would be equal to their width. For square rooms with vaulted ceilings, their height would be one-third greater than their width. For other rooms, Palladio used Pythagoras' theory of means to determine their heights. Accordingly, there were three types of means: arithmetic, geometric, and harmonic.

1. ARITHMETIC : $\dfrac{c-b}{b-a} = \dfrac{c}{c}$ eg. 1, 2, 3.. or 6, 9, 12.

2. GEOMETRIC : $\dfrac{c-b}{b-a} = \dfrac{c}{b}$ eg. 1, 2, 4.. or 4, 6, 9.

3. HARMONIC : $\dfrac{c-b}{b-a} = \dfrac{c}{a}$ eg. 2, 3, 6.. or 6, 8, 12.

In each, the mean (b) between the two extremes of the room's width (a) and length (c) was the room's height.

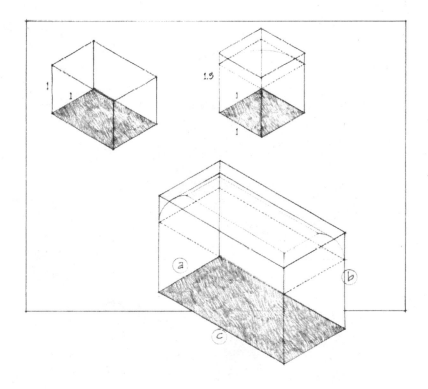

RENAISSANCE THEORIES

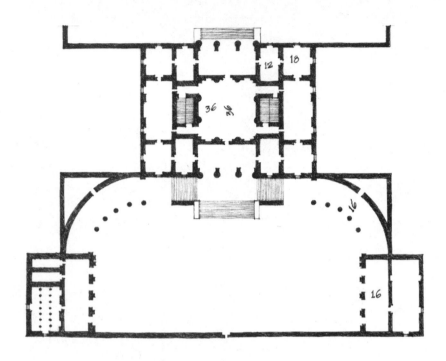

VILLA THIENE: Cicogna, 1549. Andrea Palladio

18 × 36, 36 × 36, 36 × 18, 18 × 18, 18 × 12

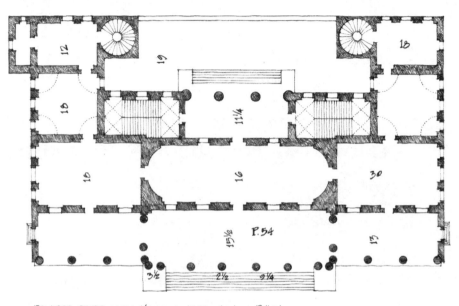

PALAZZO CHIERICATI: Vicenza, 1550. Andrea Palladio

54 × 16 (18), 18 × 30, 18 × 18, 18 × 12

"Beauty will result from the form and correspondence
of the whole, with respect to the several parts, of
the parts with regard to each other, and of these
again to the whole; that the structure may appear
an entire and complete body, wherein each member
agrees with the other, and all necessary to compose
what you intend to form." Andrea Palladio, The Four Books on Architecture, Book I, Chapter 1.

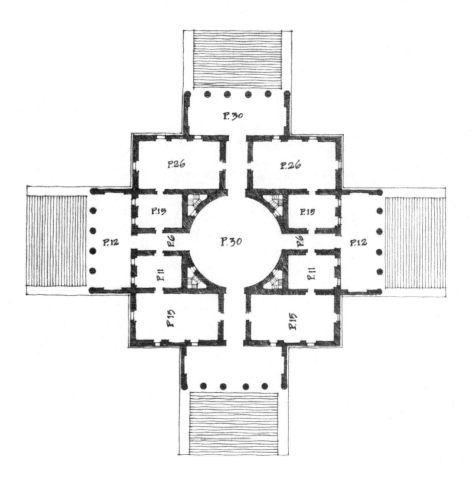

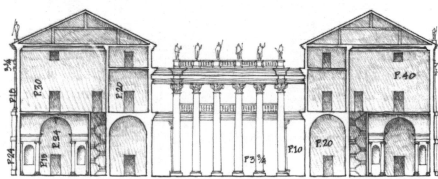

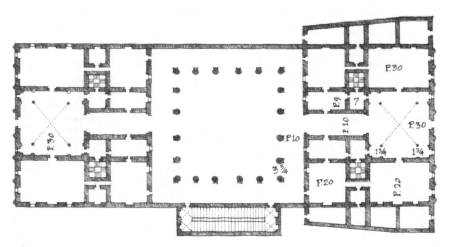

VILLA CAPRA, (THE ROTONDA): Vicenza. 1552-
Andrea Palladio

12 x 30, 6 x 15, 30 x 30

PALAZZO ISEPPO PORTO: 1552
Andrea Palladio

30 x 30, 20 x 30, 10 x 30, 45 x 45

THE MODULOR

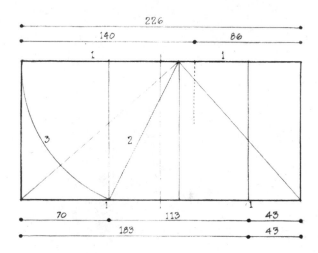

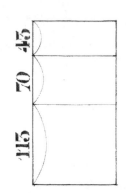

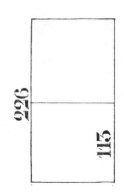

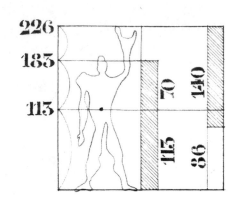

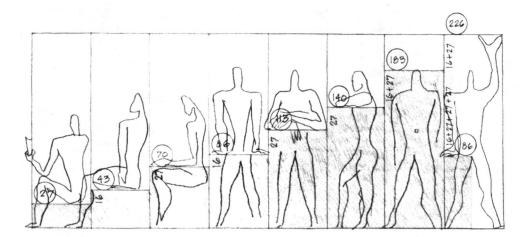

Le Corbusier developed his proportioning system, the Modulor, to order "the dimensions of that which contains and that which is contained." He saw the measuring tools of the Greeks, Egyptians, and other high civilizations as being "infinitely rich and subtle because they formed part of the mathematics of the human body, gracious, elegant, and firm, the source of that harmony which moves us, beauty." He therefore based his measuring tool, the Modulor, on both mathematics (the aesthetic dimensions of the Golden Section and the Fibonacci Series), and the proportions of the humany body (functional dimensions).

Le Corbusier began his study in 1942, and published The Modulor: A Harmonious Measure to the Human Scale Universally Applicable to Architecture and Mechanics in 1948. A second volume, Modulor II, was published in 1954.

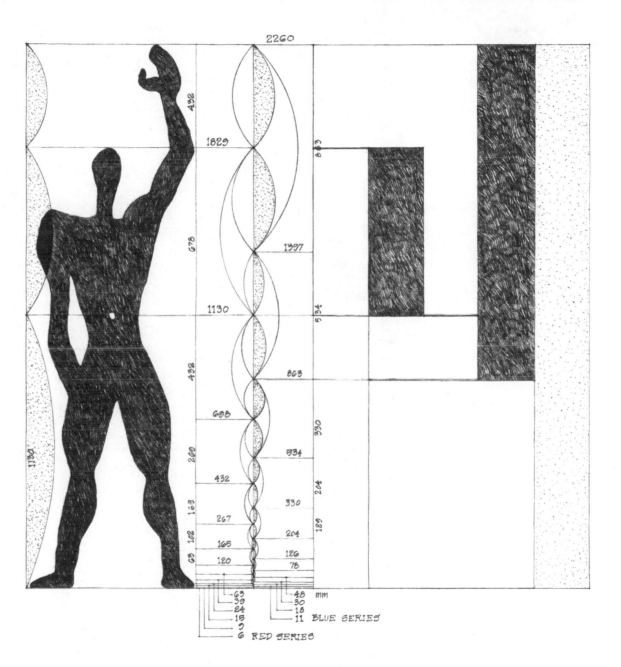

Le Corbusier saw the Modulor not merely as a series of numbers with an inherent harmony, but as a system of measurements that could govern lengths, surfaces, and volumes, and "maintain the human scale everywhere." It could "lend itself to an infinity of combinations; it ensures unity with diversity.... the miracle of numbers."

The basic grid consists of three measures:
113, 70, 43 (cm), proportioned according to the Golden Section.

$$43 + 70 = 113$$
$$113 + 70 = 183$$
$$113 + 70 + 43 = 226 \quad (2 \times 113)$$

113, 183, 226 define the space occupied by the human figure. From 113 and 226, Le Corbusier developed the Red and Blue series, diminishing scales of dimensions that were related to the stature of the human figure.

THE MODULOR

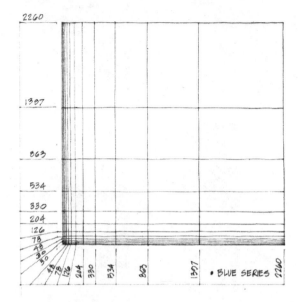

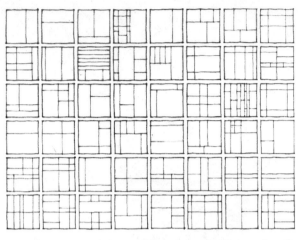

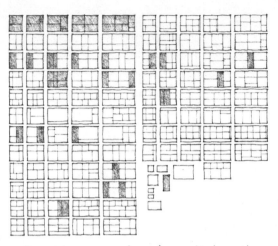

Le Corbusier used these diagrams to illustrate the diversity of panel sizes and surfaces that could be obtained with the proportions of the Modulor.

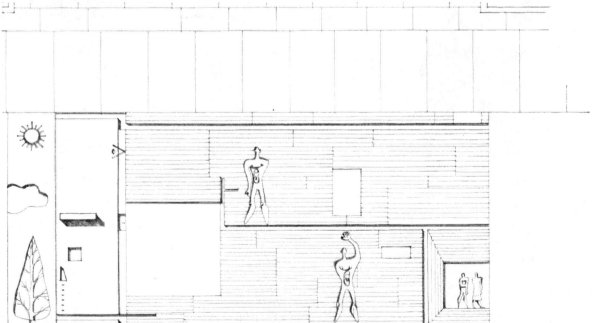

FACADE DETAIL: UNITE' D'HABITATION, Firminy-Vert, France. 1960-68   Le Corbusier

The principle work of Le Corbusier that exemplefied the use of the Modulor was his Unite' d'habitation at Marseilles, 1946-52. It uses 15 measures of the Modulor to bring human scale to a building that is 140 meters long, 24 meters wide, and 70 meters high.

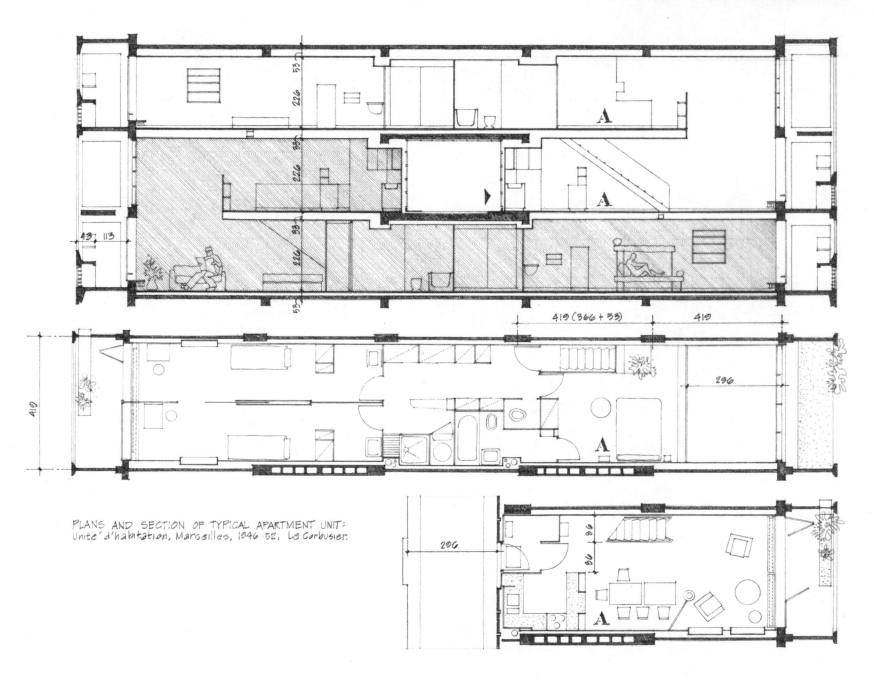

PLANS AND SECTION OF TYPICAL APARTMENT UNIT:
Unité d'habitation, Marseilles, 1946-52, Le Corbusier.

THE 'KEN'

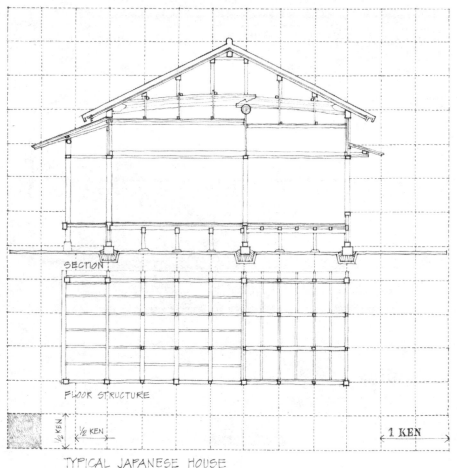

SECTION

FLOOR STRUCTURE

1/2 KEN   1/2 KEN

1 KEN

TYPICAL JAPANESE HOUSE

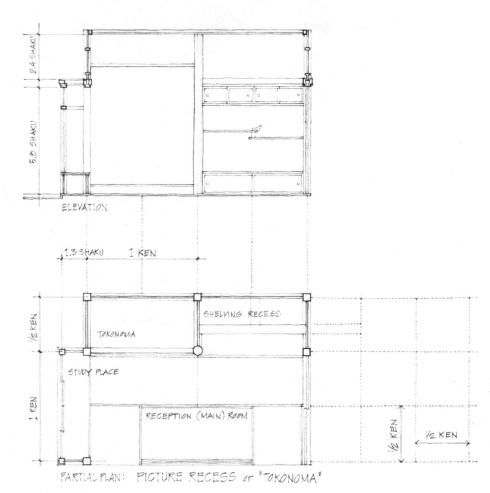

2.4 SHAKU

5.8 SHAKU

ELEVATION

1.3 SHAKU   1 KEN

1/2 KEN

1 KEN

TOKONOMA

SHELVING RECESS

STUDY PLACE

RECEPTION (MAIN) ROOM

1/2 KEN   1/2 KEN

PARTIAL PLAN: PICTURE RECESS or "TOKONOMA"

The traditional Japanese unit of measure, the Shaku, was originally imported from China. It is almost equivalent to the English foot, and divisible into decimal units. Another unit of measure, the Ken, was introduced in the latter half of Japan's Middle Ages. Although it was originally used simply to designate the interval between two columns, and varied in size, the Ken was soon standardized for residential architecture. Unlike the module of the Classical Orders, the diameter of a column, varied with the size of a building, the Ken became an absolute measurement.

The Ken, however, was not only a measurement for the construction of buildings. It evolved into an aesthetic module that ordered the structure, materials, and space of Japanese architecture.

Two methods of designing with the Ken modular grid developed that affected its dimension. In the Inaka-ma method, the Ken grid (6 shaku) determined the center-to-center spacing of columns. The standard tatami floor mat, (3 x 6 shaku, or ½ x 1 ken), therefore, varied slightly to allow for the thickness of columns.

In the Kyō-ma method, the floor mat remained constant, (3.15 x 6.30 shaku), and the column spacing (Ken module) varied according to the size of the room, and ranged from 6.4 to 6.7 shaku.

Room sizes are designated by the number of its floor mats. The size of the floor mat was originally designed to accommodate two persons sitting, or one sleeping. As the ordering system of the Ken grid developed, however, the floor mat lost its dependence on human dimensions, and was subjected to the demands of the structural system and its column spacing.

Because of their 1:2 modularity, the floor mats can be arranged in a number of ways for any given room size. And for each room size, a different ceiling height is determined according to the following: ceiling height (shaku) = no. of mats x .03.

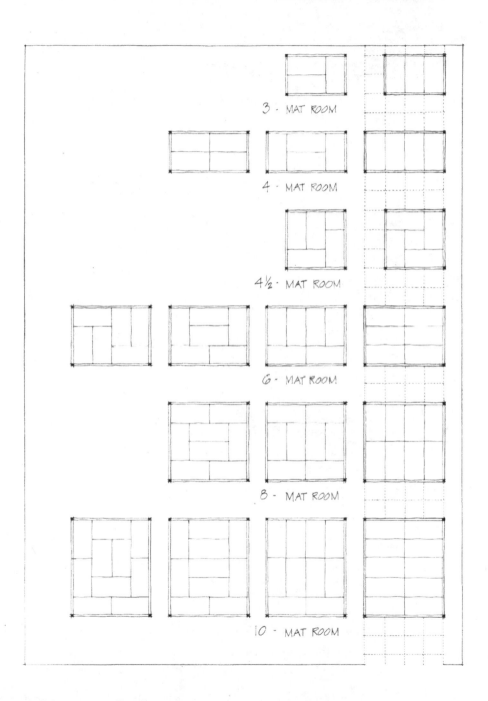

3 - MAT ROOM

4 - MAT ROOM

4½ - MAT ROOM

6 - MAT ROOM

8 - MAT ROOM

10 - MAT ROOM

THE 'KEN'

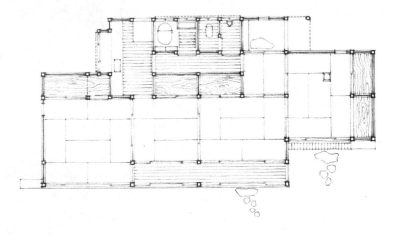

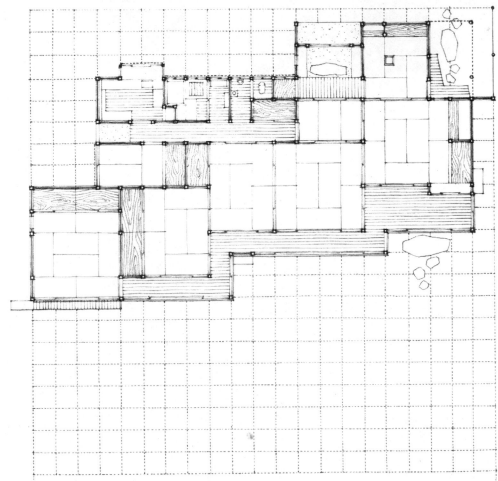

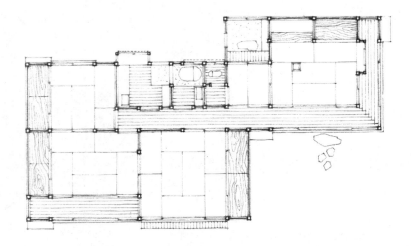

In a typical Japanese residence, the Ken grid orders the structure as well as the additive, space-to-space sequence of rooms. The relatively small size of the module allows the rectangular spaces to be freely arranged in linear, staggered, or clustered patterns.

THE 'KEN'

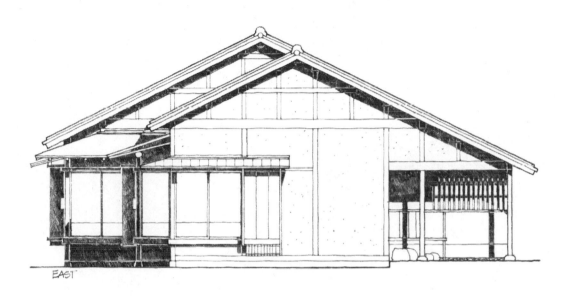

EAST

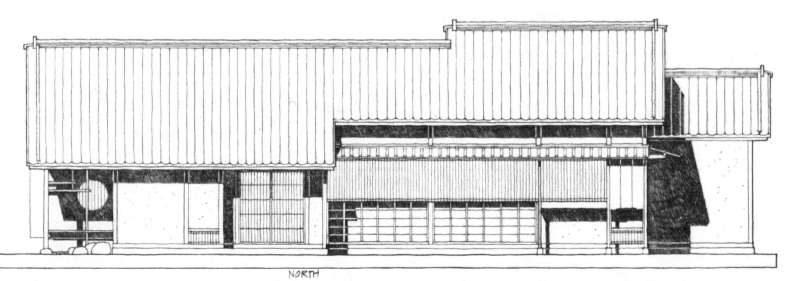

NORTH

ELEVATIONS OF A TYPICAL JAPANESE RESIDENCE

ANTHROPOMORPHIC PROPORTIONS

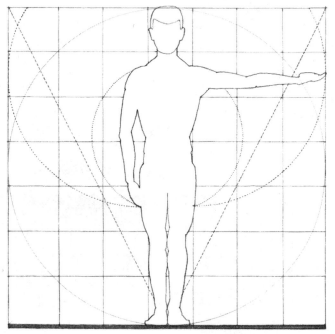

Anthropomorphic proportioning systems are based on the dimensions and proportions of the human body. While the architects of the Renaissance saw the proportions of the human figure as a reaffirmation that certain mathematical ratios reflected the harmony of their universe, anthropomorphic proportioning methods seek not abstract or symbolic ratios, but functional ones. They are predicated on the theory that forms and spaces in architecture are either containers or extensions of the human body and should, therefore, be determined by its dimensions.

The difficulty with anthropomorphic proportioning is the nature of the data required for its use. For example, the dimensions given here, in millimeters, are average measurements and are merely guidelines. Average dimensions must always be treated with caution since the actual dimensions of the people to be served will vary according to age, sex, and race.

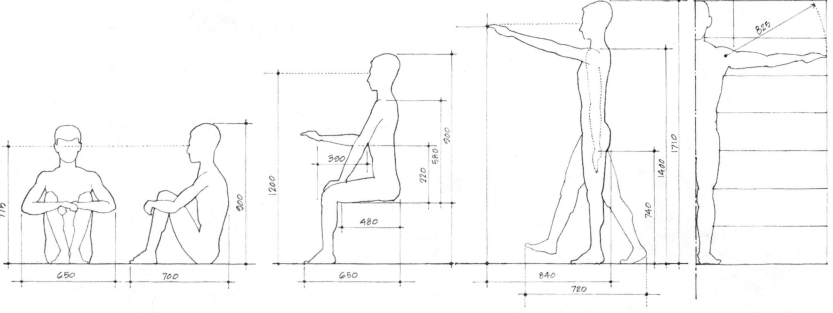

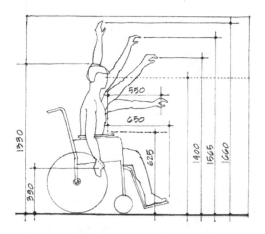

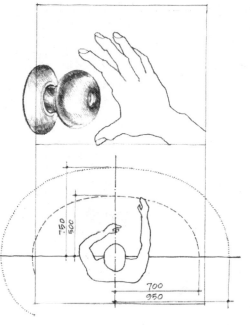

The dimensions and proportions of the human body affect the proportion of things we handle, the height and distance of things we must reach, the dimensions of the furniture we use for sitting, working, eating, and sleeping.

In addition to these elements that we use in a building, the dimensions of the human body also affect the volume of space we require for movement, activity, and rest.

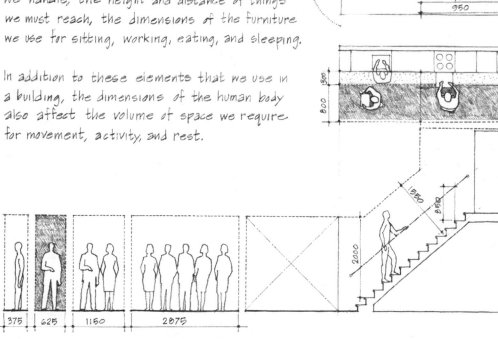

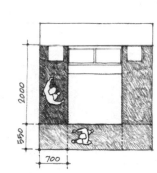

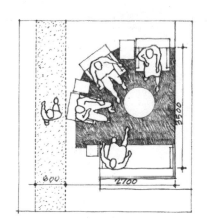

SCALE

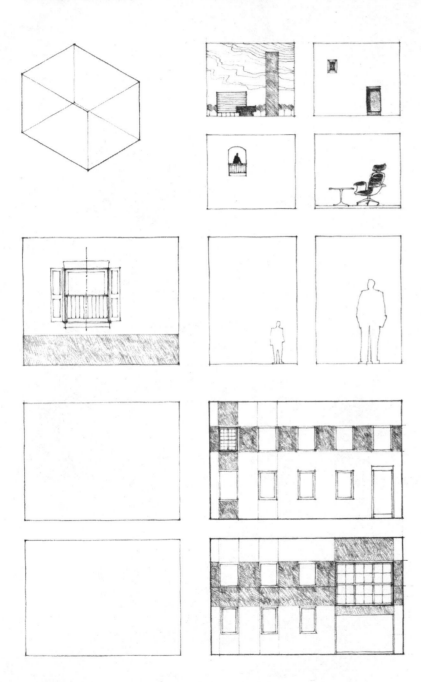

While proportion refers to the mathematical relationships among the real dimensions of a form or space, scale refers to how we perceive the size of a building element or space relative to other forms. In visually measuring the size of an element, we tend to use other elements of known size in their context as measuring devices. These are known as scale-giving elements, and fall into two general categories: building elements whose size and characteristics are familiar to us through experience, and the human figure. In architecture, therefore, we are concerned with two types of scale:

1. GENERIC SCALE:
The size of a building element relative to other forms in its context;

2. HUMAN SCALE:
The size of a building element or space relative to the dimensions and proportions of the human body.

All building elements have a certain size. It may be predetermined by the manufacturer, or it may be selected by the designer from a range of choices. Nevertheless, the size of each element is perceived relative to the sizes of other elements around it. For example, the size and proportion of windows in a building facade are usually related to one another, as well as to the spaces between them and the overall dimensions of the facade. If the windows are all of the same size and shape, they establish a scale relative to the size of the facade. If, however, one of the windows is larger than the others, it would create another scale within the composition of the facade. The jump in scale could indicate the size or significance of the space behind the window, or it could alter our perception of the size of the other windows or the dimensions of the facade.

Many building elements have sizes that are familiar to us, and can, therefore, be used to help us gauge the sizes of other elements around them. Such elements as residential window units and doorways can give us an idea of how large a building is, and how many stories it has. Stairs and handrails can help us measure the scale of a space. Because of their familiarity, these elements can also be used to deliberately alter our perception of the size of a building form or space.

Some buildings and spaces have two scales operating simultaneously. The entrance portico of the Rotunda at the University of Virginia, (1820. Thomas Jefferson) is scaled to the overall building form, while the doorway and windows behind it are scaled to the size of the spaces within the building.

The recessed entry portals of Reims Cathedral (1211-1290) are scaled to the dimensions of the facade, and can be seen and recognized at a distance as the building's entrances. As we get closer, however, we see that the actual entrances are really simple doors within the larger portals, and are scaled to our dimensions, to a human scale.

REIMS CATHEDRAL: 1211-1290

SCALE

Vitruvian figure by Franceso di Giorgio. 16th Century

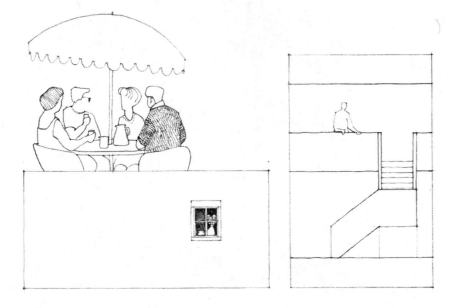

Human scale in architecture is based on the dimensions and proportions of the human body. It has already been mentioned in the section on anthropomorphic proportioning that our dimensions vary from individual to individual and, therefore, cannot be used as an absolute measuring device. We can, however, measure a space whose width is such that we can reach out and touch its walls. Similarly, we can measure its height if we can reach up and touch the ceiling plane overhead. Once we can no longer do these things, we must rely on other visual rather than tactile clues to give us a sense of the scale of a space.

For these clues we can use elements that have human meaning, and whose dimensions are related to our own dimensions. Such elements as furnishings— a table, sofa, or chair— or stairs, a window or a doorway, not only help us judge the size of a space but also give it a human scale or feeling.

Intimate settings of tables and lounge chairs in a large hotel lobby will tell us something about the expansiveness of the space as well as define comfortable, human-scale areas within it. A stairway leading up to a second-story balcony or loft will give us an idea of the vertical dimension of a room as well as suggest a human presence. A window in a blank wall can tell us something about the space behind it as well as leave the impression that it is inhabited.

Of a room's three dimensions, its height has a greater effect on its scale than either its width or length. While the walls of the room provide enclosure, the height of the ceiling plane overhead determines its qualities of shelter and intimacy.

Raising the ceiling height of a 12x16-foot room from 8 to 9 feet will be more noticeable, and affect its scale more, than if its width were increased to 13 feet, or its length to 17 feet. While the 12x16-foot room with a 9-foot ceiling would feel comfortable to most people, a 50x50-foot space with the same ceiling height might begin to feel oppressive.

In addition to the vertical dimension of a space, other factors that will affect its scale are:
• the shape, color, and pattern of its bounding surfaces,
• the shape and disposition of its openings,
• the nature and scale of the elements placed within it.

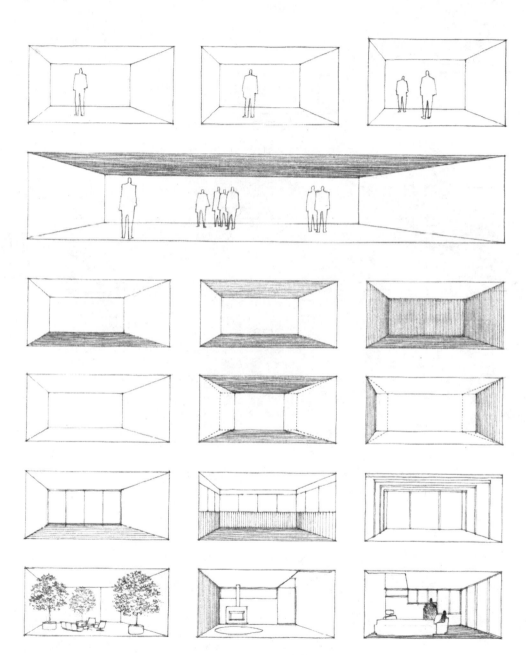

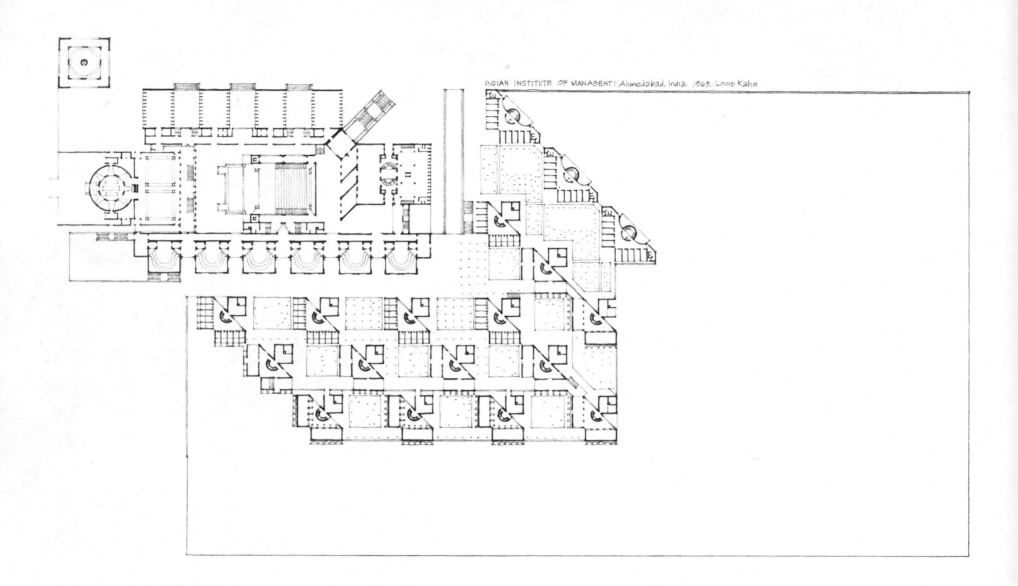

INDIAN INSTITUTE OF MANAGEMENT: Ahmedabad, India. 1963. Louis Kahn

7
PRINCIPLES

ORDERING PRINCIPLES

In Chapter 4, a geometric basis was used to formalize the relationships among the forms and spaces of a building organization. This chapter discusses additional organizational principles that can be utilized to create order in an architectural composition.

There exists a natural diversity and complexity in the program requirements for buildings. Their forms and spaces must acknowledge the hierarchy inherent in the functions they accommodate, the users they serve, the purposes or meaning they convey, the scope or context they address. It is in recognition of this natural diversity, complexity, and hierarchy in the program and substance of buildings that ordering principles are discussed.

Order without diversity can result in monotony or boredom; diversity without order can produce chaos. The following ordering principles are seen as visual devices that allow the diverse forms and spaces of a building to co-exist perceptually and conceptually within an orded and unified whole.

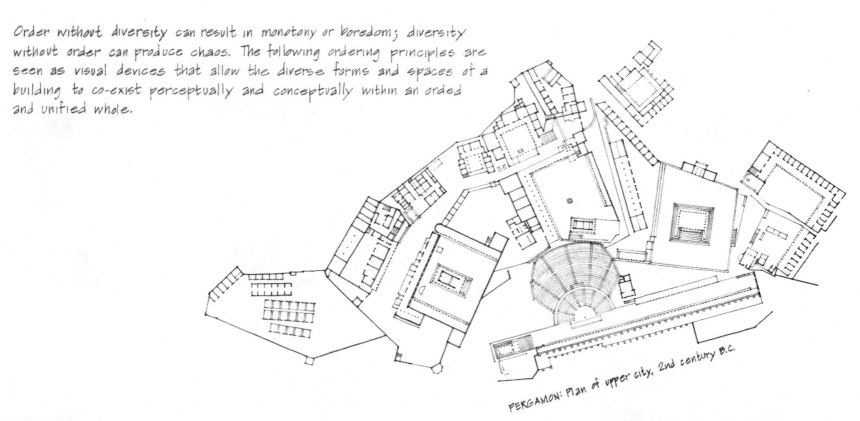

PERGAMON: Plan of upper city, 2nd century B.C.

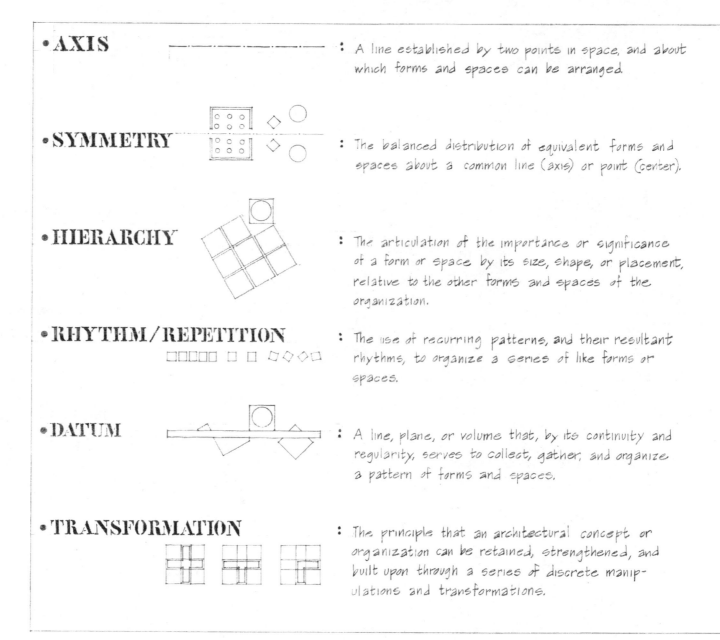

- **AXIS** : A line established by two points in space, and about which forms and spaces can be arranged.

- **SYMMETRY** : The balanced distribution of equivalent forms and spaces about a common line (axis) or point (center).

- **HIERARCHY** : The articulation of the importance or significance of a form or space by its size, shape, or placement, relative to the other forms and spaces of the organization.

- **RHYTHM/REPETITION** : The use of recurring patterns, and their resultant rhythms, to organize a series of like forms or spaces.

- **DATUM** : A line, plane, or volume that, by its continuity and regularity, serves to collect, gather, and organize a pattern of forms and spaces.

- **TRANSFORMATION** : The principle that an architectural concept or organization can be retained, strengthened, and built upon through a series of discrete manipulations and transformations.

AXIS

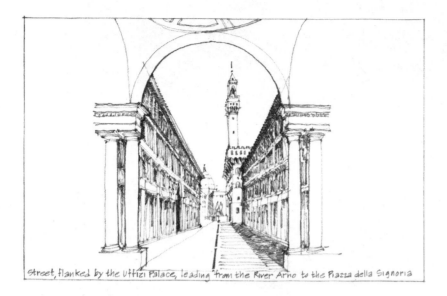

Street, flanked by the Uffizi Palace, leading from the River Arno to the Piazza della Signoria

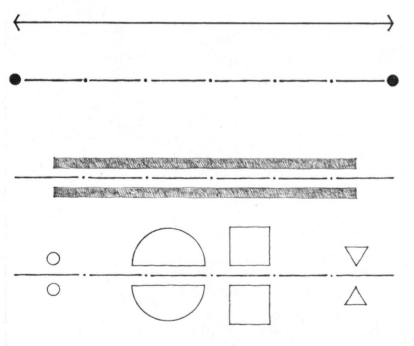

The axis is perhaps the most elementary means of organizing forms and spaces in architecture. It is a line established by two points in space and about which forms and spaces can be arranged in a regular or irregular manner. Although imaginary and not visible, an axis is a powerful, dominating, regulating device. Although it implies symmetry, it demands balance. The specific disposition of elements about an axis will determine whether the visual force of an axial organization is subtle or overpowering, loosely structured or formal, picturesque or monotonous.

Since an axis is essentially a linear condition, it has qualities of length and direction, and induces movement and views along its path.

For its definition, an axis must be terminated at both of its ends.

The notion of an axis can be reinforced by defining edges along its length. These edges can be simply lines on the ground plan, or vertical planes that define a linear space coincidental with the axis.

An axis can also be established by a symmetrical arrangement of forms and spaces.

The terminating elements of an axis serve to both
send and receive its visual thrust. These terminating
elements can be any of the following:

1. Points in space established by vertical, linear
   elements or centralized building forms.

2. Vertical planes, such as a symmetrical building
   facade or front, preceded by a forecourt or other
   similar open space.

3. Well-defined spaces, generally centralized or
   regular in form.

4. Gateways that open outward toward a view or
   vista beyond.

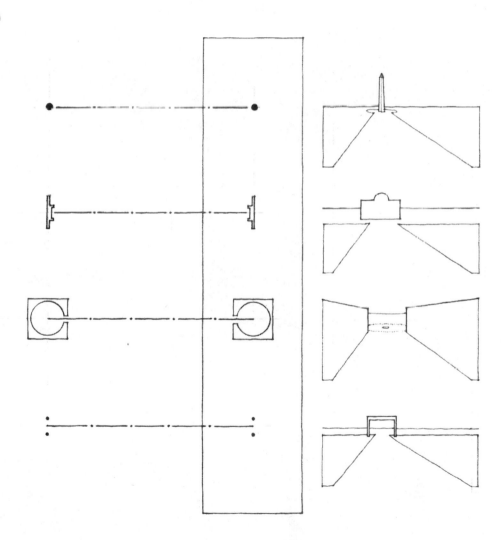

AXIS

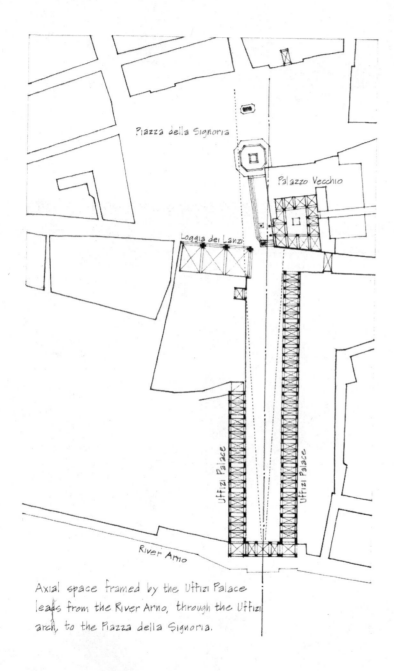

Piazza della Signoria

Palazzo Vecchio

Loggia dei Lanzi

Uffizi Palace

Uffizi Palace

River Arno

Axial space framed by the Uffizi Palace
leads from the River Arno, through the Uffizi
arch, to the Piazza della Signoria.

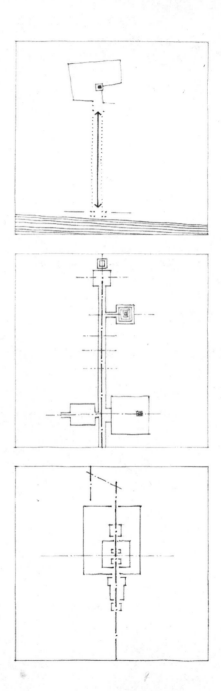

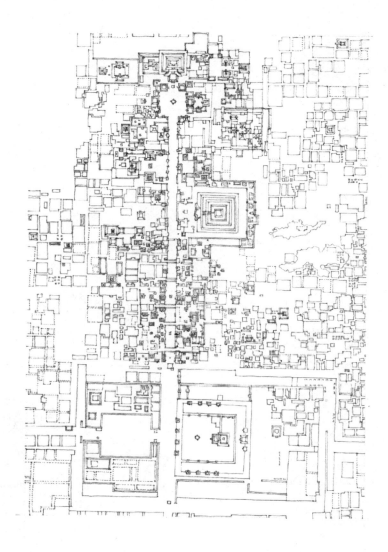

TEOTIHUACÁN: Pre-Columbian city in Central America.

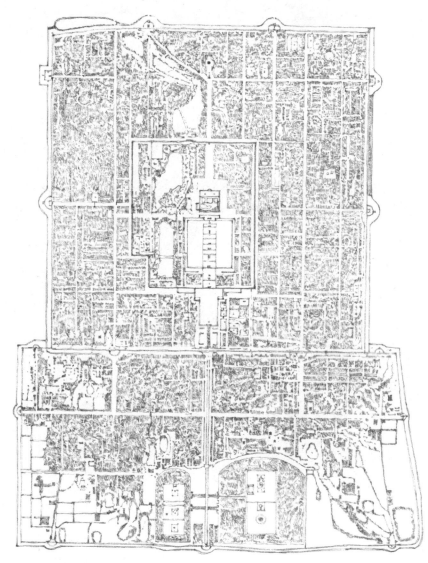

PLAN OF PEKING, CHINA.

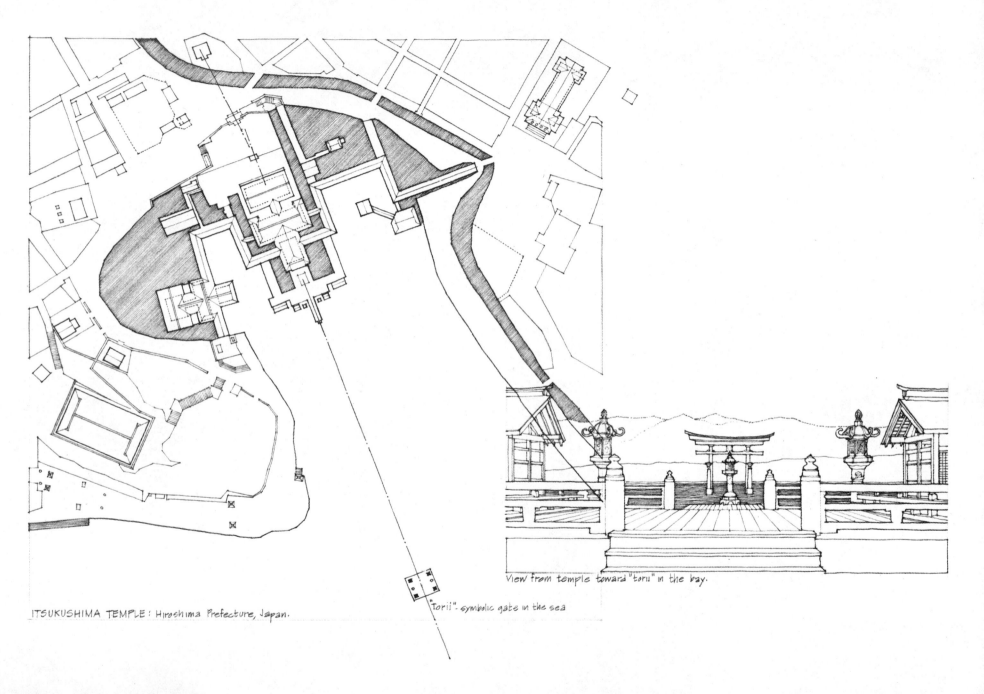

ITSUKUSHIMA TEMPLE: Hiroshima Prefecture, Japan.

"Torii". symbolic gate in the sea

View from temple toward "torii" in the bay.

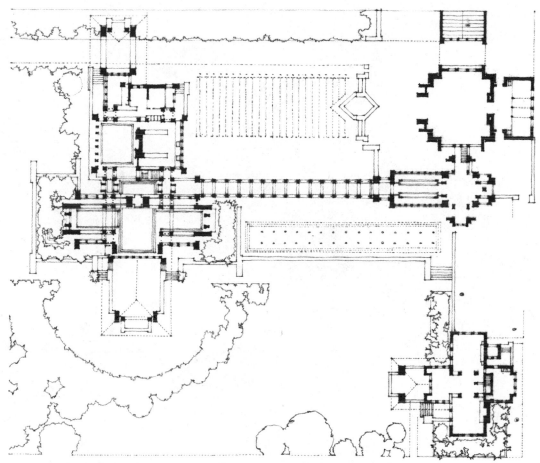

DARWIN D. MARTIN HOUSE & ESTATE: Buffalo, New York. 1904. Frank Lloyd Wright.

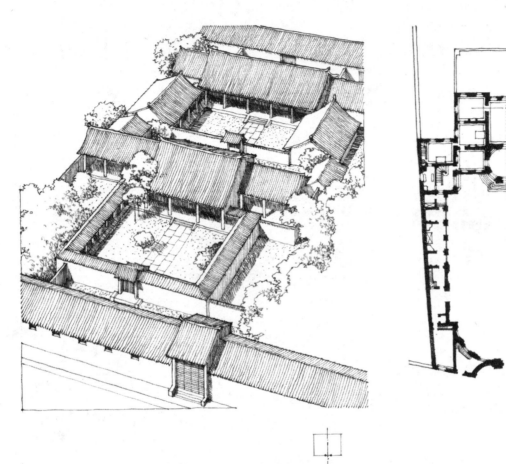

CHINESE COURTYARD HOUSE: Peking, China.

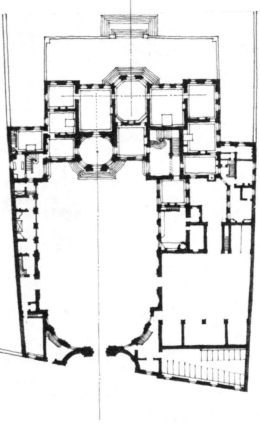

HOTEL DE MATIGNON: Paris. 1721. J. Courtonne

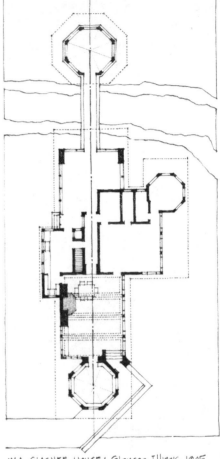

W.A. GLASNER HOUSE: Glencoe, Illinois. 1905
Frank Lloyd Wright

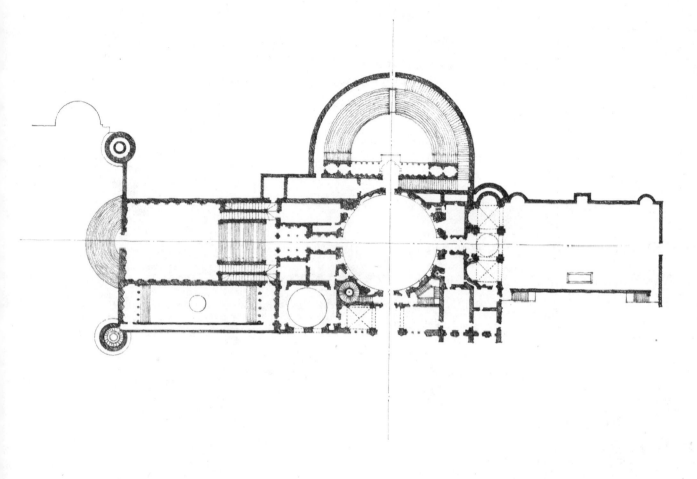

VILLA MADAMA: Rome. 1517. Raphael Sanzio

FORUMS OF TRAJAN, AUGUSTUS, CAESER, & NERVA: Rome

TRAJAN

CAESAR

AUGUSTUS

NERVA

SYMMETRY

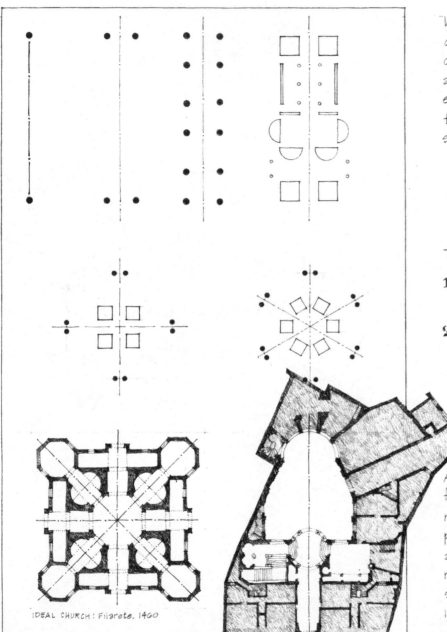

IDEAL CHURCH: Filarete. 1460

HÔTEL DE BEAUVAIS: Paris, 1656. Antoine le Pautre

While an axial condition can exist without a symmetrical condition being simultaneously present, a symmetrical condition cannot exist without implying the existence of an axis or center about which it is structured. An axis is established by two points; a symmetrical condition requires the balanced arrangement of equivalent patterns of form and space about a common line (axis) or point (center).

There are basically two types of symmetry:

1. Bilateral symmetry refers to the balanced arrangement of equivalent elements about a common axis.

2. Radial symmetry consists of equivalent elements balanced about two or more axes that intersect at a central point.

An architectural composition can utilize symmetry to organize its forms and spaces in two ways. An entire building organization can be made symmetrical. Or a symmetrical condition can occur in only a portion of the building, and organize an irregular pattern of forms and spaces about itself. This latter case allows a building to respond to exceptional conditions of its site or program. The regular, symmetrical condition itself can be reserved for significant or important spaces in the organization.

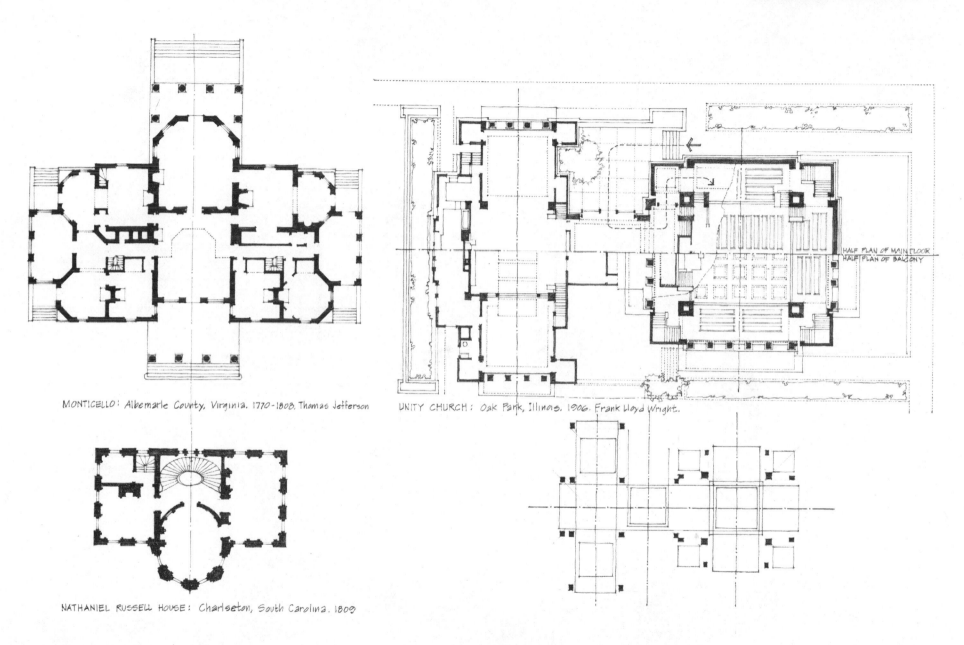

MONTICELLO: Albemarle County, Virginia. 1770-1808, Thomas Jefferson

UNITY CHURCH: Oak Park, Illinois. 1906. Frank Lloyd Wright.

HALF PLAN OF MAIN FLOOR
HALF PLAN OF BALCONY

NATHANIEL RUSSELL HOUSE: Charleston, South Carolina. 1809

SYMMETRY

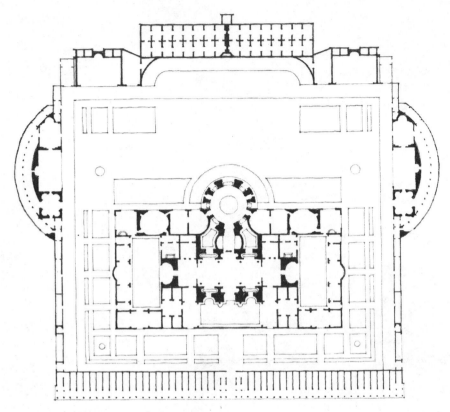

BATHS (THERMAE) OF CARACALLA: Rome. 211-17 A.D.

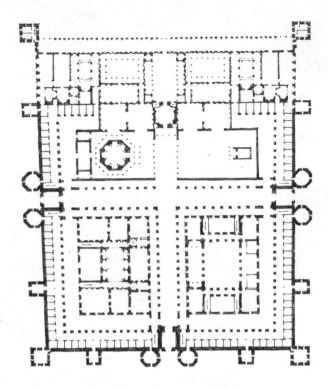

PALACE OF DIOCLETIAN: Spalato (Yugoslavia) C. 300 A.D.

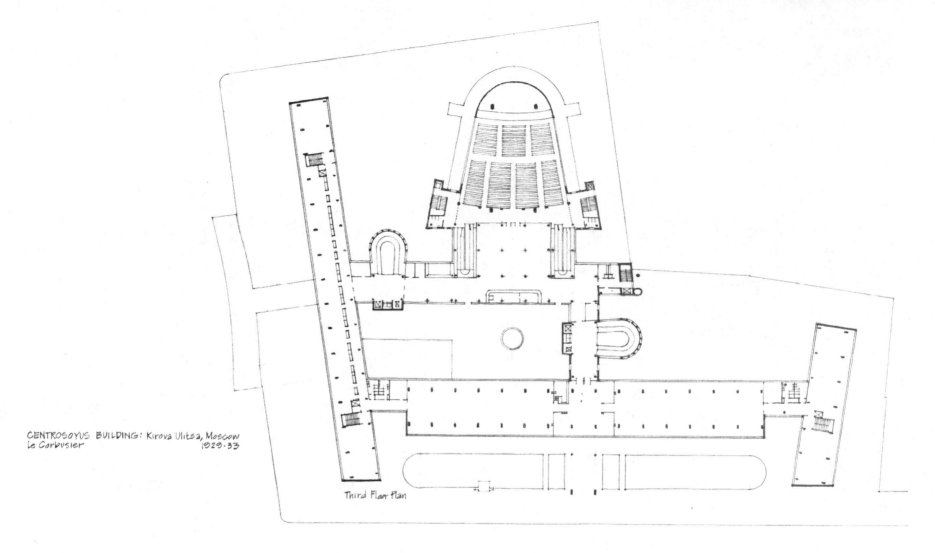

CENTROSOYUS BUILDING: Kirova Ulitsa, Moscow
Le Corbusier   1928-33

Third Floor Plan

SYMMETRY

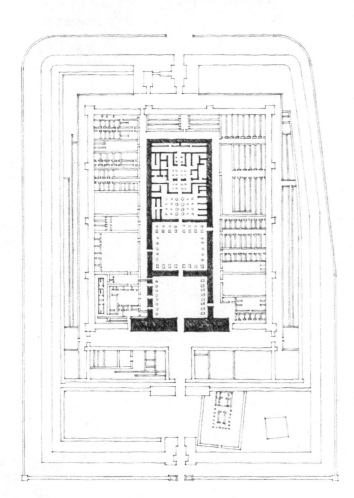

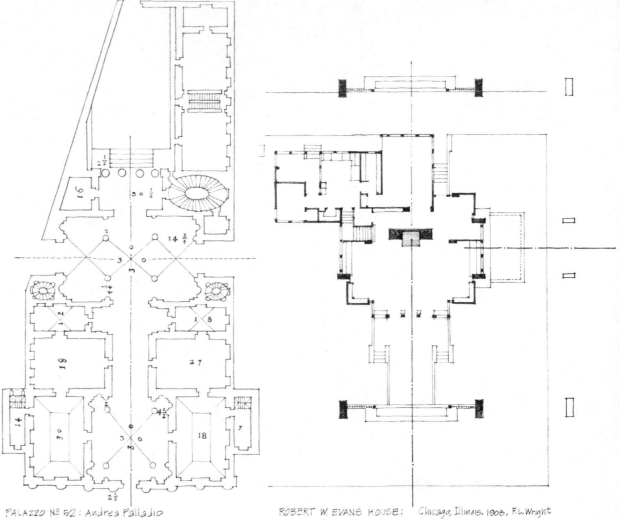

FUNERARY TEMPLE of RAMESSES III : Medinet-Habu. 1198 B.C.   PALAZZO Nº 52 : Andrea Palladio   ROBERT W. EVANS HOUSE : Chicago, Illinois. 1908. F.L. Wright

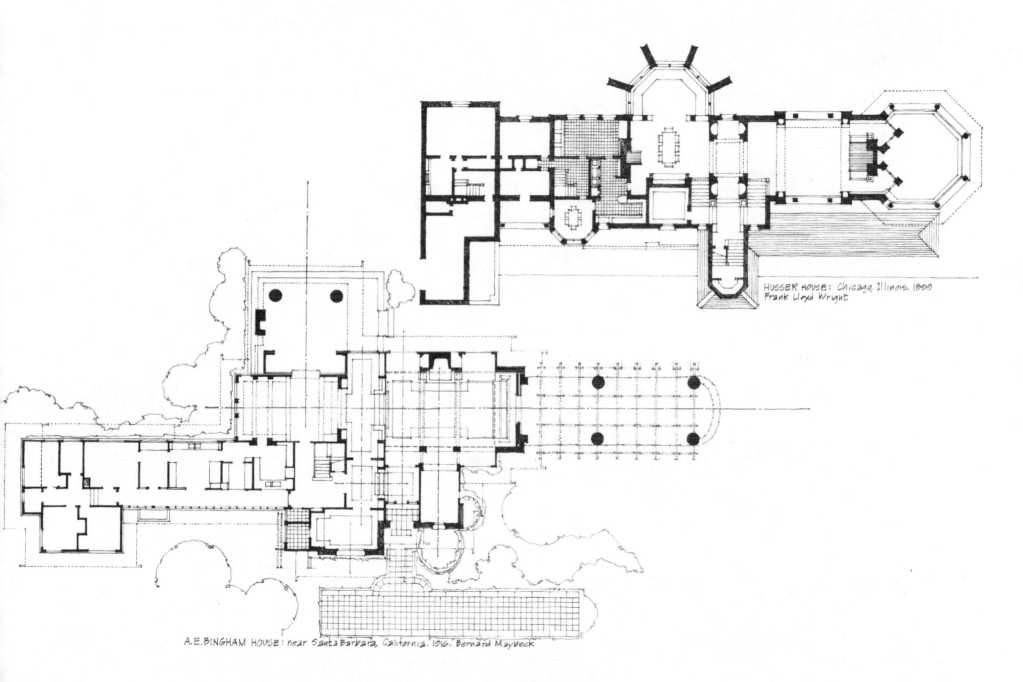

HUSSER HOUSE: Chicago, Illinois. 1800
Frank Lloyd Wright

A.E. BINGHAM HOUSE: near Santa Barbara, California. 1916. Bernard Maybeck

SYMMETRY

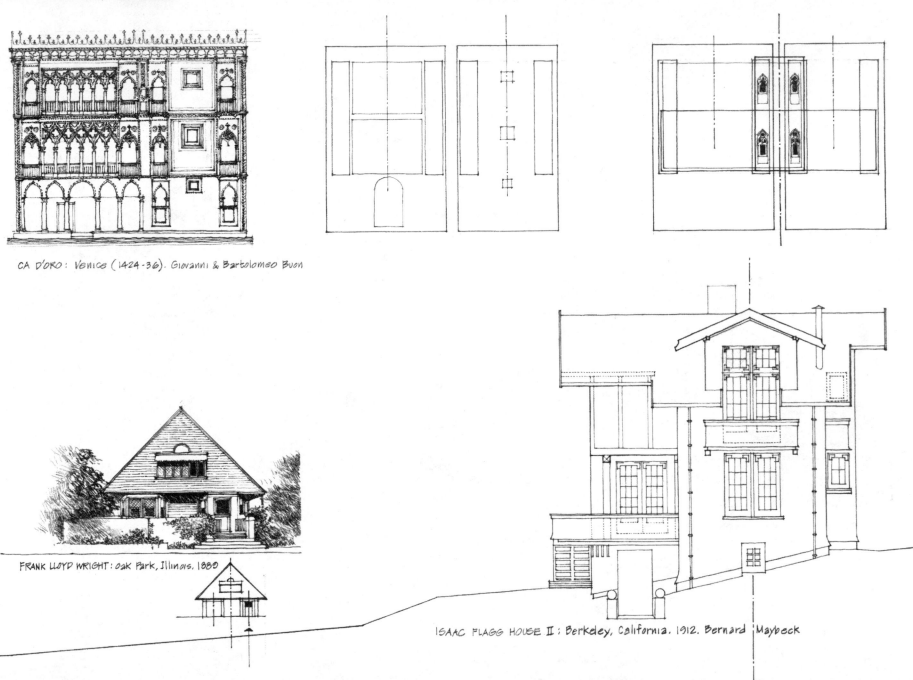

CA D'ORO: Venice (1424-36). Giovanni & Bartolomeo Buon

FRANK LLOYD WRIGHT: Oak Park, Illinois. 1889

ISAAC FLAGG HOUSE II: Berkeley, California. 1912. Bernard Maybeck

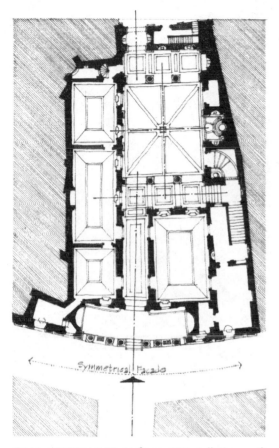

PALAZZO PIETRO MASSIMI: Rome. 1532-6. Baldasare Peruzzi

Symmetrical Facade

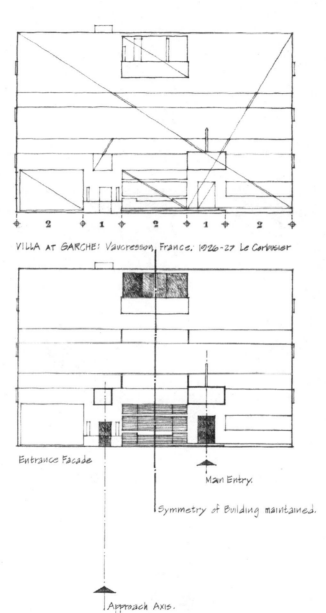

VILLA AT GARCHE: Vaucresson, France. 1926-27 Le Corbusier

Entrance Facade

Main Entry.

Symmetry of Building maintained.

Approach Axis.

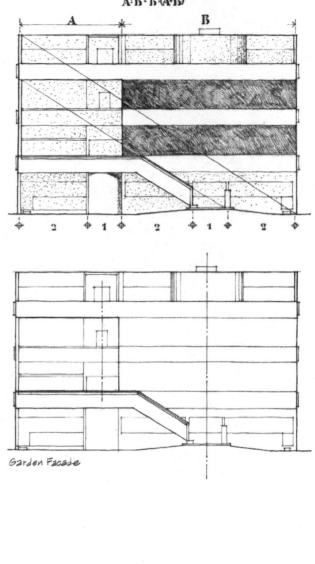

Garden Facade

HIERARCHY

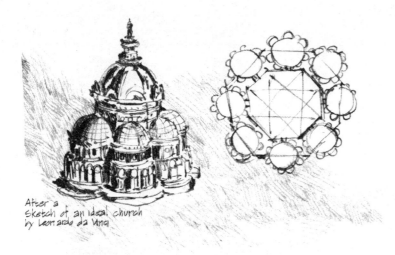

After a
sketch of an ideal church
by Leonardo da Vinci

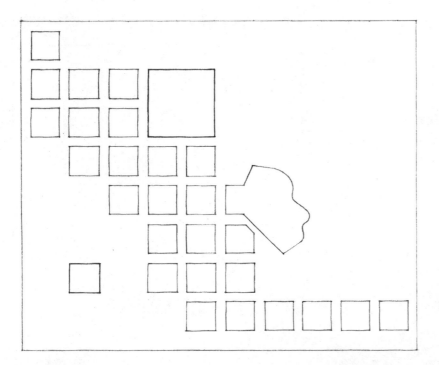

The principle of hierarchy implies that in most, if not all, architectural compositions, real differences exist among their forms and spaces. These differences reflect, in a sense, the degree of importance of these forms and spaces, and the functional, formal, and symbolic roles they play in their organization. The value system by which their relative importance is measured will, of course, depend on the specific situation, the needs and desires of the users, and the decisions of the designer. The values expressed may be individual or collective, personal or cultural. In any case, the manner in which these functional or symbolic differences among a building's elements are revealed is critical to the establishment of a visible, hierarchical order among its forms and spaces.

For a form or space to be articulated as being important or significant to an organization, it must be made visibly unique. This can be achieved by endowing a form or shape with:

• exceptional size
• a unique shape
• a strategic location

In each case, the hierarchically important form or space is given meaning and significance by being an exception to the norm, an anomaly within an otherwise regular pattern.

A form or space may dominate an architectural composition by being significantly different in size than all the other elements in the composition. Normally, this dominance is made visible by the sheer size of an element. In some cases, an element can also dominate by being significantly smaller than the other elements in the organization, and placed in a well-defined setting.

BY SIZE

Forms and spaces can be made visually dominant, and thus important, by clearly differentiating their shape from that of the other elements in the composition. A discernible contrast in shape is critical, whether the differentiation is based on a change in geometry or regularity. Of course, it is also important that the shape selected for the hierarchically important element be compatible with its function and use.

BY SHAPE

Forms and spaces may be strategically placed to call attention to themselves as being the important elements in a composition. Hierarchically important locations for a form or space include:

- the termination of a linear sequence or axial organization;
- the centerpiece of a symmetrical organization;
- the focus of a centralized or radial organization;
- offset, above, below, or in the foreground of a composition.

BY PLACEMENT

HIERARCHY

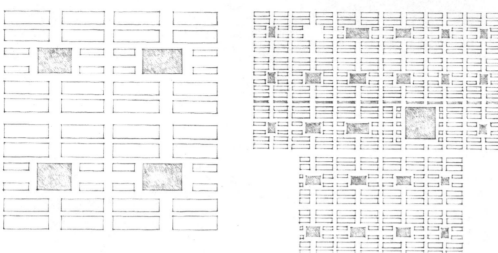

PLAN FOR SAVANNAH, Georgia. James Oglethorpe, 1733

Savannah Plan, after 1856

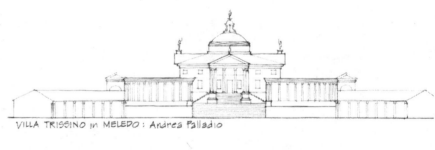

VILLA TRISSINO in MELEDO: Andrea Palladio

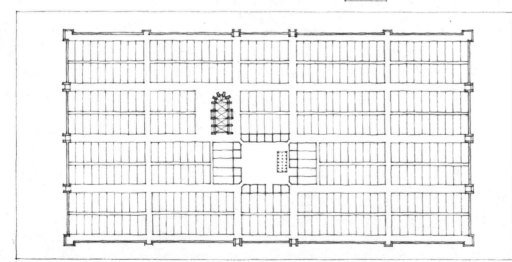

PLAN OF MONTPAZIER: A regularly laid-out Medeival town in France, founded in 1284

CHAPEL

DATUM FORMED BY MONK'S CELLS

Fourth-floor Plan:
MONASTERY of Sainte-Marie-de-la-Tourette,
near Lyons, France, 1956-59. Le Corbusier

View of Florence illustrating the dominance of the cathedral over the urban landscape.

HIERARCHY

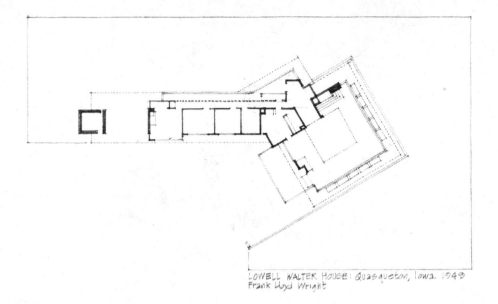

LOWELL WALTER HOUSE: Quasqueton, Iowa. 1949
Frank Lloyd Wright

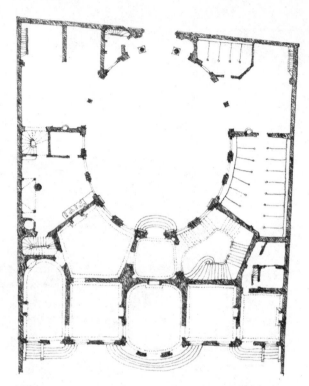

HÔTEL AMELOT: Paris. 1710-13. Germain Boffrand.

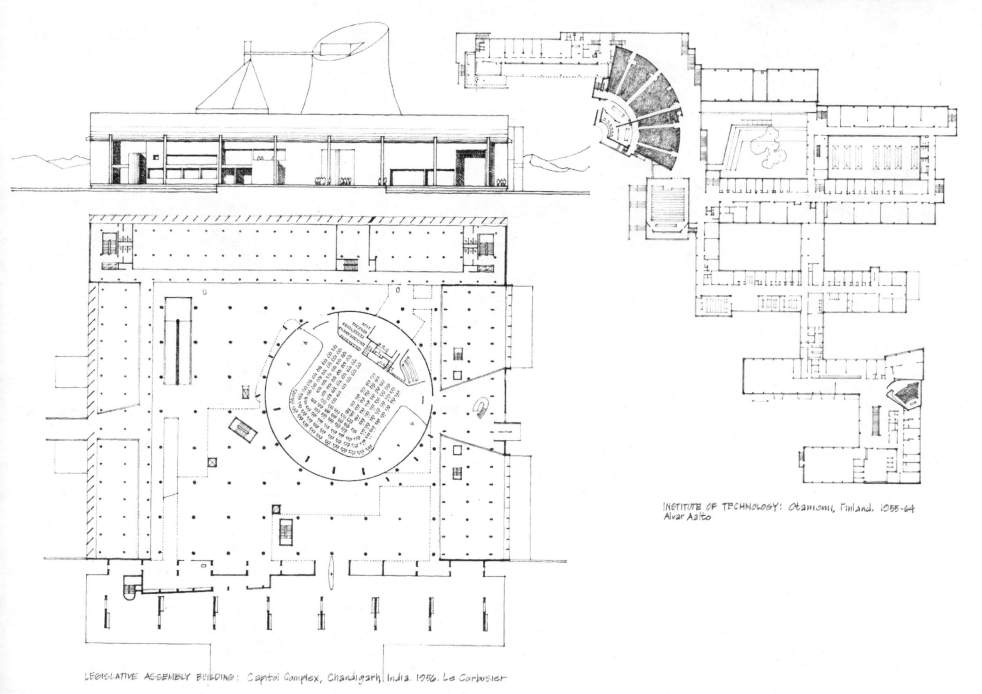

INSTITUTE OF TECHNOLOGY: Otaniemi, Finland. 1955-64
Alvar Aalto

LEGISLATIVE ASSEMBLY BUILDING: Capitol Complex, Chandigarh, India. 1956. Le Corbusier

HIERARCHY

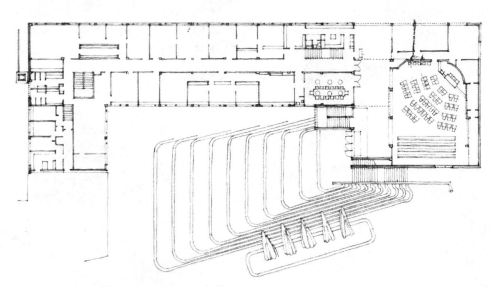

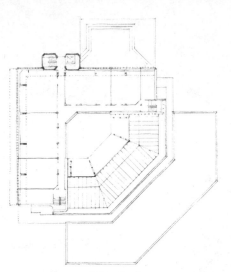

HISTORY FACULTY BUILDING
Cambridge University, England. 1964-67
Jame Stirling

TOWN HALL, Seinäjoki. 1961-65. Alvar Aalto

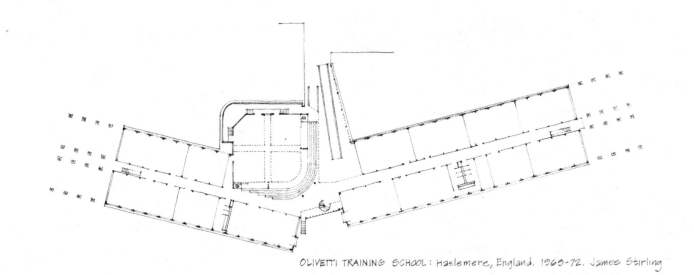

OLIVETTI TRAINING SCHOOL: Haslemere, England. 1969-72. James Stirling

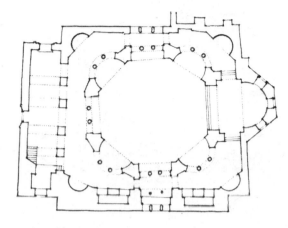

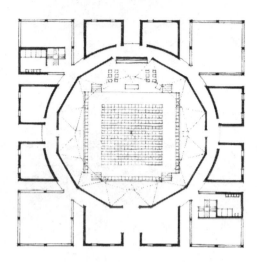

IDEAL CHURCH: c.1490 Leonardi da Vinci

S.S. SERGIUS and BACCHUS: Constantinople (Istanbul)
Erected by Justinian.   525-30 A.D.

FIRST UNITARIAN CHURCH: Rochester, New York. 1959
First Design. Louis Kahn

DATUM

From GAVOTTE 1, SIXTH CELLO SUITE, by Johann Sebastian Bach (1685-1750). Transcribed for classical guitar by Jerry Snyder.

A datum refers to a line, plane or volume of reference to which other elements in a composition can relate. It organizes a random pattern of elements through its regularity, continuity, and constant presence. For example, the lines of a musical staff serve as a datum in providing the visual basis for reading notes and the relative pitches of their tones. The regularity of their spacing and their continuity organizes, clarifies, and accentuates the differences between the series of notes in a musical composition.

In a preceding section, the ability of an axis to organize a series of elements along its length was illustrated. The axis was serving, in effect, as a datum. A datum, however, need not be a straight line. It can also be planar or volumetric in form.

To be an effective ordering device, a datum line must have sufficient visual continuity to cut through or by-pass all of the elements being organized. If planar or volumetric in form, a datum must have sufficient size, closure, and regularity to be seen as a figure that can embrace or gather together the elements being organized within its field.

Given a random organization of dissimilar elements, a datum can organize these elements in the following ways:

A line can cut through or form a common edge for the pattern; a grid of lines can form a neutral, unifying field for the pattern.

LINE

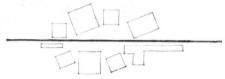

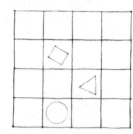

A plane can gather the pattern of elements beneath it, or serve as a background and enframe the elements in its field.

PLANE

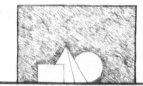

A volume can collect the pattern within its boundries, or organize them along its perimeter.

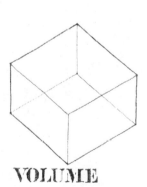

VOLUME

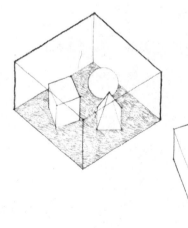

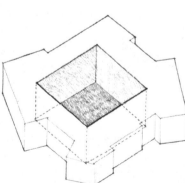

Arcades unify the facades of houses that front the town square of Telč, Czechoslovakia.

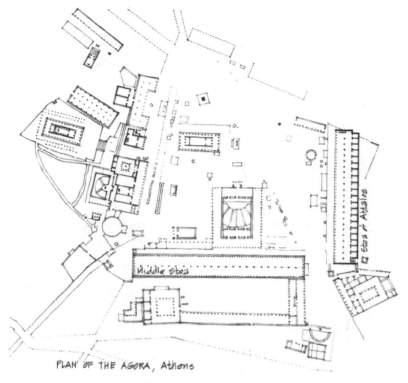

PLAN OF THE AGORA, Athens

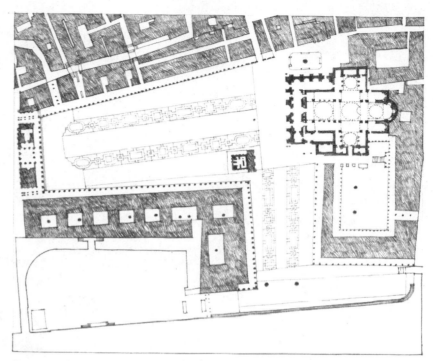

PIAZZA SAN MARCO, Venice

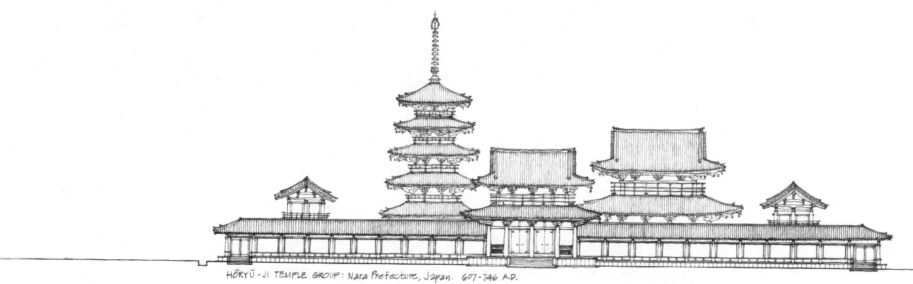

HŌRYŪ-JI TEMPLE GROUP: Nara Prefecture, Japan. 607-746 A.D.

DATUM

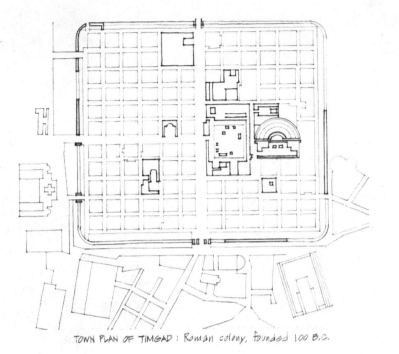

TOWN PLAN OF TIMGAD : Roman colony, founded 100 B.C.

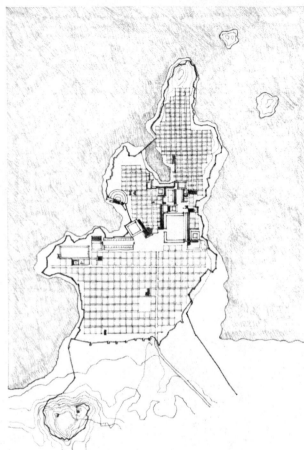

PLAN OF MILETUS : 5th Century, B.C.

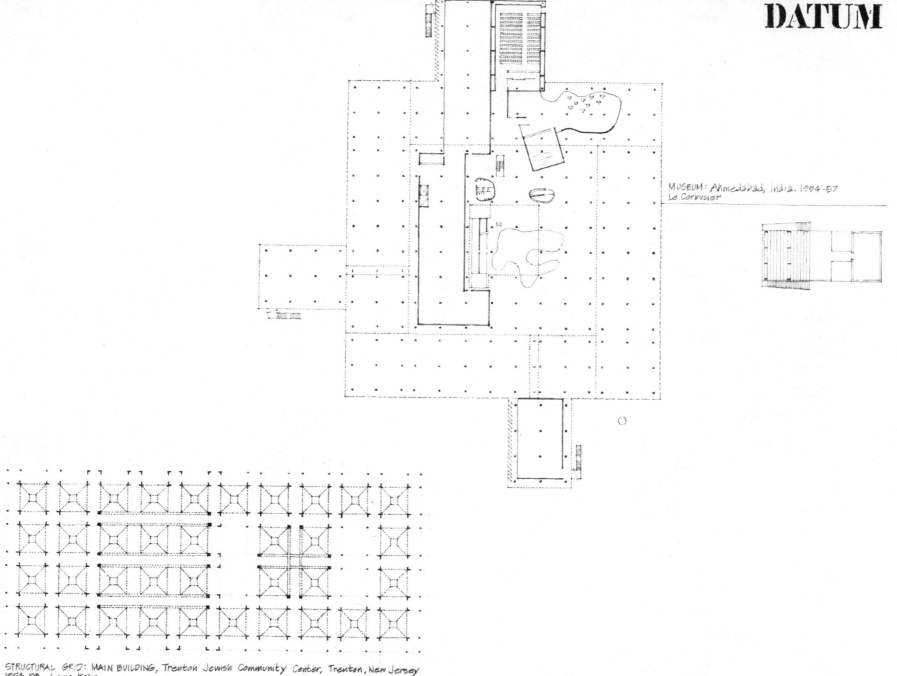

MUSEUM: Ahmedabad, India. 1954-57
Le Corbusier

STRUCTURAL GRID: MAIN BUILDING, Trenton Jewish Community Center, Trenton, New Jersey 1954-59. Louis Kahn.

DATUM

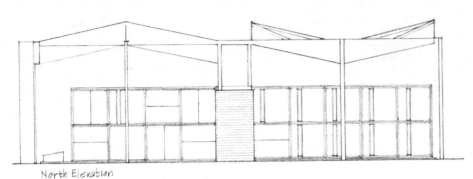

North Elevation

CENTRE LE CORBUSIER: Zurich. 1963-67. Le Corbusier

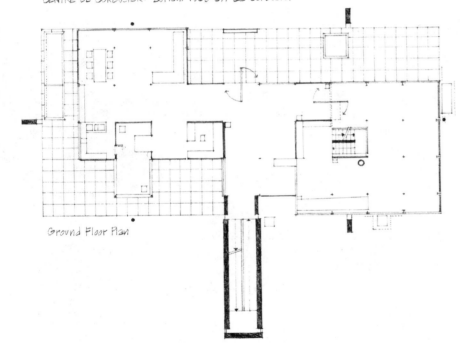

Ground Floor Plan

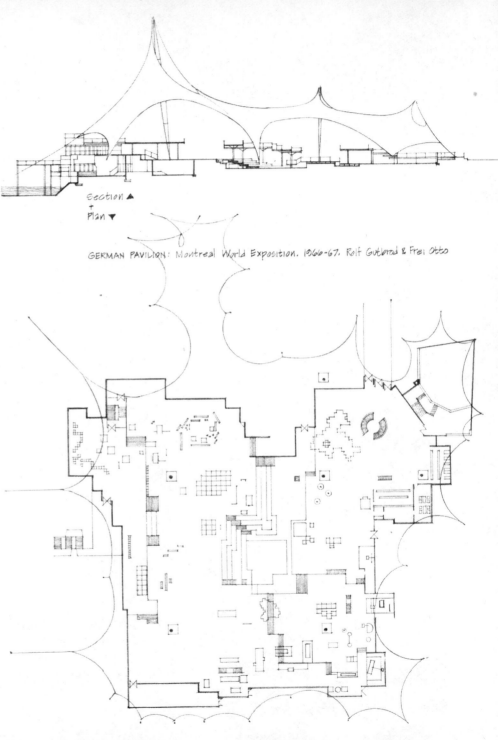

Section ▲
+
Plan ▼

GERMAN PAVILION: Montreal World Exposition. 1966-67. Rolf Gutbrod & Frei Otto

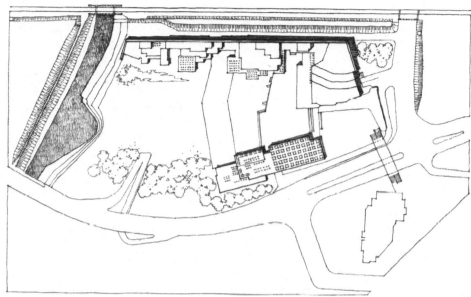

CULTURAL CENTER; Leverkusen, Germany. 1962. (Competition) Alvar Aalto

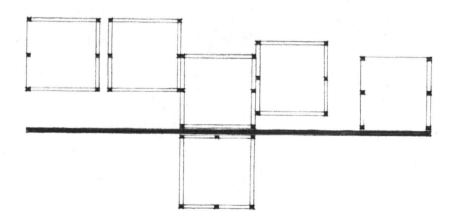

DeVore House: Montgomery County, Pennsylvania. (Project) 1954. Louis Kahn

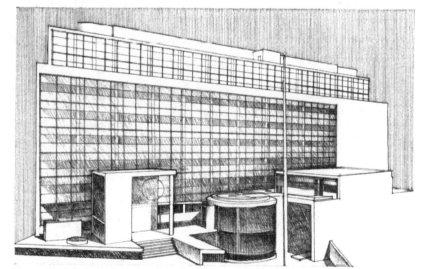

SALVATION ARMY HOSTEL: Paris, 1929-33, Le Corbusier

DATUM

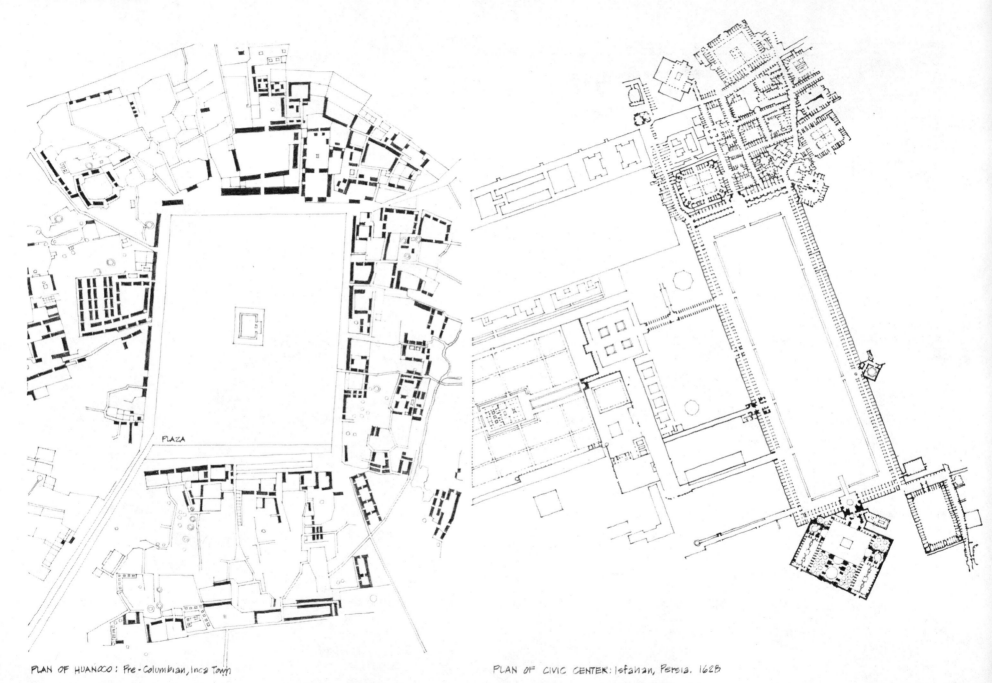

PLAN OF HUANOCO: Pre-Columbian, Inca Town

PLAN OF CIVIC CENTER: Isfahan, Persia. 1628

PLAZA

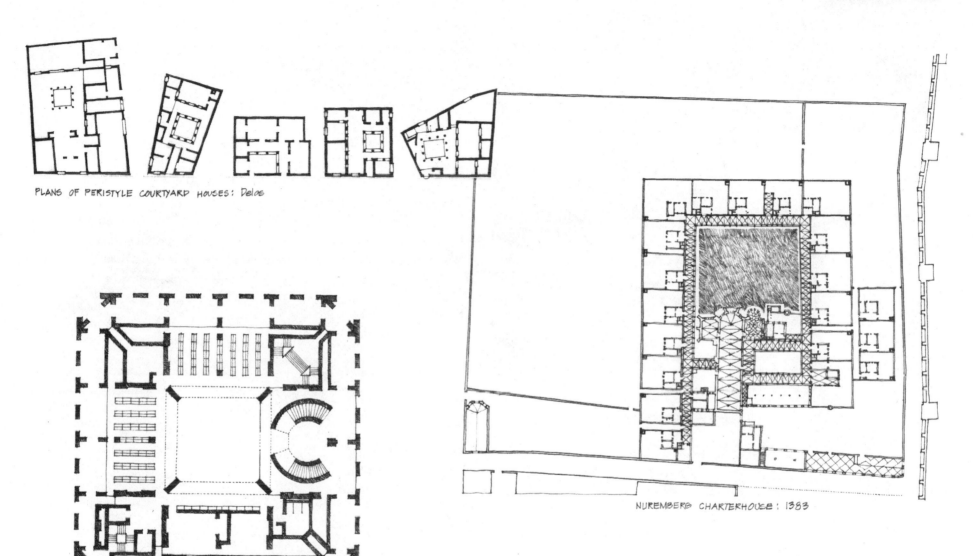

PLANS OF PERISTYLE COURTYARD HOUSES: Delos

LIBRARY: Philip Exeter Academy, Exeter, New Hampshire
1967-72. Louis Kahn.

NUREMBERG CHARTERHOUSE: 1383

RHYTHM

COLUMN DETAILS: Notre Dame la Grande, Poitiers, France. 1130-45

Rhythm refers to the regular or harmonious recurrence of lines, shapes, forms, or colors. It incorporates the fundamental notion of repetition as a device to organize forms and spaces in architecture. Almost all building types incorporate elements that are, by their nature, repetitive. Beams and columns repeat themselves to form repetitive structural bays and modules of space. Windows and doors repeatedly puncture a building's surface to allow light, air, views, and people to enter its interiors. Spaces often recur to accommodate similar or repetitive functional requirements in the building program. This section discusses the patterns of repetition that can be utilized to organize a series of recurring elements, and the resultant visual rhythms these patterns create.

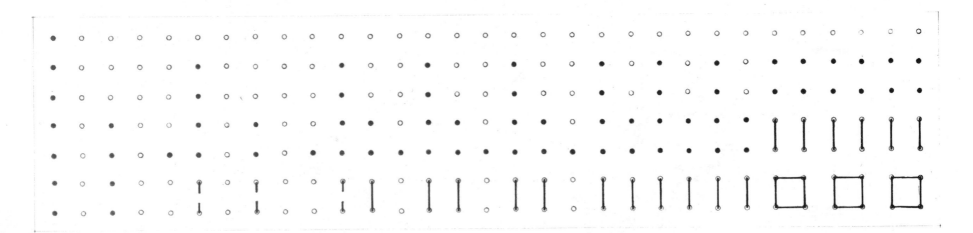

We tend to group elements in a random composition according to:

1. their closeness or proximity to one another, and
2. the visual characteristics they share in common.

The principle of repetition utilizes both of these concepts of perception to order recurring elements in a composition.

The simplest form of repetition is a linear pattern of redundant elements. Elements need not be perfectly identical, however, to be grouped in a repetitive fashion. They may merely share a common trait, a common denominator, allowing each element to be individually unique, yet belong to the same family.

Physical traits by which architectural forms and spaces can be organized in a repetitive fashion are:

• **SIZE**

• **SHAPE**

• **DETAIL CHARACTERISTICS**

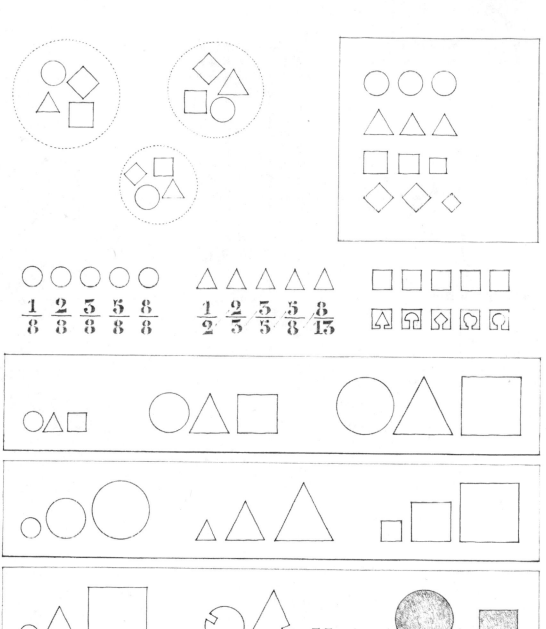

REPETITION

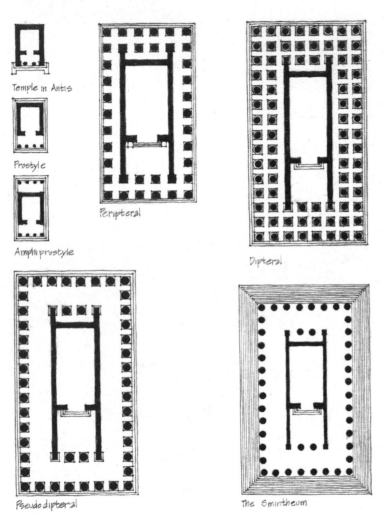

Temple in Antis

Prostyle

Amphi prostyle

Peripteral

Dipteral

Pseudo dipteral

The Smintheum

CLASSIFICATION OF TEMPLES ACCORDING TO THE ARRANGEMENTS OF THE COLONNADES : From Vitruvius' Ten Books on Architecture, Book III, Chapter II.

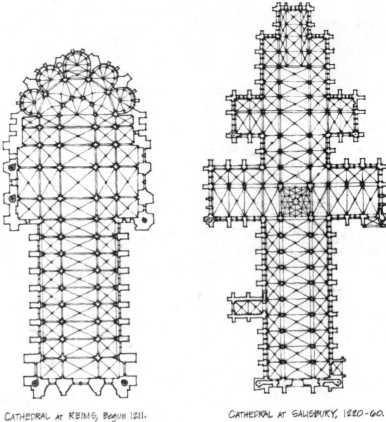

CATHEDRAL at REIMS, Begun 1211.

CATHEDRAL at SALISBURY, 1220-60.

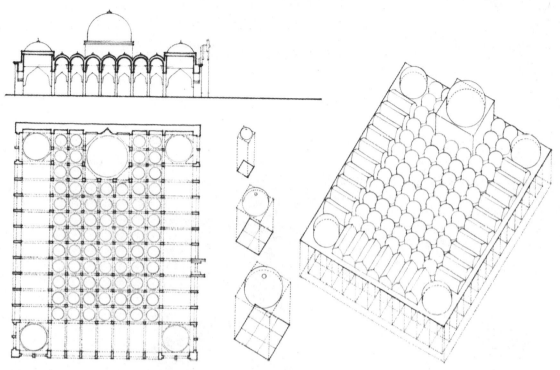

THE JAMI' MASJID : Gulbara, India. 1567

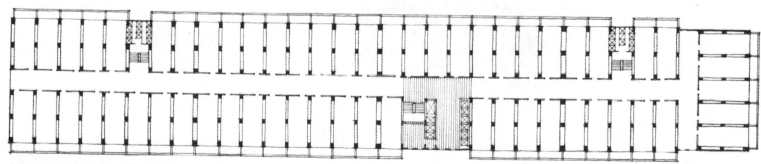

TYPICAL FLOOR PLAN : Unite d'habitation, Marseilles, 1046-52. Le Corbusier

REPETITION

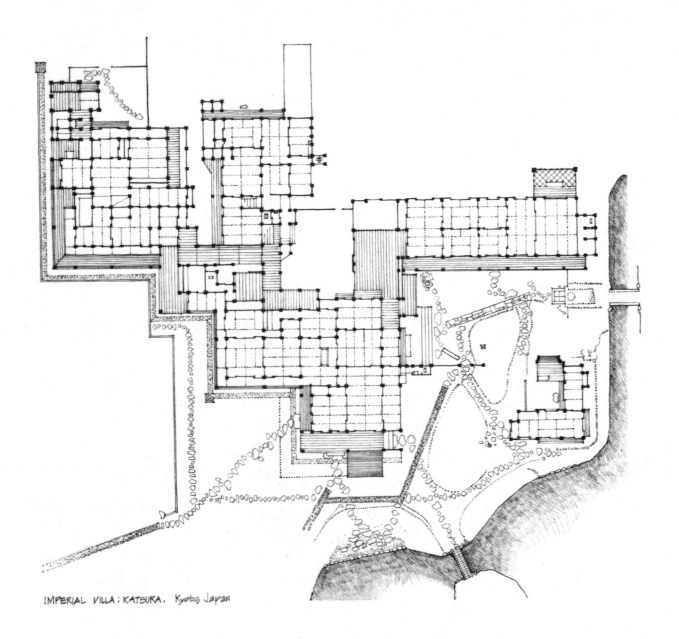

IMPERIAL VILLA; KATSURA. Kyoto, Japan

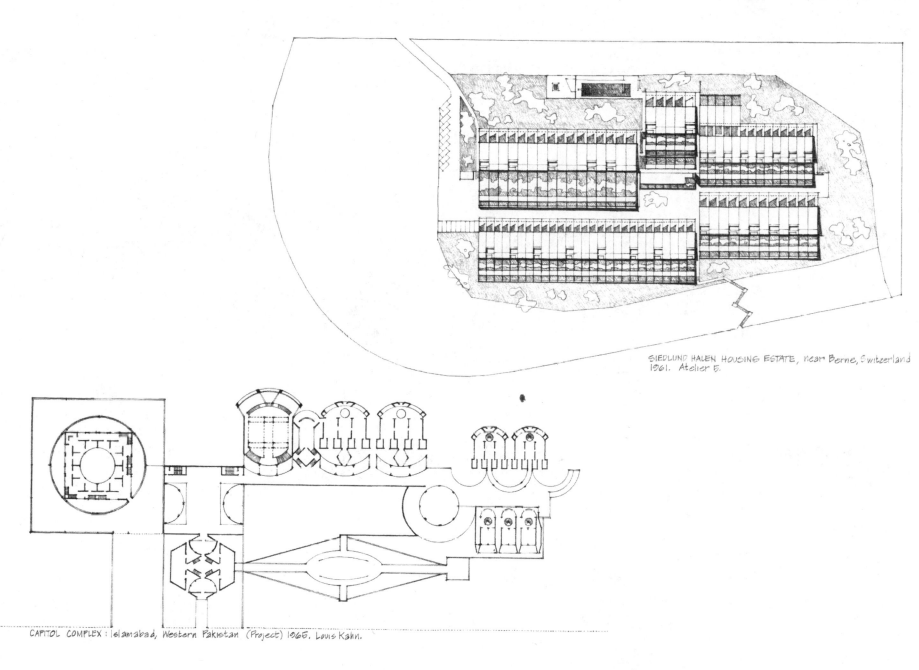

SIEDLUND HALEN HOUSING ESTATE, near Berne, Switzerland 1961. Atelier 5.

CAPITOL COMPLEX: Islamabad, Western Pakistan (Project) 1965. Louis Kahn.

REPETITION

VIEW OF SPANISH HILLTOWN OF MOJACAR

VIEW OF TOWN OF APANOMERIA

THE KÜLLIYE of BEYAZID II: Bursa, Turkey. 1398-1403

TRULLI - FARMHOUSE COMPLEX: near Cisternino, Italy.

After Edward Allen, Stone Shelters, © M.I.T. Press. 1969.

REPETITION

Victorian facades fronting a San Francisco street.

View of Villa Hermosa, Spain

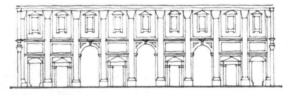

a · b · a · b · a · b · a · b · a . . . .

a · a · b · a · b · a · b · a · a . . . .

A B C B C B C B A

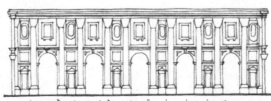

a · b · b · b · b · b · b · a . . . .

c · a · b · a · b · a · b · a · c . . . .

A B C B C B C B A

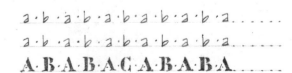

a · b · a · b · a · b · a · b · a · b · a . . . . .

a · b · a · b · a · b · a · b · a · b · a . . . . .

A B A B A C A B A B A . . . . . .

Studies of internal facade of a basilica by Borromini

376

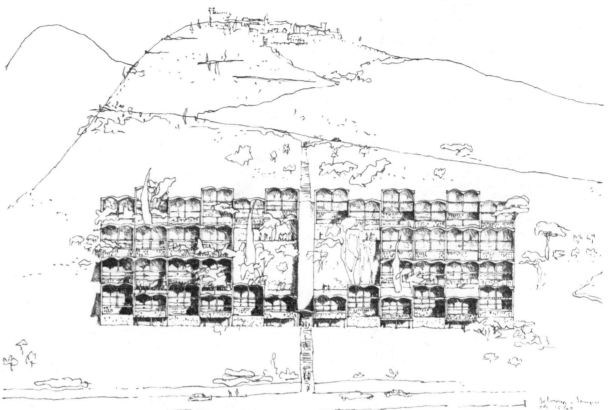

"ROQ" HOUSING PROJECT : Cap Martin, below the town of Roquebrune. 1949. Le Corbusier.

Arcade fronting town square of Garrovillas, Spain.

REPETITION

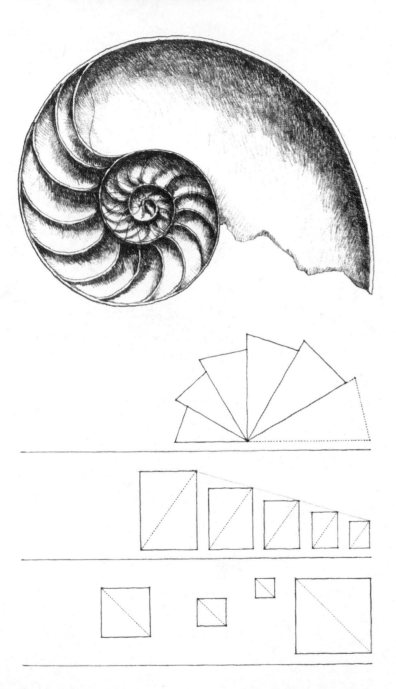

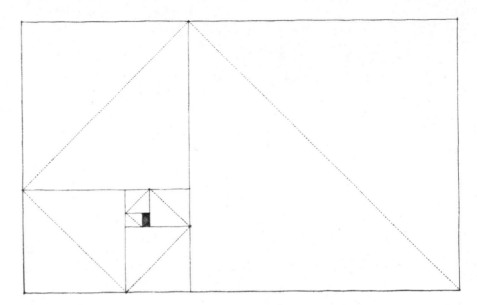

The radial segments of a nautilus shell spiral outward in a reverberating manner from its center, and maintain the shell's organic unity through its additive growth. Using the mathematical ratio of the Golden Section, a series of rectangles can be generated to form a unified organization wherein each rectangle is proportionately related to the others as well as to the overall structure. In each of these examples, the principle of reverberation allows a group of elements that are similar in shape but hierarchically graded in size to be ordered.

Reverberating patterns of forms and spaces can be organized in the following ways:

* in a radial or concentric manner about a point;
* sequentially according to size in a linear fashion;
* randomly, but related by proximity as well as similarity of form.

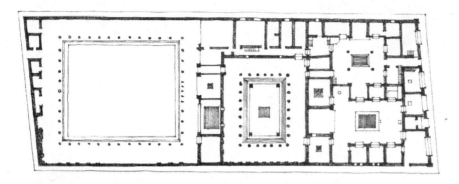

'HOUSE of the FAUN': Pompeii. C.2nd Century B.C.

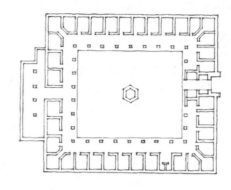

BEY-HAN: Istanbul

HASAN PASHA HAN: Istanbul

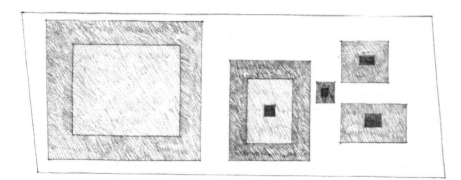

JESTER HOUSE: Palos Verdes, California. (Project) 1938. Frank Lloyd Wright

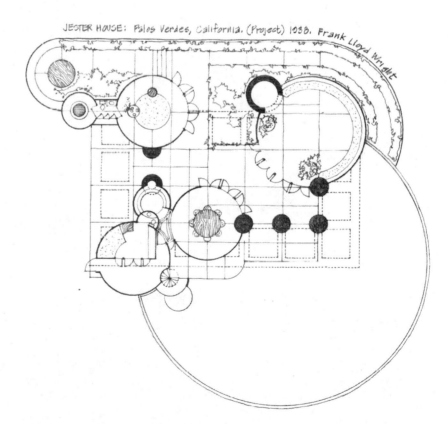

SYDNEY OPERA HOUSE: Sydney, Australia. Designed 1957. Completed 1973. Jørn Utzon

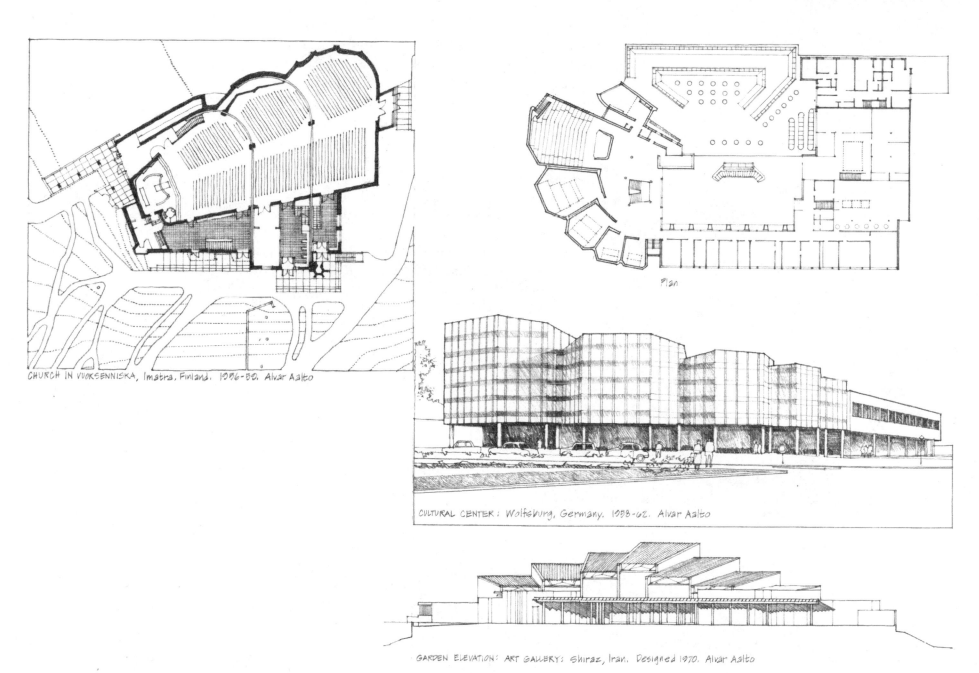

CHURCH IN VUOKSENNISKA, Imatra, Finland. 1956-59. Alvar Aalto

Plan

CULTURAL CENTER: Wolfsburg, Germany. 1958-62. Alvar Aalto

GARDEN ELEVATION: ART GALLERY: Shiraz, Iran. Designed 1970. Alvar Aalto

TRANSFORMATION

The study of architecture, as in other disciplines, should legitimately involve the study of its past, of prior experiences, of endeavors and accomplishments from which much can be learned and emulated. The principle of transformation accepts this notion; this book, and all of the examples it contains, is predicated on it.

The principle of transformation allows a designer to select a prototypical architectural model whose formal structure and ordering of elements might be appropriate and reasonable, and to transform it through a series of discrete manipulations to respond to the specific conditions and context of the design task at hand. Transformation requires first that the ordering system of the prior or prototypical model be perceived and understood so that, through a series of finite changes and permutations, the original design concept can be clarified, strengthened, and built upon, rather than destroyed.

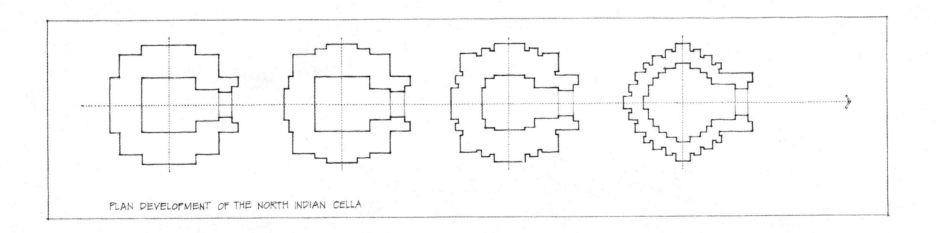

PLAN DEVELOPMENT OF THE NORTH INDIAN CELLA

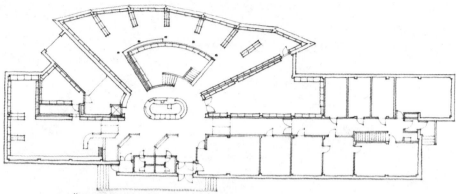

LIBRARY: Seinäjoki, Finland. 1963-65.

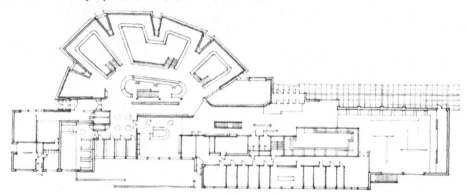

LIBRARY: Rovaniemi, Finland. 1963-68

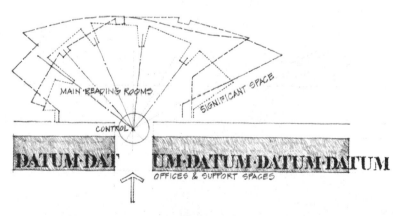

MAIN READING ROOMS

SIGNIFICANT SPACE

CONTROL

DATUM·DATUM·DATUM·DATUM·DATUM

OFFICES & SUPPORT SPACES

SCHEME FOR 3 LIBRARIES by Alvar Aalto

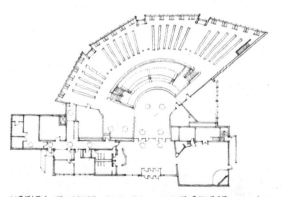

LIBRARY OF MOUNT ANGEL BENEDICTINE COLLEGE; Mount Angel, Oregon. 1965-70.

TRANSFORMATION

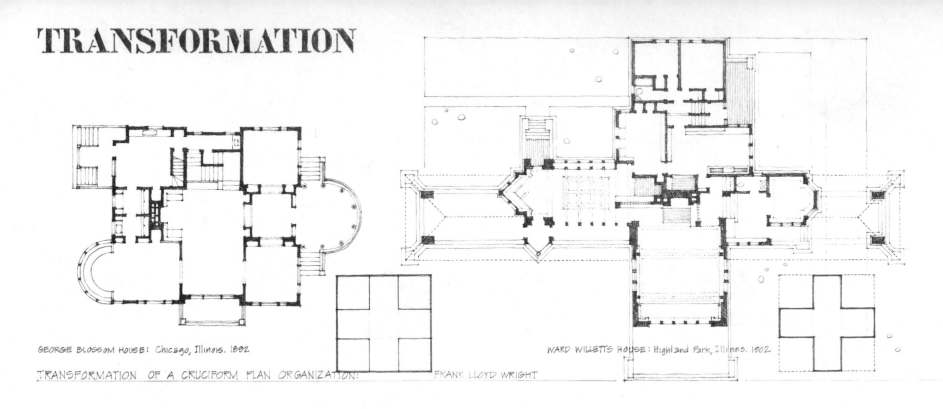

GEORGE BLOSSOM HOUSE: Chicago, Illinois. 1892.

WARD WILLETTS HOUSE: Highland Park, Illinois. 1902.

TRANSFORMATION OF A CRUCIFORM PLAN ORGANIZATION: FRANK LLOYD WRIGHT

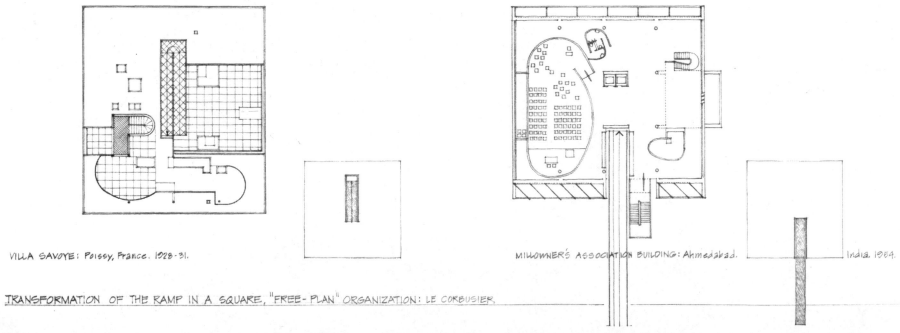

VILLA SAVOYE: Poissy, France. 1928-31.

MILLOWNER'S ASSOCIATION BUILDING: Ahmedabad. India. 1954.

TRANSFORMATION OF THE RAMP IN A SQUARE, "FREE-PLAN" ORGANIZATION: LE CORBUSIER

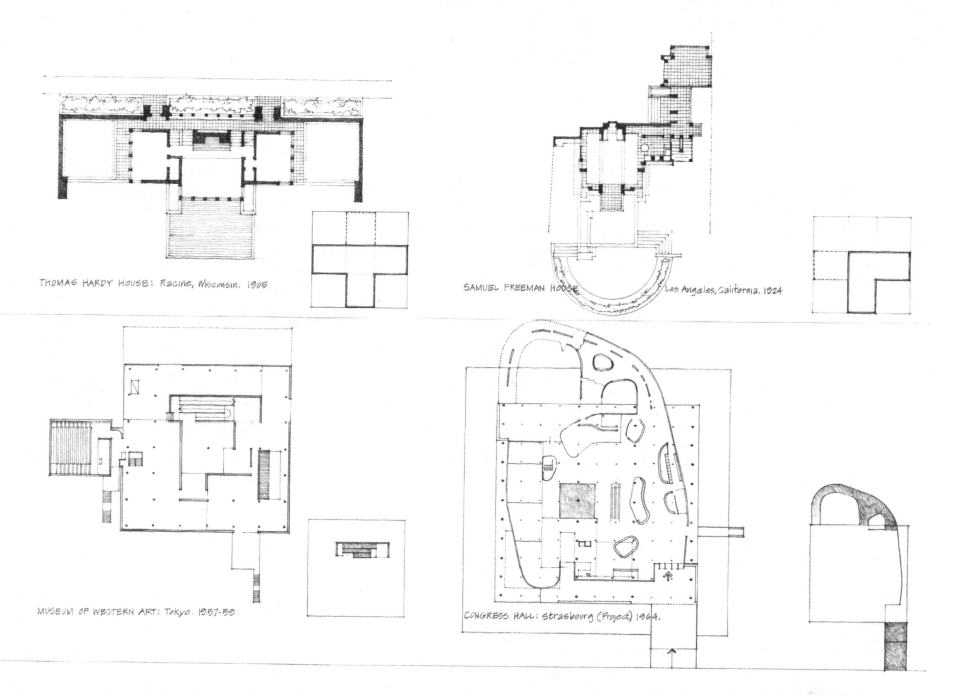

THOMAS HARDY HOUSE: Racine, Wisconsin. 1905

SAMUEL FREEMAN HOUSE   Los Angeles, California. 1924

MUSEUM OF WESTERN ART: Tokyo. 1957-59

CONGRESS HALL: Strasbourg (Project) 1964.

CONCLUSION

This book, throughout its presentation of the elements of form and space, has been concerned primarily with the visual aspects of their physical reality in architecture. Points, moving through space, defining lines, lines defining planes, planes defining volumes of form and space. Beyond these visual functions, these elements, by their relationships to one another and the nature of their organization, also communicate notions of domain and place, entrance and path of movement, hierarchy and order. These are presented as the literal, denotative meanings of form and space in architecture.

As in language, however, architectural forms and spaces also have connotative meanings – associative values and symbolic content that is subject to personal and cultural interpretation, and can change with time. The spires of a Gothic cathedral can stand for the realm, values, or goals of Christianity. The Greek column can convey the notion of democracy, or, as in America in the early 19th century, the presence of civilization in a new world.

Although the study of connotative meanings, of semiotics and symbology in architecture, is beyond the scope of this book, it should be noted here that architecture, in combining form and space into a single essence, not only facilitates purpose but communicates meaning. The art of architecture makes our existence not only visible but meaningful.

"You employ stone, wood, and concrete, and with these materials you build houses and palaces. That is construction. Ingenuity is at work.

"But suddenly, you touch my heart, you do me good, I am happy and I say: 'This is beautiful.' That is architecture. Art enters in.

"My house is practical. I thank you, as I might thank Railway engineers, or the Telephone service. You have not touched my heart.

"But suppose that walls rise toward heaven in such a way that I am moved. I perceive your intentions. Your mood has been gentle, brutal, charming, or noble. The stones you have erected tell me so. You fix me to the place and my eyes regard it. They behold something which expresses a thought. A thought which reveals itself without word or sound, but solely by means of shapes which stand in a certain relationship to one another. These shapes are such that they are clearly revealed in light. The relationships between them have not necessarily any reference to what is practical or descriptive. They are a mathematical creation of your mind. They are the language of Architecture. By the use of raw materials and starting from conditions more or less utilitarian, you have established certain relationships which have aroused my emotions. This is Architecture."

Le Corbusier

A SELECTED BIBLIOGRAPHY

Aalto, Alvar. Complete Works. 2 volumes. Zurich: Les Editions d'Architecture Artemis, 1963.

Arnheim, Rudolf. Art and Visual Perception. Berkeley: University of California Press, 1965.

Ashihara, Yoshinobu. Exterior Design in Architecture. New York: Van Nostrand Reinhold Co., 1970.

Bacon, Edmund. Design of Cities. New York: The Viking Press, 1974.

Collins, George R., gen. ed. Planning and Cities Series. New York: George Braziller, 1968 –.

Engel, Heinrich. The Japanese House: A Tradition for Contemporary Architecture. Tokyo: Charles E. Tuttle, Co., 1964.

Fletcher, Sir Banister. A History of Architecture. 18th ed. Revised by J.C. Palmes. New York: Charles Scribner's Sons, 1975.

Giedion, Siegfried. Space, Time and Architecture. 4th ed. Cambridge: Harvard University Press, 1963.

Giurgola, Romaldo and Mehta, Jarmini. Louis I. Kahn. Boulder: Westview Press, 1975.

Halprin, Lawrence. Cities. Cambridge: The MIT Press, 1972.

Hitchcock, Henry Russell. In the Nature of Materials. New York: Da Capo Press, 1975.

Jencks, Charles. Modern Movements in Architecture. Garden City, N.Y.: Anchor Press, 1973.

Le Corbusier. Oeuvre Complète. 8 Volumes. Zurich: Les Editions d'Architecture, 1964–70.

  Towards a New Architecture. London: The Architectural Press, 1946.

Martienssen, Heather. The Shapes of Structure. London: Oxford University Press, 1976.

Moore Charles; Allen, Gerald; Lyndon, Donlyn. The Place of Houses. New York: Holt, Rinehart and Winston, 1974.

Mumford, Lewis. The City in History. New York: Harcourt, Brace & World, Inc., 1961.

Norberg-Schulz, Christian. Meaning in Western Architecture. New York: Praeger Publishers, 1975.

Palladio, Andrea. The Four Books of Architecture. New York: Dover Publications, 1965.

Pevsner, Nikolaus. A History of Building Types. Princeton: Princeton University Press, 1976.

Rasmussen, Steen Eiler. Experiencing Architecture. Cambridge: The MIT Press, 1964.

  Towns and Buildings. Cambridge: The MIT Press, 1969.

Rowe, Colin. The Mathematics of the Ideal Villa and Other Essays. Cambridge: The MIT Press, 1976.

Rudofsky, Bernard. Architecture Without Architects. Garden City, N.Y.: Doubleday & Co., 1964.

Simonds, John Ormsbee. Landscape Architecture. New York: McGraw Hill Book Co., Inc., 1961.

Stierlin, Henri, gen. ed. Living Architecture Series. New York: Grosset & Dunlap, 1966 –.

Venturi, Robert. Complexity and Contradiction in Architecture. New York: The Museum of Modern Art, 1966.

Vitruvius. The Ten Books of Architecture. New York: Dover Publications, 1960.

Wilson, Forrest. Structure: the Essence of Architecture. New York: Van Nostrand Reinhold Co., 1971.

Wittkower, Rudolf. Architectural Principles in the Age of Humanism. New York: W.W. Norton & Co., Inc., 1971.

Wong, Wucius. Principles of Two-Dimensional Design. New York: Van Nostrand Reinhold Co., 1972.

Wright, Frank Lloyd. Writings and Buildings. New York: Meridian Books, 1960.

Zevi, Bruno. Architecture as Space. New York: Horizon Press, 1957.

INDEX

INDEX OF BUILDINGS

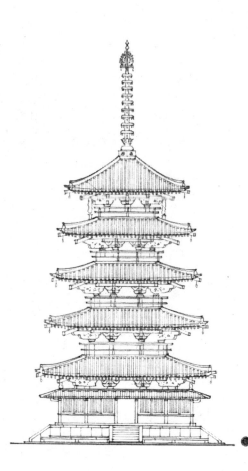